Windows in Buildings

Bodies like crystal, houses made of glass
Sunlight spread across, yet shadow not to be found
Urdu verse by Baqar Naqvi

Without a glass palace
Life becomes a burden.
Glass opens up a new age
Brick building only does harm.

Scheerbart

Windows in Buildings: Thermal, Acoustic, Visual and Solar Performance

(CD-ROM with MS-Excel workbooks included)

T. Muneer, N. Abodahab, G. Weir and J. Kubie
Napier University, Edinburgh

with a chapter on Solar Radiation and Daylight Data
by D. Kinghorn

Architectural Press

OXFORD AUCKLAND BOSTON JOHANNESBURG MELBOURNE NEW DELHI

Architectural Press
An imprint of Butterworth-Heinemann
Linacre House, Jordan Hill, Oxford OX2 8DP
225 Wildwood Avenue, Woburn, MA 01801-2041
A division of Reed Educational and Professional Publishing Ltd

℞ A member of the Reed Elsevier plc group

First published 2000

British Library Cataloguing in Publication Data
A catalogue record for this book is available from the British Library

Library of Congress Cataloguing in Publication Data
A catalogue record for this book is available from the Library of Congress

ISBN 0 7506 4209 2

Printed and bound in Great Britain by
Biddles Ltd, www.Biddles.co.uk

CONTENTS

FOREWORD

The window is more than a link between the inside and outside of a building, architecturally it defines the character of the building. The transparent building, which is seen as very desirable by many, offers great challenges to the engineer in terms of satisfying building regulations, minimizing energy consumption and providing glare-free daylighting. Modern glazing systems using selective coatings and cavities containing inert gases assist. However, to take full advantage of these systems it is essential to understand how windows work.

Professor Muneer and his co-authors, who between them cover a wide range of expertise in the field, have brought together significant quantities of data related to the overall performance of windows, together with the techniques necessary for the calculation of external irradiance and illuminance. Additionally some of the latest research in these areas is included.

A novel feature of the book is that calculations are backed up by software tools operating within the environment of the Excel spreadsheet. These will be of great value to the student, practising engineer and researcher. The value is further enhanced in that the authors have taken a holistic approach that extends into the issues of sustainability and whole life costs. It can be expected that this book will become a much quoted reference source.

Professor Michael Holmes
ARUP R&D

PREFACE

If daylight is the 'form giver' of a building, the window is the daylight provider. Glazing systems lie at the heart of the window design and it is therefore logical to explore the interaction of windows and buildings.

The object of this book is to present the state of the art of high-efficiency glazing systems and their energetic and environmental impact on modern buildings. The book is written with a view to provide easy-to-use charts, tables and software for the design and selection of glazing system for their appropriate incorporation in modern buildings. The target audience are the architects, builders and building designers, building services engineers, students, educators and researchers working in the area of energy efficiency in buildings.

Glass offers a high degree of functionality. It may be made to blend with the desired building architecture. Due to recent engineering developments it is now possible to design and build buildings with glass walls which keep the weather out and warmth in. Properly selected glazing can save energy, help reduce the environmental impact on heating and lighting without compromising acoustical protection, safety or comfort. In effect the large-scale use of glass in modern buildings implies its 'rediscovery'. Consequently, new algorithms and tools have to be provided which incorporate the emerging knowledge-base. This was the reason for the production of this book.

Another contributing factor to the present development is the emerging use of computer spreadsheets for engineering computation. To quote E. M. Forster, 'The only books that influence us are those for which we are ready, and have gone a little farther down our particular path than we have yet gone ourselves.' The simplicity of data entry and its manipulation afforded by spreadsheets makes it an ideal design and analysis tool. Modern spreadsheet software offer very powerful numerical and decision-making facilities. Almost every engineering professional has a spreadsheet loaded on his or her computer. This book exploits this situation to fill the gap between the ability to perform involved calculations and the desire to do so without the tedium of writing one's own software.

Another advantage offered by the spreadsheet medium is that each formula is readable, and fits in its appropriate position, i.e. the spreadsheet cell. This enables the user to easily follow the algorithmic chain. On the other hand, commercially available software, while powerful, does not allow the user the facility to examine or alter the computer code. In many cases such commercial or shareware software, due to its very design, may take several weeks and months of training. Owing to their widespread use and user-friendly layout, spreadsheets require only a few minutes' training before the user is fully in charge of the situation. This point will be demonstrated in Chapter 2 where more sophisticated features of Microsoft Excel are introduced.

The book covers the main design aspects of windows – thermal insulation, solar heat transmission, daylight, sound insulation and life cycle assessment. The necessary rigour for understanding the physical principles and analysis is backed up with a number of computer workbooks, each dealing with a given computational aspect. To quote Robert Goddard, 'No matter how much progress one makes, there is always the thrill of just beginning.' The hard–soft combination of material presented here is, we hope, 'just the beginning'. In due course there is bound to be much more activity for this type of presentation where the boundary between the author and the reader starts to become blurred. The reader may then be able to take the book onward to a different plane!

The following program-copying policy is to be maintained. Copies are limited to a one person/one machine basis. Each individual reader may keep backup copies as required. However, further distribution of the programs constitutes a violation of the copyright agreement and hence is illegal. Although prepared with great care and subject to rigorous quality control checks, neither the author nor the publisher warrants the performance or the results that may be obtained by using the enclosed suite of computer spreadsheets or programs. Accordingly, the accompanying programs are licensed on an 'as-is' basis. The purchaser or user of this book assumes their performance or fitness for any particular purpose.

The authors welcome suggestions for additions or improvements.

ACKNOWLEDGEMENTS

The present text is the culmination of research and review undertaken by the authors during the past decade. Many organisations have either sponsored or actively supported this programme of work. Noteworthy among them are Napier University, Edinburgh; Strathclyde University, Glasgow; The Royal Academy of Engineering, London; the Chartered Institute of Building Services Engineers, Balham; Nordan (UK), Lanarkshire; Living Design, Glasgow; Interpane, Germany; Fraunhofer Institute for Solar Energy Systems, Freiburg; Pilkington plc, Merseyside; the UK Meteorological Office, Bracknell and the Lawrence Berkeley Laboratory, Berkeley. Their contributions are gratefully acknowledged.

The present text was undoubtedly enriched by the inclusion of material from a number of sources. In this respect acknowledgement is given herein to the relevant sources of information; the names of authors are followed by their publications. G.D. Ander: *Daylighting*, Van Nostrand Reinhold; R.E. Boltz and G.L. Tuve: *CRC Handbook of tables for applied engineering science*, CRC Press; J. Carmody et al.: *Residential windows*, W.W. Norton & Company; CIBSE: *Energy efficiency in buildings*; T.E. Johnson: *Low-e glazing design guide*, Butterworth Architecture; P.J. Littlefair: *Solar radiation and daylight data for Garston*; Meteorological Office (UK): *Solar radiation data*; H. Nakamura and Y. Koga: *Solar radiation and daylight data for Fukuoka*; Pilkington plc: *Glass in building*; D.C. Pritchard: *Lighting*, Longman; Royal Greenwich Observatory: *Data for solar declination and equation of time*; and P.R. Tregenza: *Solar radiation and daylight data for Manchester and Sheffield*.

The following individuals are thanked for their support: Daruish Arasteh, Ken Butcher, John Fulwood, Alistair Gilchrist, Baolei Han, Mike Holmes, Yasuko Koga, Geoff Levermore, Paul Littlefair, Kerr MacGregor, John Mardaljevic, Helen Rose, Stephen Selkowitz and Peter Tregenza.

The help extended by the publishers Neil Warnock-Smith, Mike Cash and Marie Milmore is particularly appreciated. The authors are grateful to George Pringle for his assistance in artwork.

The authors would like to extend special thanks to their partners for the patience and forbearance provided throughout the length of this project.

MICROSOFT EXCEL WORKBOOKS ON COMPACT DISK
Folder names given within square brackets

2 The Microsoft Excel computing environment [Chap2]

Calc2-01	*U*-value for single-glazing (sequential computation)
Calc2-02	Glazing *U*-value as a function of wind speed (dynamic graphs)
Calc2-03	Thermal properties of infill gases (lookup tables)
Calc2-04	Finding the window aspect for a desired solar energy budget (Goal Seek)
Calc2-05	Day of the week (Visual Basic for Applications)
Calc2-06	Solar geometry for any tilted window (FORTRAN-based DLL [Fr206.dll])
Calc2-07	Optimisation of window aspect and tilt for maximising solar energy capture (Solver)
Fr206.dll	FORTRAN-based DLL for Calc2-06
Prog16.for	FORTRAN program for Calc2-06

3 Thermal properties of windows [Chap3]

Calc3-01a	*U*-value of double-glazed window using air, Ar, Kr, Xe or SF_6 infill (approximate solution)
Calc3-01bAir	*U*-value of double-glazed window using Air (precise solution)
Calc3-01bAr	*U*-value of double-glazed window using Ar (precise solution)
Calc3-01bKr	*U*-value of double-glazed window using Kr (precise solution)
Calc3-01bXe	*U*-value of double-glazed window using Xe (precise solution)
Calc3-02	*U*-value of triple-glazed window using air, Ar, Kr, Xe or SF_6 infill
Calc3-03	Temperature stratification in a double-glazed window
Calc3-04	Combined conduction, convection and radiation analysis
Calc3-05	Psychrometery – dew point temperature determination (FORTRAN-based DLL [Prog72.dll])
Data3-01	Psychrometric chart
Prog72.dll	FORTRAN-based DLL for Calc3-05

4 Windows and solar heat [Chap4]

Calc4-01	Equation of time and solar declination angle
Calc4-02	Time conversion: LCT to AST and vice versa
Calc4-03	Sunrise, sunset and day-length

5 Windows and daylight [Chap5]

6 Acoustic properties of windows [Chap6]
Calc6-01   Sound-reduction calculation for a given facade

8 Solar radiation and daylight data *D Kinghorn* [Chap8]
Calc8-01   Sky luminance data transposition
Data8-01   Slope illuminance and irradiance data for Fukuoka, Japan (1994)
Data8-02   Slope illuminance and irradiance data for Garston, UK (1991/2)
Data8-03   Slope illuminance and irradiance data for Edinburgh (Heriot-Watt), UK (1993/4)
Data8-04   Slope illuminance and irradiance data for Manchester, UK (1993)
Data8-05   Slope illuminance and irradiance data for Edinburgh (Napier), UK (1992/3)
Data8-06   Slope illuminance and irradiance data for Sheffield, UK (1994)
Data8-07   Sky luminance distribution data for Fukuoka, Japan (1994)
Data8-08   Sky luminance distribution data for Garston, UK (1993)
Data8-09   Sky luminance distribution data for Sheffield, UK (1993)
Data8-10   Sky radiance distribution data for Fukuoka, Japan (1994)

Total number of workbooks = 53. Total number of DLLs and FORTRAN programs = 9

Windows 95/98/NT4 Executable files on CD [FORTRAN, Exe and other files]
LD_Fill.exe: Sky luminance distribution plotter – colour raster
LD_Numbr.exe: Sky luminance distribution recording scheme (UK system)
LD_Vals.exe: Sky luminance distribution plotter – luminance values
Plot_XY.exe: X-Y plotter

LD_Fill.for: Sky luminance distribution plotter – colour raster
LD_Numbr.for: Sky luminance distribution recording scheme (UK system)
LD_Vals.for: Sky luminance distribution plotter – luminance values
Plot_XY.for: X-Y plotter

Data_XY.txt: Data file for Plot_XY.exe
LD_Indat.csv: Data file for LD_Fill.exe and LD_Vals.exe

GINO files required for the execution of the above exe files:
Ggraflib.dll, Ginlibmp.dll, Mwinerr.dll and GINO.con

Total number of FORTRAN, Exe and other files = 14

Total number of files on CD = 76

INSTRUCTIONS ON THE USE OF WORKBOOKS AND EXECUTABLE FILES

The CD accompanying this book contains 53 Microsoft Excel workbooks, four directly executable files, two text files which provide data for the executable programs and four GINO graphics software files (three 'DLL' and one 'con' file). GINO is a versatile graphics environment which has been used to produce the above-mentioned executable files. The output of such files is beyond the sophistication of the graphic facilities available within Excel.

Chapter 2 provides detailed instructions on the use of Excel workbooks and it is recommended that that material be read before using the workbooks. The workbooks are categorised on a chapter basis and are therefore placed within the respective folders. Chapters 1 and 7 contain no electronic material.

All the 76 files included in the CD-ROM are naturally 'read only' and thus protected from any accidental deletion. The files may be copied on the user's PC and used directly. If any changes are made to the workbooks then the user should use the 'Save As' command and use a different file name to save the altered version of the file(s). Note that some of the workbooks contain multiple worksheets with interlinking formulae. Care must therefore be exercised not to alter the cell addresses.

Some of the workbooks use dynamic-linked libraries (DLLs). The present authors developed the DLLs using FORTRAN software. DLLs are powerful tools that take away the tedium of large, sequential number crunching using the power of programming languages. Care must be exercised when handling DLL-based workbooks. Step-by-step instructions are therefore provided in the box below.

For all DLL-based workbooks the following procedure **MUST** be used:
- Launch Excel software
- Open the DLL-based workbook
- Enter data in the relevant worksheet(s)
- Simultaneously press ALT + F8 keys
- Select the relevant macro from the dialog box
- Either click the Run button or simultaneously press ALT + R keys

The exe files enable graphical representation of large and varied data sets. The respective input data files are also included. It is important that the user conform to the format of the given files if they wish to import their own data in the given files LD_Indat.csv and Data_XY.txt. Note that the latter files may be created from any of the popular spreadsheet software.

Finally, care must be exercised in using the present electronic files. If any changes are made within the files, they must be resaved under different names. In any case, the original set of files may always be retrieved from the CD-ROM.

The following procedure may be used to remove the READ only flag from all the files thus enabling any edits to be performed:

- Copy the file(s) from the CD onto the hard disk in any suitable directory (say in the 'C' drive)
- After changing over to the above directory, use the MS-DOS command: ATTRIB -R *.*

1 INTRODUCTION

Windows, as a key element of buildings, are essential architecturally, socially, psychologically as well as environmentally. Today more attention is being given to the performance of windows and they are being designed to do exactly what we require of them. Windows have very appropriately been described as being the eyes, the ears and the nostrils of a building.

Recently, higher levels of insulation, lower infiltration rates and larger areas of glazed aperture have been required in the design of buildings. In view of this increasing demand, the conventional window has become the weakest thermal fabric in a building. For example, studies have shown that 6% of the United Kingdom's energy consumption is due to heat losses from domestic glazings alone. In addition to their poor thermal performance, conventional windows can create comfort problems and damaging accumulations of condensation. These malfunctions have strengthened the demands for windows with higher thermal performance. The use of double-glazed windows is still the most common method of providing a reasonable level of thermal resistance. Various technologies have been introduced to double-glazed windows to further enhance their performance. Examples of these new advances include spectrally selective low-emissivity coatings on glass and on thin plastic films, solar control coatings, infrared transparent glazings, anti-reflective surface treatments, low-conductivity infill gases, honeycombs, silica aerogels, multi-layer film suspension systems, holographic coatings, optically switchable glazings, polarised glazings and evacuated enclosures.

Most double-glazed windows currently manufactured consist of two panes of glass separated from each other by an edge-seal. The edge-seal isolates the cavity between the glazings, thereby creating an enclosure suitable for non-durable coatings and/or substitute infill gases. However the edge-seal creates a thermal bridge, termed cold bridging, between internal and external environments. It causes energy loss at the perimeter of the window hence reducing the window's overall thermal performance. Cold bridging may also cause condensation occurrence on the bottom part of the window inner pane. Better window glazing calls for a parallel development in edge-seal and frame technology.

Windows provide humans with a variety of functions which include the supply of the interior spaces of buildings with light, solar energy, air and view according to the desires of the occupants and to shield them from dust, noise, rain and excessive heat or cold. Windows also provide the passers-by with attractive views into buildings that can be used effectively in the design of commercial premises. Some of the functions which are of importance to architects and building services engineers are considered briefly in the following sections.

1.1   Windows and life

Humans spend the greater part of their lives in shelters. From the earliest times, they have made structures which, however rough and crude, were meant to protect them from the dangers and discomforts of the external environment.

Humans, in seeking shelter, need to be able to remain in touch with the outside world, that is, the shelter must have some form of visual contact. The oldest way of bringing light into a shelter is to let the natural light enter through openings and at the same time, the opening is also expected to admit fresh air. How much light is to be introduced depends on what the shelter is used for, and how much is admitted will depend on the climate, the material and the external environment. Similarly, some regulating device is needed to keep out excessive noise, dust and smells and to protect the inside from the inclement conditions of the prevailing weather. The admittance of air, rain, snow, heat and cold can thus be prevented or regulated. The greatest problem is how to admit what is wanted and keep out what is not. Modern technology is able to overcome what seems to be an insurmountable problem, but the dominant link is achieved through the sense of sight. It is a window in a building that allows humans to look out of or look into a building, to see or to be seen, to watch the activities of others, or simply to observe the outside world. In a nutshell, people must have windows in their buildings.

1.2   Windows and energy conservation

Most of the energy used today originates from fossil fuels (gas, oil and coal). Burning fossil fuels emits pollutants, including carbon dioxide and gases that cause acid rain. As carbon dioxide and other gases build up in the atmosphere, more of the sun's heat is trapped giving rise to what has been termed the greenhouse effect. This could potentially result in the earth becoming hotter, and could increase the risk of storms, coastal flooding and drought. Using energy more efficiently is one of the most cost-effective means of reducing emissions of carbon dioxide and, additionally, helps to conserve fossil fuels.

Buildings account for the bulk of the energy budget of the OECD countries. At least one-quarter of the domestic heating bill in these countries is due to the thermal energy loss through glazings because they are the weakest thermal component in a building. Therefore, improving the thermal insulation of the window will contribute to energy conservation and environmental improvement.

Heat is lost through windows by conduction, convection and radiation. Detailed analysis of the mechanism of heat loss through single- and double-glazed windows will be presented in Chapter 3. It is convenient to combine all types of heat loss in a single parameter that describes the behaviour of a glazed window. This parameter, which will be discussed later, is called the thermal transmittance or *U*-value. The lower the window *U*-value, the better is its thermal insulation and the more energy it can conserve. Better *U*-values can be achieved by using modern technology. Examples of this technology are given later in this book.

1.3   Windows as daylight providers

Daylight is one of the largest concerns for both architects and residents. Traditionally, the main purpose of a window is to admit daylight and many houses are still designed on the assumption that daylight will be the working light for a greater part of the day. For example, electrical lighting in the UK accounts for an estimated 5% of the total primary energy consumption and office buildings may consume up to 60% of their total energy in the form of electric lighting. Therefore, by reducing reliance on artificial lighting, daylight can be an effective means of saving energy and reducing the environmental impact. However, lighting cannot be provided by daylight alone for the entire working day throughout the year. Daylight and artificial light may need to be integrated to avoid lack of proper lighting within a building. Daylight is also required to enhance the appearance of an interior and its contents by admitting areas of light and shade that give shape and detail for objects. The inclusion of daylight in the workplace provides workers with social and physiological benefits. Daylight, for instance, may increase the ability of office workers to do deskwork.

Low-emissivity (low-e) coatings are invisible, but they are remarkably well suited for increasing thermal comfort and controlling solar impact. Using a low-emissivity coating to improve a double-glazed window's performance has little effect on daylight transmissivity. The daylight transmissivity of a double-glazed window with 4 mm thick float glass is 80% and if one low-e coating is added, while other conditions remain the same, the transmissivity becomes 75%. However, as a consequence of using the low-e coating, the *U*-value is reduced by about half.

Daylight can, however, be troublesome in some situations. For example, occupants may feel discomfort by glare due to the excess of illumination in their field of view. If the level of glare becomes very high, it may impair, for example, our ability to read. Interior objects such as furniture and paintwork may suffer visual degradation and fading if subjected to daylight for longer periods of time. The use of excessive glazed areas in an attempt to admit more daylight may give rise to solar overheating. Some windows using special low-emissivity coatings, especially in commercial buildings, can reflect solar energy while admitting the worthwhile daylight, thus reducing cooling loads without increasing the lighting load.

For example, in the UK buildings have traditionally been designed using daylight data recorded from the National Physical Laboratory in Teddington near London between 1933 and 1939. More recently new building constructions have employed illuminance data from Kew, about 10 miles from Teddington. The age of the data may not create any serious concern, although the clean air Acts passed in major towns and cities across the country could possibly influence present daylight levels. There is, however, concern for the lack of illuminance data for the rest of the country. It has been shown that values of average horizontal illuminance in the northern part of the UK are about two-thirds of those reported for Kew. These differences have far-reaching consequences for the performance of windows.

As a consequence of the absence of adequate measured illuminance data, building designers have to rely on predictive tools and models. These models should be capable of accurately predicting illuminance values from meteorological parameters such as solar radiation. There are algorithms that allow the prediction of illuminance when solar irradiation is provided as an input parameter. Thus validated insolation models will provide information not only on the interception of irradiation, but also on daylight.

1.4   Therapeutical aspects of daylight

People react to changing seasons with altered moods and behaviour. This problem is exacerbated in high-latitude locations where, seasonally, there is lack of sufficient daylight indoors. This common disorder among people living near high latitudes, such as Northern Europe, is diagnosed as seasonal affective disorder (SAD). Within Britain around half a million people have been reported to show symptoms of SAD. Research has shown that daylight has an important bearing on the human brain's chemistry. Light entering via eyes stimulates the nerve centres within the brain which controls daily rhythms and moods. During the night, the pineal glands produce melatonin, which causes drowsiness and thus sleepiness. At daybreak the incident daylight affects the glands in such a way that they cease production of melatonin. If the receipt of the dosage of daylight is not high enough, the above process is not halted completely and this causes drowsiness. Further research has indicated a link between human exposure to light and serotonin, a substance identified as a neurotransmitter. Lack of serotonin is known to be a cause of depression. With the advent of superinsulated windows it is possible to provide much larger glazed areas thus exploiting daylight and passive solar heat gains.

1.5   Windows as solar energy providers

During the past quarter-century many building air-conditioning systems were overdesigned. For example, the resulting plant capacity in the UK building stock exceeds the true requirements by as much as 30%. The World Energy Council has estimated that the overall efficiency of some air-conditioning systems is as low as 5%. Thus, an overdesigned air-conditioning system imposes a serious penalty on the environment.

The instrument of the Kyoto Protocol on global warming has been used to challenge building services engineers to become involved in a CO_2 permit scheme. This scheme is being used by the UK government to implement the Kyoto Protocol. Solar energy may be considered as a serious candidate to reduce the use of fossil fuels for building energy consumption. With reference to the European Union member states the receipt of solar energy within the United Kingdom is towards the lower end. Even then the annual energy incident on UK buildings (1614 TWh) exceeds the country's oil production (1504 TWh).

1.6   Windows as sound insulators

Noise is defined as unwanted sound and has many effects on human beings. It causes annoyance or dissatisfaction, affects communication, leads to damage to hearing, influences performance of tasks, and results in permanent changes in the normal functioning of the human organism which causes mental and/or physical deterioration.

Sound insulation within a building is as important as other building services, such as heating, ventilation and lighting. Noise is communicated to rooms within a building via many different paths, from noise sources elsewhere in the building and/or from noise sources outside it. Examples of these sources are road traffic, railways, aircraft, industry and building mechanical services. Modern architecture using light-weight structures, often with large windows, allows more sound to be transmitted into the building compared with the heavy, load-bearing walls of older buildings.

Sound insulation does not mean eliminating all sources of sound. Humans do need contact with the outside world through hearing desired sound.

Factors contributing to the sound insulation of a multiple glazed window are its mass, air-tightness, the gap width of the window cavity, and the acoustical isolation of the absorbent material around the edges of the air space. With each doubling of glass thickness, the corresponding sound insulation is increased by about 4 dB. A well-designed double-glazed window can provide over 40 dB of sound insulation. The best air gap for sound insulation has a width of at least 150 mm. Ideally, for best thermal insulation and lower cost, the optimum air gap should only be around 20 mm, but for larger widths there is no serious degradation in the thermal performance. Thus a compromise is needed between thermal and acoustic considerations.

1.7   Window technology

During the last decade window technology has seen more dramatic changes than any other building technology. In the past, the addition of extra glazing was the only option for improving window thermal performance. Recently, modern technology has introduced low-emissivity coatings, inert infill gases, insulating edge spacers and low conductive frames in window design. Windows having the combination of these technologies are referred to as superinsulated windows. For instance, a German window company, Interpane, has brought onto the market a window with a *U*-value which is as good as an insulated wall.

In addition to reducing energy loss from buildings, superinsulated windows also offer the following advantages:

- The improvement in comfort through the elimination of cold down-draughts and radiation exchange.
- Better noise-attenuation performance.
- An increase in the total light admission in residential and other buildings by allowing greater window areas to be employed without increasing the overall energy losses.
- With appropriate selective coatings, a reduction in overheating problems in temperate and tropical zones in summer, leading to a reduction in the need for indoor cooling.
- Greater flexibility and freedom for architects, designers and users.
- A reduction in condensation problems at the window edge area.

Research in all aspects of windows is very active and new technology in material, design, manufacture and installation is being developed. The following are some of window technologies presently in the marketplace.

1.7.1   Wavelength selective coatings

Transparent wavelength selective coatings on glazing substrates can be used to reflect or absorb certain bands of radiation while allowing the transmission of others. Some of the technologies utilising coating techniques are summarised below.

1.7.1.1   Low-emissivity coatings

A low-emissivity (low-e) coating is a low absorptive coating to suppress infrared radiation exchange. Transmission in the longwave infrared (far infrared) is nearly zero for the commonly used materials. However, their reflectivity for the shortwave infrared is low. Most of the solar energy is shortwave infrared while the energy radiated from warm objects is in the far infrared band. A low-e glazing, therefore, acts as a selective reflector

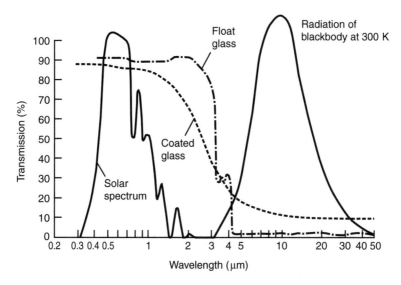

Figure 1.7.1 *Transmittance of float and low-e coated glass (Source: Pilkington plc)*

where solar transmission is quite high, solar reflectance is low and the reflectance of the far infrared emitted from internal objects is very high. Figure 1.7.1 shows the spectral transmittance of low-e coatings. These characteristics are appreciated by building occupants as in winter more daylight and solar energy are welcome and less heat loss from the interiors is required. Sixty per cent of the heat lost through ordinary windows is through longwave infrared radiation. A low-e window essentially doubles a window's thermal resistance because the low-e coating nearly shuts down the infrared conduit.

Low-emissivity films are generally of the type dielectric/metal/dielectric or dielectric/metal. The wavelength selective properties of dielectric/metal/ dielectric films are derived from both the optical properties of the metal and dielectric layers and the interference effects caused by the film stack. Metal films are approximately less than 10 nm thick and exhibit partial visibility and solar transparency. The dielectric film, when used to overcoat a metal, must exhibit high infrared transmittance in order to preserve the infrared reflectance of the metal. The preferred metals are silver, gold and copper, although silver is the most widely used. Traditionally, aqueous tin chloride, tin organometallic liquid or powder is sprayed onto the surface of the glass as it leaves the float bath. The spray reacts with the glass surface at about 600°C forming tin oxide in the air. This is probably the most efficient process for glass coating. These coatings have been improved by Pilkington by the use of a two-layer coating to reduce the iridescence of thicker tin oxide coatings.

1.7.1.2   Spectral splitting and cold mirrors

Spectral splitting coatings can be used to divide the solar spectrum into different broadband regions. In this way various glazings can be tailored to particular photovoltaic or photothermal needs. Spectral splitting coatings allow for multiple photovoltaic and combined photovoltaic–photothermal systems. By tailoring the solar energy to that of the photovoltaic response, the overall system efficiency can be increased. The cold mirror coating has the opposite spectral response to that of the transparent low-e film. The cold mirror exhibits a high reflectance in the visible region and transmits highly in the infrared. Cold mirrors are generally multilayer dielectric interference films. A simple design utilising a conventional dielectric/metal/dielectric low-e coating might be used to separate the visible and the near infrared portions of the solar spectrum. The visible portion could be used for photovoltaic conversion and the infrared portion could be used for photothermal conversion. Also, the photovoltaic will operate more efficiently if infrared heating is eliminated. If transparent low-e coatings with different spectral characteristics were used, the solar spectrum could be partitioned from low to high energy as the low-e transition wavelengths become shorter.

1.7.1.3   Holographically coated glazings

Holographic coatings can be tuned to reflect any waveband in the solar spectrum while allowing 75–80% transmittance in the visible waveband. The holographically coated film would be laminated between two glazing substrates for protection. These coatings are already used in head-up displays for cockpit and automobile windscreens where instrument information is projected optically onto the screen and reflected to the pilot or the driver.

1.7.2   Superwindows

Superwindows are glazing systems comprising multiple panes of glass or plastic films, with one or more low-emissivity coatings, gas cavity fillings and insulating frame and spacers.

The window U-value is defined as the rate of heat loss per square metre, under steady-state conditions, for a temperature difference of one Kelvin between the inner and outer environments separated by the glazing system. For triple-glazing with two low-e coatings of emissivity $= 0.1$, the U-value is approximately 1.0 W/m^2K. Filling the gap between glazing layers with gases such as krypton or xenon increases the insulating value of the unit sufficiently to make it possible to reduce the size of the gaps and to build units with an overall thickness of 25 mm or less. This allows the superwindows to be used in conventional double-glazing sash designs and framing systems and makes them viable for building retrofit. Superwindows are commercially available now and the range will continue increasing.

1.7.3 Transparent insulation materials

Transparent insulation material (TIM) are materials which allow solar energy to be readily transmitted, but minimise the heat loss through the surface.

1.7.3.1 Aerogel windows

The air space between window panes can be filled with aerogel, a microporous silicate foam material which reduces thermal transmission. Two forms of aerogel exist for use in windows, monolithic (in the form of continuous slabs) and granular (in the form of granules). Monolithic aerogel has excellent properties, being both highly transparent and having thermal properties approaching that of an opaque wall. It is predicted that only a slight vacuum would be required to achieve a U-value of 0.37 W/m^2K for a double-glazed window with a 2 cm layer of aerogel. Granular aerogel, on the other hand, can be poured into the space between double-glazing. The resulting heat loss coefficient for a 2 cm thick space of granules between glass panes is about 1 W/m^2K depending on the size of the granules. However, the translucent nature of this design makes it less suited for normal windows than monolithic aerogel.

1.7.3.2 Xerogel

Xerogel is a material similar to aerogel resulting from attempts to avoid the expensive supercritical drying process involved in monolithic aerogel manufacture. It has a higher diffuse transmittance but also a higher thermal conductivity.

1.7.3.3 Geometric media

Geometric media is a term used to describe glazings in which the geometric composition of the material gives rise to advantageous insulating and solar transmission properties. The capillary and honeycomb types are most commonly made of polycarbonate or acrylic plastic. These materials are, however, translucent rather than transparent.

1.7.4 Vacuum windows

Evacuated windows circumvent the high cost of gas filling. These windows utilise a vacuum in combination with a low-emissivity coating on one of the internal surfaces, an approach which eliminates cavity gas convection and most of the radiant heat transfer. Conduction through the spacers then becomes the major vehicle of heat transfer. This technology is currently being developed to overcome the following problems:

- The seal must be able to maintain the vacuum required. The pressure within the cavity has to be maintained to extremely low values, e.g. of the order of 10^{-8} bar. Table 1.7.1 shows the percentage loss for different gases/gas mixtures through various sealants after twenty years' service.
- The exceptionally low heat transfer across the glazing requires special attention be given to the frame of the glazing unit.
- The temperature difference between the outer and inner panes will be large, producing thermal expansion that could overstress rigid edge seals.
- Spacers are needed in the evacuated cavity to keep the glass layers from collapsing.

More work is needed to optimise, test and develop manufacturing processes to commercialise the concept.

Table 1.7.1 Per cent gas loss through various sealants after 20 years

	Ar / SF_6	Ar	Ar	Ar	SF_6
Single seal					
Polysulphide	8 to 10	13 to 15		6 to 13	0 to 1
Polyurethane	8 to 10	13 to 15	15 to 20	33 to 45	3 to 5
Silicone			> 45		
Butyl			5 to 7		
Polyisobutylene			4 to 5		
Permapol P-2			5 to 10		
Permapol LPM			1 to 4		
Thikol LP			3 to 9		
Dual seal					
Polysulphide	5 to 6				
Polyurethane	2 to 5				
Silicone	12 to 15				

1.8   Condensation in buildings

Condensation might be described as the modern disease of buildings. In high-latitude countries millions of households are affected by it. Condensation is a natural phenomenon which occurs when warm moist air comes into contact with a cold surface, which cools the air below its saturation point, causing its water vapour to condense. In dwellings, condensation on glazings may obstruct the view through windows and, if it becomes so excessive and no means for drainage is provided within the window frame, condensed water will run off causing damage to window frame, furniture and paintwork.

Single-glazed windows are the weakest thermal elements in building. In winter, the temperature of the glass pane of the single-glazed window approaches the outside ambient temperature. The indoor air which is in contact with the glass surface discards some of its water vapour, forming condensation.

1.8.1 The causes of surface condensation

Condensation results from a series of relatively simple and well-understood physical factors. Its occurrence should, therefore, be thoroughly predictable. The factors that effect the formation of condensation are as follows.

1.8.1.1 The effect of infiltration

In cold weather, the temperature of the external air is usually so low that its moisture content is also very low even if the air is saturated. Thus, if cold air infiltrates inside the building, the moisture increase within the building will be insignificant. However, the 'warm weather condensation' phenomenon may become the cause for condensation. When there is a sudden change from cold to warm humid weather, there will be a short period when condensation can form on cold structural surfaces until they have had a chance to warm up. It usually affects high thermal capacity structures which are very slow to respond to an increase in temperature.

The amount of rainfall does not affect the risk of condensation. External humidity in temperate climates (with the exception of warm weather condensation) has little influence on internal condensation.

1.8.1.2 The effect of internal environment

The internal humidity is the most important factor in condensation occurrence. Considerable amounts of water vapour are generated within dwellings by the occupants and their activities. It has been estimated that four persons living in a house for 12 hours will, merely by the process of breathing, add 2.5 kg of water vapour to the internal air. An average person engaged in sedentary activities will exhale more than a litre of water vapour in 24 hours. More energetic activities can increase this amount by up to four times. Typical family activities, e.g. breathing, cooking, washing and drying clothes, produce about 12 litres of water vapour per day. Flueless heating appliances that depend on combustion to produce their heat are the bulk producers of water vapour, e.g. natural gas produces 1.5 kg of moisture for each m^3 burned.

The most susceptible parts of a dwelling to condensation are those areas which are not heated or are heated inadequately. Heating of a building is important in many respects. Firstly, internal warm air can carry more water vapour than cold air. Therefore water vapour which cold air cannot carry will become suspended in the warm air instead of being condensed on building furniture and structure. The moisture-laden air can then be removed by ventilation. Secondly, if heating of a building is supplied in consistent levels, it will keep the internal surfaces warm and above dew point. Intermittent heating most frequently obtained by switching the heating systems off during periods of unoccupancy and switching them on during habitation hours will increase the condensation rate.

1.8.1.3   The effect of ventilation

In temperate climates, the outdoor air is likely to be at lower moisture content than the indoor air. Therefore, it is theoretically possible to avoid all condensation by adequate ventilation.

In the past, dwellings were naturally ventilated by means of less well-fitted doors and windows, suspended floors, flues or chimneys. New construction techniques generally reduce natural ventilation. Opening windows and doors is being discouraged because of anticipated increased energy costs. In addition, occupants are sensitive to the discomfort of draughts created especially by open windows.

The paradox that faces building services engineers nowadays is that, on the one hand, the greater the ventilation, the greater the heat necessary to replace that which is lost by ventilation, and consequently the greater the cost. On the other hand, the less the ventilation and the heat input to the building, the more likely the condensation occurrence.

Ventilation should be consistent throughout the whole building and ventilators should be incorporated into windows. Such ventilators provide a controlled amount of fresh air in a small but adequate quantity which circulates around the window area keeping condensation at a minimum.

1.8.1.4   The effect of room surface temperature

Surface condensation will occur if the temperature of the surfaces of the internal space falls below the dew point of the neighbouring air. Therefore, the internal surface temperature should be maintained within a few degrees below the internal air temperature. This is also a requirement for thermal comfort, i.e. for humans to be thermally comfortable surface temperature should never fall more than 5°C below the air temperature.

To completely eliminate the risk of surface condensation, consistent, standard levels of temperature throughout the building and the internal air should be maintained. Also, the building shell has to have reasonable levels of thermal insulation. However, surface condensation may occur in areas where cold-bridging is possible.

Adequate insulation can minimise the risk of surface condensation by maintaining the surface temperature at a reasonable level. However, no amount of thermal insulation can make an unheated room warm. Insulation must always be complemented with a reasonable heating system if its effectiveness is to be realised.

1.8.2   The avoidance of condensation

Condensation is very much related to the way in which buildings are heated, ventilated and insulated. By control of humidity, temperature and air movement, much of the inconvenience of condensation can be prevented. Condensation problem should be seriously addressed during the initial design of a dwelling. Means for the removal of moisture from within the house by ventilation must therefore be provided. Moist air should be removed at source, in kitchen, bathroom or shower and should not be allowed to move to cooler areas such as bedrooms. The air extraction can be done either by natural means through open windows or other vents, or mechanically by fitting an extraction fan.

1.9   Life cycle assessment of multi-glazed windows

Life cycle assessment (LCA) is a systematic approach to assessment of environmental impacts associated with a product, process or activity, adopting a holistic or whole life approach to design methodologies. This book addresses a continuing need to focus on sustainable development, using LCA as an assessment tool to develop a greater understanding of the window life cycle, and to highlight improvements which are necessary to lessen its environmental impact and make the processes involved more benign. To do this successfully requires that the demands of modern living, and the comfort conditions expected, be incorporated into design criteria, while ensuring that the needs of future generations are not compromised by today's activities. Along with rising demands to improve efficiency and decrease energy consumption in buildings comes an expectation for continual improvement in building interiors. To this end, both the aural and visual characteristics of window installations become paramount, in addition to the well-researched thermal performance criteria.

Optimum window design includes the impact of energy consumption, global environmental impact and occupant comfort. Optimisation of energy consumption incorporates embodied energy, thermal performance and electric lighting demand over the life cycle of a window. Global environmental impact optimisation is similar, but evaluation is based on energy generation, and greenhouse gas production. Occupant comfort optimisation guides the user towards a glazing solution which offers sufficient noise attenuation, while minimising thermal losses and electric lighting demand. Each of the above objectives provides loose guidance, leaving room for judgement and is not intended to be prescriptive.

1.10   Legislation and regulations

In order to ensure that a window functions properly, much legislation and many regulations on energy conservation and other areas have been imposed in many countries. The strict legislation and regulations have made it impossible for house builders to use single-glazed windows, and they have to incorporate double-glazed or triple-glazed windows into their new houses to meet the requirements of the legislation, especially in the northern countries such as the UK, Canada, Norway, the USA and Germany. This has led to the use and innovation of double-glazed windows and thus increased the quality of the indoor environment of buildings.

The regulations related to windows address the following issues: minimum window area for daylighting; maximum U-value for window thermal characteristics; maximum window area in combination with solar transmittance for summer conditions; maximum infiltration through windows; minimum acoustic insulation; minimum fire and safety requirements. In some countries these regulations are only recommended by the government but in others they are mandatory. For example, the UK legislation now precludes the use of single-glazed windows.

1.11   Use of computers in window design

Use of computers to predict the performance of building elements is now widespread. Computer modelling offers one way of assessing complex transport mechanisms and the interaction of these in buildings. This technique is being used increasingly in the building services industry.

Computational fluid dynamics (CFD) can be described as the use of computers to model and evaluate the behaviour of fluids in given situations. The use of CFD modelling in window research areas is well documented. The CFD modelling results obtained in this book have been verified and validated by a variety of methods. Use of CFD and other microprocessor-intensive applications is bound to grow as a result of the developments taking place in the hardware and software technologies.

1.12   Scope of the present book

This book aims to provide building professionals with the necessary information to enable analysis and design of multiple-glazed windows. Thermal, aural and shortwave energetic transfer characteristics of windows are addressed here.

The book is written with a view to provide easy-to-use charts, tables and software for the design and selection of glazing system for their appropriate incorporation into modern buildings. The target audience is architects, builders and building designers, building services engineers, students, educators and researchers working in the area of energy efficiency in buildings.

The ever-falling price and increasing processing power of personal computers has led to a significantly increased sophistication in building energy analysis. A study by the US-based Semiconductor Industry Association has shown that by the year 2001, integrated circuits of 256 **MB RAM** will be commonly available. Such computers would easily be able to handle detailed hourly databases of solar radiation, daylight illuminance and other weather parameters. In turn, the databases will be used to analyse the interaction of window and the building. The Microsoft Excel-based applications provided in the present text enable large amounts of computation using desktop or laptop computers.

2 THE MICROSOFT EXCEL COMPUTING ENVIRONMENT

Modern engineering design and analysis demands for increased productivity, reduced costs, faster time to work completion, improved quality and world-wide access to information. In just ten years, information technology (IT) advances have been a catalyst to significant changes in the way design practices are run. Undoubtedly the key drivers of this change have been the explosive breakthrough in the design and development of integrated circuit chips and the emergence of computer aided design (CAD) software. Computer processor technology is one of the most important areas of growth. The Institution of Mechanical Engineering's *Professional Engineering* magazine (*PE*, 1998) predicts that by the year 2005 complete systems, with the storage and processing power of a 1997 personal computer, will be available on a single chip. Chips with the respective capacities of a gigabit and one terabit memory will be commonly available by the years 2002 and 2010. This will no doubt transform the way in which engineering design and analysis is undertaken. It would be possible to use palm-sized computers and large numerical databases for undertaking numeric-intensive calculations. The real, and perhaps only, barrier to the use of computer hardware would be the software requiring a long training period.

While larger, more complex engineering application packages such as those used for undertaking finite element analysis (FEA) or computational fluid dynamic (CFD) work present the top end of the market, many people would argue that it is the smaller software applications that have had the most immediate effect on their work environments. The advantage of using a spreadsheet-based computing environment such as Microsoft Excel is that the training times are of the order of, at most, a few hours compared to several weeks that may be required for some of the above-mentioned applications. Further, the learning curve for Excel is very gentle and easy. Help is available in the form of well-written texts, study guides and training videos. There are very many such texts available and those readers who have not had the opportunity of using Excel in the past may refer to Hallberg et al. (1997) and Liengme (1997). The former text provides a basic drill in the use of Excel whereas the latter includes more focused applications directly to be used for engineering applications.

In general terms, there are some very compelling reasons to switch from a manual (calculator-based) to computer-based engineering design. These are:

- Cheaper: Very significant savings in the person-hours required for basic design calculations and optimisation.
- Faster: The results are available at once, without long waiting periods. Any new models made available in the scientific journals can be rigorously tested and applied.
- Ease of analysis: The ability to perform 'what-if analysis' is significantly improved.
- Use of graphics: Information can be displayed, copied and printed in an easy-to-understand manner thus making it easy to communicate with clients who may not have a scientific background.
- Ease of communication: Design information may be transmitted through the World Wide Web easily and cheaply. Discussion can then take place for design scenarios.
- Ease of updating: Newer databases may be linked-up quite easily and thus the design process can be kept abreast of rapid technological changes.
- Mainstream activity: Although some organisations take pride in being 'early adopters', most prefer to use only the mainstream technology. Now with the wider adaptability of computer-based applications in the industry and academia, organisations not using this technology would fall into the 'obsolete' class.

2.1   Excel – A user-friendly environment for number crunching

The history of the development of computer spreadsheets may be traced to VisiCalc which in the early 1970s created a significant impact in the corporate field. Prior to the launch of spreadsheets scientists and engineers had looked down on PCs. However, VisiCalc changed that image. Some journals claim that without the spreadsheet the PC would never have developed so rapidly in the early 1980s.

The chances are that most people who perform any work with numbers do have recourse to a spreadsheet. VisiCalc was rapidly replaced by Lotus 1-2-3 in the 1980s, which was faster, smarter and easier to use. But Lotus were slow in transferring their product to the Microsoft Windows environment and consequentially lost ground to their nearest rival, Microsoft Excel. Today with over 50 million users world-wide the sales of Excel are only second to the Web browser software. Excel comes with a range of templates and on-screen training tips. For most science and engineering students it requires only a few hours' training to master the software at an intermediate level. It is also the corporate standard for spreadsheets.

The average Excel user probably employs only a tenth of its power, which now extends well beyond calculating lists of figures or making colourful charts. The power of Excel for engineering use is exploitable through its multitude of functions, i.e. macros (to perform repeatedly a chain of commands or operations), lookup tables (for performing interpolations on large property tables and data querying), goal seek (for solving non-linear equations), solver (for solution of a given set of non-linear equations and optimisation) and inter-linked graphs (for performing what-if and other analyses).

In this respect new books are emerging which highlight the computing potential of Excel. However, this field is very virgin and a lot more development is bound to take place in the near future. Due to their very nature engineering subjects easily lend themselves to the use of spreadsheets. In this respect packages such as Mathcad, Mathematica or Matlab face strong competition from spreadsheets, which in contrast require only a fraction of the training time.

British Petroleum is one of the world's largest oil and petrochemical corporations. Annually, they publish their *Statistical Review of World Energy* on their home page on the Internet. The information can be loaded as Microsoft Excel spreadsheets. This example clearly demonstrates the position of Excel in the world market as the premier tool for analysing tabular and graphical information.

2.2 The functionality of Excel – an example-based tour

This chapter is designed to give readers a very focused introduction to the potential of Excel as a CAD tool. Only those **functions**, **tools** and **procedures** are included here which are of direct relevance to the present text. This book reviews the current window technology and the associated knowledge base. However, since all examples and computational tools provided in the companion CD use Excel as the problem-solving environment it was felt that a brief tour of the most essential features of Excel would be of benefit to the reader. The relevant material is presented in the following sections. It may be worthy of note that all examples and workbooks available on the companion CD run in the Microsoft Excel 97 software and are equally effective within the Microsoft Windows 95/98 or the Microsoft NT environments. As stated above, it is assumed that the reader has a basic familiarity with the Excel package. Those who would like to gain the basic skills for using Excel are referred to the texts mentioned above.

2.2.1 Sequential computation

Sequential computation is the most fundamental and perhaps one of the most useful properties of Excel. Demonstration of this feature is provided in the form of the following example using the Calc2-01.xls workbook contained in the CD accompanying this book.

Example 2.2.1

It was pointed out in Chapter 1 that the overall heat transfer coefficient (*U*-value) of windows and other building components is a convenient index to evaluate their thermal transmission characteristics. U-values take into account the conduction through the fabric together with the convective and radiative heat transfer processes taking place at the internal and external surface of the building element. A steady-state heat transfer condition is assumed for the determination of the respective U-values and these are used widely by design engineers to estimate fabric heat flows in buildings.

The U-value of an element is the reciprocal of the sum of the individual resistances of the material layers which compose it. For a typical building component:

$$U = (R_{si} + \Sigma R_j + R_{so})^{-1} \tag{2.2.1}$$

R_{si} is the combined radiative–convective internal surface resistance (m^2K/W), ΣR_j the thermal resistances of structural components and R_{so} the combined radiative–convective external surface resistance (m^2K/W). R_{so} is defined as

$$R_{so} = (\varepsilon h_{ro} + h_{co})^{-1} \tag{2.2.2}$$

ε is the emissivity factor, h_{ro} the longwave radiation heat transfer coefficient and h_{co} the convective transfer coefficient.

Develop an Excel worksheet to ease the following tasks:

(a) Computation of U-value for varying glass thickness and external wind speed.
(b) Determination of the critical heat transfer paths (thermal resistance) which have the most significant effect on U-value.
(c) Investigation into the influence of the external heat transfer coefficient (h_{so}) models, recently made available in the scientific journals. Compare the effect of these models on the U-value against calculations based on the CIBSE (1982) and ASHRAE (1993) recommended models.
(d) Investigation into the influence of the wind direction, windward or leeward, on U-value.

Open the Calc2-01.xls workbook either by double-clicking the file icon from the Windows 95/98 or NT environment, or by opening the workbook once the Excel software has been launched. At this stage it would be useful to explain the layout of all the workbooks provided with this text. The top and the left part of the sheet confirm the name and title of the workbook and any 'global' parameters, such as glass thickness and thermal conductivity. If the global parameters are too numerous or where the computation demands such a structure they may be provided via an additional worksheet, as will be shown in other example workbooks. Independent variables such as wind speed may be provided in a column so that the effect of its variation on the overall heat-loss coefficient may be explored. This feature will be demonstrated via Calc2-02.xls (Cells D9:D15 in Sheet 'Main').

A red border divides the inputs from the outputs. Sequential computations of the individual thermal resistance are then undertaken leading up to the U-value estimate.

Note that Excel has a 15-digit precision and hence it surpasses the accuracy of the usual (single precision) FORTRAN codes.

Tasks (a) and (b) above can be addressed by changing the input variables. For example, if the glass thickness is doubled from the given 4 mm to 8 mm an insignificant change takes place in the U-value. However, if the wind speed is halved or the internal heat transfer coefficient is doubled, progressively significant changes in the U-value result. The most critical resistance in a single-glazed window is the internal heat transfer coefficient.

Tasks (c) and (d) require further information. Loveday and Taki (1998) have undertaken field measurements of the heat loss coefficients of walls. Their research suggests that the CIBSE (Eq. (2.2.3)) and ASHRAE (Eq. (2.2.4)) procedures result in lower U-value estimates. Note that ASHRAE (1993) does not explicitly provide an expression of the form given in Eq. (2.2.4). Rather, they provide design values of 22.7 W/m^{2}K and 34 W/m^{2}K, respectively for the summer and winter months. Equation (2.2.4) has been developed by Loveday and Taki (1998) to enable a comparison of R_{so} with other work.

$$h_{so} = 5.8 + 4.1v \tag{2.2.3}$$

$$h_{so} = 7.1 + 3.42v \tag{2.2.4}$$

v is the mean wind speed, expressed in m/s. The model proposed by Loveday and Taki, based on an up-to-date review of all notable studies, is given by

$$h_{so} = 16.7v^{0.5} \tag{2.2.5}$$

Other models are given below.

$$\text{Ito et al. (1972):} \quad h_{so} = 18.6v^{0.605} \tag{2.2.6}$$

$$\text{Cole and Sturrock (1977):} \quad h_{so} = 5.7 + 6.0v \tag{2.2.7}$$

$$\text{Sharples (1982):} \quad h_{so} = 1.9 + 0.65v \tag{2.2.8}$$

The reader may easily incorporate any of the above-mentioned models into cell B10 of the 'Main' worksheet in Calc2-01.xls. The effect on U-value may then be investigated for a number of wind speed values.

Research on the effect of wind direction on U-value of walls has been undertaken by Ito et al. (1972) and Sharples (1982). The model recommended by Ito et al. (1972) for leeward direction of wind is:

$$h_{so} = 8.3 + 0.725v \tag{2.2.9}$$

Once again, this model may be incorporated within the worksheet as discussed above and its influence investigated. This type of analysis is presented in the following section.

2.2.2   Dynamic graphs

An interesting feature of Excel is that it provides a dynamic link between numeric and graphic environments. While spreadsheet tables are essential for querying information expressed in numerical format, often, graphical outputs are also sought by designers to provide an insight into the overall picture. Example 2.2.2 will demonstrate this feature of Excel.

Example 2.2.2

In Section 2.2.1 models were presented for the external (exterior to the building or window surface) convective heat transfer coefficient. Using Calc2-01.xls compute the U-value of a single-glazed window for a variation of wind velocity from 0 to 3 m/s and display your results graphically for the following models:

CIBSE (1982)
ASHRAE (1993)
Loveday and Taki (1998)
Ito et al. (1972) model for leeward direction

Use the embedded graph facility to explore the variation of U-value as a function of the glass thickness, for a range of, say, from 3 to 12 mm.

Using Calc2-01.xls as the starting point, Calc2-02.xls was thus created to perform the above numerical experiments. Within Calc2-02.xls the minimum and maximum value of wind speed may be provided in the sheet entitled 'Main'. Any change in these parameters will automatically change the graph. The change in the window heat loss, resulting from a windward to a leeward condition, may also be examined quite conveniently.

2.2.3   Lookup tables

Excel provides a very useful facility for creating lookup tables. Through this facility the user may find one piece of information that is based on another. A lookup table consists of a column or row of ascending values, called

Table 2.2.1 Thermophysical properties for xenon (Hanley et al., 1974)

T (K)	ρ (kg/m^3)	$\mu \times 10^7$ (kg/m.s)	$k \times 10^3$ (W/m.K)	Cp (kJ/kg.K)	$\nu \times 10^7$ (m^2/s)	$\alpha \times 10^6$ (m^2/s)	Pr
250	6.40	195.8	4.69	0.161	30.591	4.560	0.671
255	6.27	199.6	4.78	0.161	31.809	4.740	0.671
260	6.15	203.4	4.87	0.161	33.050	4.924	0.671
265	6.04	207.2	4.96	0.161	34.315	5.112	0.671
270	5.93	211.0	5.05	0.161	35.603	5.303	0.671
275	5.82	214.8	5.14	0.161	36.916	5.497	0.672
280	5.71	218.6	5.23	0.161	38.252	5.695	0.672
285	5.61	222.3	5.31	0.161	39.594	5.885	0.673
290	5.52	226.1	5.40	0.161	40.977	6.090	0.673
295	5.42	229.9	5.49	0.161	42.385	6.298	0.673
300	5.33	233.6	5.58	0.161	43.797	6.510	0.673
310	5.16	241.1	5.76	0.161	46.710	6.944	0.673
320	5.00	248.5	5.93	0.161	49.696	7.380	0.673
330	4.85	255.9	6.10	0.161	52.775	7.828	0.674
340	4.71	263.3	6.28	0.161	55.947	8.304	0.674
350	4.57	270.6	6.45	0.161	59.189	8.779	0.674

'compare values', and corresponding data for each compare value, as shown in Table 2.2.1 which gives the thermophysical properties of xenon. In this illustration, the first column (temperature of the gas) contains data for the compare values. The corresponding data are the thermophysical property values.

Lookup tables are encountered by design engineers very frequently. For example, a large number of window glass selection tables are available from most manufacturers. In the present context, demonstration is provided by including lookup tables for thermophysical properties for three inert gases, i.e. argon, krypton and xenon. The analysis of any multi-glazed window heat loss involves calculation of the convective heat transfer within the window cavity. This in turn requires estimation of the thermophysical properties of the gas at the mean cavity temperature, which is approximately the average of the corresponding cavity glazing temperature. Inevitably this requires interpolations for each of the desired thermophysical property. Help is available for the design engineer in the form of Excel's **Vlookup** function, demonstrated via the Calc2-03.xls workbook.

Example 2.2.3

Thermophysical properties of xenon gas, used as an infill material in multi-glazed windows, are available in the literature. Manual interpolation of these properties for any given value of temperature is time-consuming. Develop an Excel spreadsheet using the property matrix with a view to compute the relevant properties for a temperature of 25°C.

Open the Calc2-03.xls workbook in the usual manner (see Section 2.2.1 if any help is required). Study the layout of the 'Gas Properties' worksheet. Provide a temperature value of 25°C in cell C4. The Vlookup function performs its task in the following manner. For the given temperature of 25°C in cell C4, the corresponding absolute temperature is calculated in cell L5 (298.15). The function VLOOKUP(L5,'Gas Properties'!A7:A22,1), see cell K5, uses the arguments: lookup value, table array and column index to look in the first column to find the largest value less than or equal to 298.15 K. The corresponding values of kinematic viscosity (v), thermal conductivity (k) and Prandtl number (Pr), given in cells K6:K8 respectively, are then obtained in a likewise manner (see the worksheet under discussion for further details).

There is, however, a problem with the above procedure, i.e. properties are obtained corresponding to the largest value less than or equal to the given temperature. In this particular instance the values are obtained for a temperature of 295 K (see column K of the worksheet). To precisely obtain the properties at the given temperature, 298.15 K a more rigorous procedure is required and this is explained below.

The entire table of properties is produced in a temperature-descending manner (see cell range A24:H39). Then using the **MATCH**('Gas Properties'!L5,A24:A39,-1) function in cell I7 and the **ADDRESS**(I7 + 23,1) function in cell I8, the position of the upper bound for the given temperature is obtained. The **INDIRECT**('Gas Properties'!I8) function is then used in cell M5 to obtain the numerical value of this upper bound. Once the upper bound of the temperature (300 K) bracketing the given temperature (298.15 K) is known the corresponding values for the desired properties are obtained using the VLOOOKUP function mentioned above. These are then used along with properties obtained at 295 K to enable interpolations to be carried out.

At this stage the reader is encouraged to try out computations at other temperatures and indeed to copy into the suite of cells discussed above the property data for other gases. The properties for krypton and argon are respectively given in cell ranges A44:H66 and A71:H103.

2.2.4 Goal Seek

Design engineers often encounter a situation where the result of a formula or the final result at the end of a series of computations is known (or desired), but not the input values. To solve such a problem the Goal Seek facility may be used. Excel varies the value in the specified cell until the result in the target cell is obtained. The following example will adequately demonstrate this procedure.

Example 2.2.4

An atrium facility, adjoined to a planned office building, is to be designed for a location north of Edinburgh. The object is to provide a well-lit yet comfortable environment within the atrium. To avoid excessive overheating the window orientation is to be set to a value which will limit the incident solar radiation to a given design value. Hourly horizontal diffuse and global irradiation data for a nearby location is available for several years. As an example, only one day's hourly data is included in the Calc2-04.xls workbook. The copyright of these data resides with the UK Meteorological Office and hence the data have been suitably randomised to avoid any breach of the copyright. The data, however, do represent the approximate climate of the east of Scotland.

Use the Excel Goal Seek facility to find out the aspect for vertical windows which will result in the total energy receipt of no more than 300 Wh/m^2. It must be pointed out that the Goal Seek facility works only 'locally', i.e. the search is not exhaustive.

Refer to the Calc2-04.xls workbook. The basic data for the site, surface geometry and ground albedo (reflectance to solar radiation) are provided in cells C4:C7. For any given instance of time the incident solar radiation on any tilted window requires knowledge of horizontal diffuse and global irradiation. These basic data are provided in columns A to E while solar geometry calculations are performed in columns F to J. The slope irradiation is then computed in a sequential manner as shown in columns K to V. Note that columns 'F' to 'U' contain intermediate steps. They have therefore been hidden.

A much more compact version of the slope radiation workbook using the Visual Basic for Applications module is provided in Chapter 4. That procedure and the physics of slope radiation is explained therein. Unfortunately, the Goal Seek and Solver facilities do not work with other user-defined macros or functions and hence the sequential computations provided in columns F to V are essential.

The use of the Goal Seek procedure is now explained in a step-by-step manner.

(a) From the Tools menu select 'Goal Seek'. A dialog box such as the one shown in Figure 2.2.1 will appear. If for any reason the Goal Seek function was not originally installed with Excel software then run the setup program to install it.

(b) In the Set cell box, enter the name of the target (or results) cell. In this particular instance the cell address is V22 and the content of this cell shows that the total incident energy is 484 Wh/m^2. This quantity corresponds to the selected window aspect of south.

(c) In the To value box, enter the value of 300.

(d) In the By changing cell box, enter the reference of the cell which contains the value for window aspect, i.e. C5.

(e) Choose the OK button.

In the present context the Goal Seek procedure converges to the value of 261° from north for the window aspect. Of course, further analysis related to the transmission of short-wave energy through the specified multi-glazed

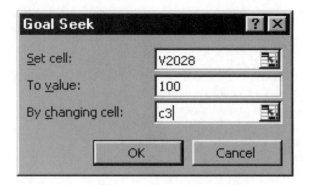

Figure 2.2.1 *The Goal Seek dialog box*

windows would be required. That topic will be the subject of discussion in Chapter 4.

2.2.5 Visual Basic for Applications

Microsoft Excel includes the Visual Basic for Applications (VBA) programming language which enables the user to write modules which may be either subroutines, functions or link-ups to user forms. A subroutine may perform repetitive tasks (macros) or enable the user to communicate with the workbook via a user form. A function, on the other hand, returns the value to a cell (or a range of cells) of a user-defined dependent variable, which may be related to either a single or several independent variables.

The example workbook Calc2-05.xls demonstrates the use of VBA.

Example 2.2.5

In order to differentiate between weekdays and weekends, modern control algorithms for energy-efficient buildings, such as the optimum start algorithm, require knowledge of the day of the week for a given date. A FORTRAN routine, Prog1-2.For, has been presented by Muneer (1997). Using this routine a Visual Basic program has been developed. This VBA program, embedded within the Calc2-05.xls workbook, is linked to the 'Main' worksheet.

To fully appreciate the mechanics of this workbook the reader is advised to undertake the following procedure:

* Open the workbook Calc2-05.xls either via a double-click on the file icon, thus launching Excel and opening the workbook in a single step, or by using the **File**, **Open** command if Excel has already been launched.

- Simultaneously press the **Alt** and **F11** keys thus launching the Visual Basic for Applications environment and the accompanying Visual Basic code. For the present example this code is displayed within the Calc205 module. It may be noted that there are three user-defined functions within the Calc205 module, i.e. *IDN*, *nwkday* and *nweek* which respectively calculate the Julian day number, weekday number and the day of the week. These functions are respectively and sequentially called upon in cells D5, E5 and F5. Further details of the computation of Julian day number and a number of other VBA routines used in this book are provided in Muneer (1997).
- You may close down the VBA environment by simultaneously pressing the **Alt** and **Q** keys.
- Try out the workbook under discussion by inputting various dates (cell range A5:C5).

Further information on the Visual Basic environment and the development of relevant codes may be obtained from Microsoft (1995a), Harris (1997) and McBride (1997).

2.2.6 FORTRAN or C-based Dynamic Linked Libraries

One of the most powerful features of Microsoft Excel operating under the Microsoft Windows environment is its ability to link with Dynamic Linked Libraries (DLLs). DLLs are in effect directly executable files, based on well-established programming languages such as FORTRAN or C. The power of such rich mediums can therefore be fully exploited. Thus, large number-crunching modules may be developed within a FORTRAN DLL and then a link provided via the Excel-VBA front-end.

A Dynamic Linked Library is an executable file, but is usually used as a library for applications (Microsoft, 1995b). A DLL contains one or more functions that are compiled, linked and stored separately from applications using them. The advantages of DLLs include:

(a) Multiple applications can access the same DLL. This reduces the overall amount of memory needed in the computer system, resulting in improved machine performance.
(b) General functions placed in the DLLs result in a small size of the applications that share these functions.
(c) Programs written in different languages can call the same DLL functions, as long as each program follows the functions' calling conventions.

The ease with which input data may be provided in Excel is second to none. Figure 2.2.2 shows the schematic of the information flows in such a scheme and the example workbook Calc2-06.xls is included to enable the user hands-on practice.

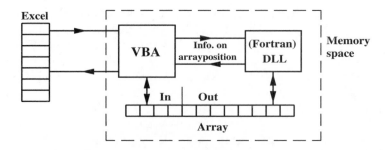

Figure 2.2.2 *A schematic of information flow for execution of a Dynamic Linked Library*

Example 2.2.6

A solar day is defined to be the interval of time from the moment the sun crosses the local meridian to the next time it crosses the same meridian. Due to the fact that the earth rotates in a diurnal cycle as well as moving forward in its orbit, the time required for one full rotation of the earth is less than a solar day by about 4 minutes. Thus, the standard time (as recorded by clocks running at a constant speed) differs from the solar time. The difference between the standard time and solar time is defined as the equation of time, EOT.

The solar declination (DEC) may be defined as the angular position of the sun at noon with respect to the equatorial plane. Computation of EOT and DEC is required for all solar energy-related analysis, such as the solar heat gain through any window system.

A high-precision algorithm and a FORTRAN routine, based on the work undertaken by the British astronomer B. D. Yallop, has been presented by Muneer (1997). Muneer's routine was also incorporated by a NASA contractor, Gronbeck (1998), to provide a web-based calculator for EOT, DEC and solar geometry.

Develop an Excel workbook which links with a suitably formatted FORTRAN DLL, based on the above code, with the view to exchanging input/output data between an Excel worksheet and the FORTRAN DLL.

Calc2-06.xls is based on the FORTRAN code Prog1-6.For: High-precision algorithm for EOT, DEC and solar geometry provided by Muneer (1997). A step-by-step procedure for using this workbook is detailed below:

(a) Open the workbook Calc2-06.xls after launching Excel. See text box on p. 31.
(b) Simultaneously press the **Alt** and **F11** keys thus launching the Visual Basic for Applications environment and the accompanying Visual Basic code.

(c) Activate the 'Compute' sheet by clicking its tab at the bottom of the workbook. Try out the workbook under discussion by inputting various date and time values (cell range A6:E17).

(d) For each change made in the date and time columns run the macro thus. Simultaneously press the **Alt** and **F8** keys to reveal the macro 'CallSolinc'. Run this macro by choosing the macro name and then click 'Run'.

Note that the terms AST (apparent solar time), SOLALT (solar altitude), SOLAZM (solar azimuth), and INC (solar inclination angle) will be introduced in Chapter 4. The relevant data for solar geometry calculations are to be provided in the 'Site geography, window geometry' sheet.

For those readers wishing to produce their own DLLs with a view to control the execution from Excel the following procedure is recommended:

Step 1 Produce the required FORTRAN code and call it, say X.For

```
Declare Sub Prog16 Lib "c:\Wi_BkMAK\Fort_Dll\Fr206.dll" Alias "_PROG16@4" _
(Myarray As Double)
Sub CallSolinc()
    Dim Myarray(1 To 16) As Double

    Myarray(1) = Sheets("Site").Cells(2, 1).Value
    Myarray(2) = Sheets("Site").Cells(2, 2).Value
    Myarray(3) = Sheets("Site").Cells(2, 3).Value
    Myarray(4) = Sheets("Site").Cells(2, 4).Value
    Myarray(5) = Sheets("Site").Cells(2, 5).Value

    For i = 6 To 17
    Myarray(6) = Sheets("Compute").Cells(i, 1).Value
    Myarray(7) = Sheets("Compute").Cells(i, 2).Value
    Myarray(8) = Sheets("Compute").Cells(i, 3).Value
    Myarray(9) = Sheets("Compute").Cells(i, 4).Value
    Myarray(10) = Sheets("Compute").Cells(i, 5).Value

    Call Prog16(Myarray(1))

    Sheets("Compute").Cells(i, 6).Value = Myarray(11)
    Sheets("Compute").Cells(i, 7).Value = Myarray(12)
    Sheets("Compute").Cells(i, 8).Value = Myarray(13)
    Sheets("Compute").Cells(i, 9).Value = Myarray(14)
    Sheets("Compute").Cells(i, 10).Value = Myarray(15)
    Sheets("Compute").Cells(i, 11).Value = Myarray(16)
    Next i
End Sub
```

Figure 2.2.3 *VBA code for linking Calc2-06.xls with Fr206.DLL*

Step 2   Using FORTRAN compiler and the code X.For produce the DLL (by compiling and then building). Say the resulting product is called Y.DLL

Step 3   Find out the alias name of the DLL by using the MS-DOS command: Dumpbin /Exports Y.DLL

Step 4   Place the Y.DLL file in a suitable folder and then change the file path address in the VBA code accordingly. This detail is further clarified by Figures 2.2.3 and 2.2.4 which respectively include the listings of

```
SUBROUTINE PROG16(comArr)
      !MS$ATTRIBUTES DLLEXPORT :: PROG16
      REAL(8) comArr(16)

      dtor=3.14159/180.0
      pi=3.14159

      NTIMES=2
      YLAT=comArr(1)
      YLONG=comArr(2)
      YRLONG=comArr(3)
      AZI=comArr(4)
      TLT=comArr(5)

      iyr=comArr(6)
      imt=comArr(7)
      idy=comArr(8)
      ihr=comArr(9)
      ime=comArr(10)
```

```
Computation of output variables eot, dec, ast,
solalt, solazm, solinc is undertaken within this
sub-module. Refer to 'Prog16.For' in Chap2
Folder for the full list.
```

```
      comArr(11)=eot/15.0
      comArr(12)=dec
      comArr(13)=ast
      comArr(14)=solalt
      comArr(15)=solazm
      comArr(16)=solinc

END    SUBROUTINE
```

Figure 2.2.4 *FORTRAN code Prog16.For, used for producing FR206.DLL. The DLL links with Calc2-06.xls via the VBA code shown in Figure 2.2.3*

the VBA and the FORTRAN source code used for developing Calc2-06.xls.

The text box below provides a step-by-step guide for the execution of all DLL-based workbooks.

For all DLL-based workbooks the following procedure **MUST** be used:
- Launch Excel software
- Open the DLL-based workbook
- Enter data in the relevant worksheet(s)
- Simultaneously press ALT + F8 keys
- Select the relevant macro from the dialog box
- Either click the Run button, or simultaneously press ALT + R keys

---

2.2.7   Microsoft Excel Solver

Microsoft Excel Solver is based on well-established numeric methods for equation solving and optimisation. These methods supply relevant numeric inputs to the candidate model and through an iterative procedure the results are generated. In Section 2.2.4 Excel's 'Goal Seek' facility was demonstrated. Solver is similar to Goal Seek, except that within Solver there is an ability to solve a family (or set) of linear or non-linear equations. Also, as mentioned above, multi-dimensional optimisation problems may also be easily handled for function maximisation or minimisation. In the authors' experience this facility of Excel is probably the most powerful feature as will be demonstrated by Example 2.2.7.

Microsoft Excel Solver can handle up to 200 independent variables with upper or lower bounds with an additional 100 constraints. However, Solver only works 'locally'. It may therefore not give all the possible solutions.

To use the Solver facility the user defines the problem that needs to be solved by identifying a **target** cell, the **changing** cells (containing the numerical values of the variables) and the **constraints** imposed upon the optimisation routine. The target cell is the cell whose value is to be maximised, minimised or made to reach a specified value. Full control of the solution process is possible via the use of the **Solver Option** dialog box. It is possible for the user to select the solution time and the desired number of iterations, precision of constraints, integer tolerance, automatic (independent-variable) scaling and the solution method used by the Solver.

Within the choice of solution method three options are available: the **Estimates**, **Derivatives** and **Search** procedures. The Estimates option enables the selection of **Tangent** option suitable for near-linear problems or the **Quadratic** option which is more suitable for problems with a high non-linearity. The Derivatives option enables a choice between **Forward differencing** (faster and yet approximate computation) and **Central differencing** (slower but precise computation). Finally, the Search option makes it possible to experiment with **Newton** (steepest descent routine which requires less processor work) and **Conjugate** gradient (routine which requires fewer iterations to obtain convergence) methods. Further information on the Solver facility is provided in Microsoft (1992) and Person (1992).

Example 2.2.7

Refer to Example 2.2.4 wherein Excel's Goal Seek procedure was used to find the value of the window orientation for the atrium facility which would limit the incident solar radiation to a specified value. Using the Excel Solver facility optimise the aspect and tilt of a given solar collector to maximise the interception of solar irradiation. Calc2-07.xls may be used for this exercise.

A brief introduction to the Solver facility was provided above. The relevant procedure is now explained in a step-by-step manner.

1 From the Tools menu select 'Solver'. A dialog box such as the one shown in Figure 2.2.5 will appear. If for any reason the Solver function was not originally installed with Excel software then run the setup program to install it.
2 In the Set Target box, enter the name of the target (or results) cell. In this particular instance the cell address is V22 and the content of this cell shows that the total incident energy is 285 Wh/m². This quantity corresponds to the selected aspect of west and tilt $= 90°$.
3 Select the Max option.
4 In the By Changing Cells box, enter the reference of the cells which contain the values for collector aspect and tilt, i.e. C5:C6.
5 Furnish any suitable constraints, as shown in the example (see Figure 2.2.5).
6 Choose the Solve button. If the 'time limit exceeded' message is displayed, click the 'continue' button.

Upon successful convergence the user has a choice of retaining the Solver solution or reverting to the original settings. Answer reports are also generated and a sample report is shown in Table 2.2.2.

Note that for a vertical collector with an aspect of due west the total energy received is 285 Wh/m². The Solver optimises the collector aspect and tilt to the respective values of 164° due north and 20° tilt, resulting in an energy yield of 660 Wh/m².

It may be possible for the Solver to reach other local maxima or minima. This may be demonstrated as follows. Launch the Solver procedure. Remove the constraints and then proceed to solve. You may find that a local maximum value has been reached.

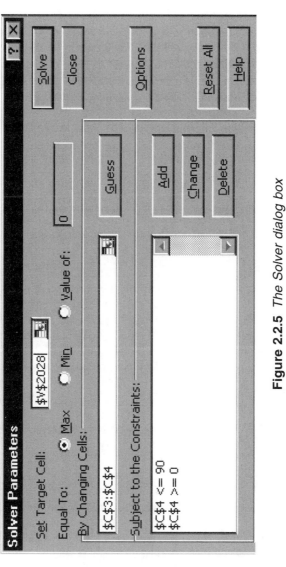

Figure 2.2.5 *The Solver dialog box*

Table 2.2.2 Answer report generated by Microsoft Excel Solver procedure
Microsoft Excel 8.0 Answer Report
Worksheet: [Calc2-07.xls]model
Target Cell (Max)

Cell	Name	Original value	Final value
V22	Total incident energy, Wh/m2	484	660

Adjustable cells

Cell	Name	Original value	Final value
C5	Aspect (due north)	180	164
C6	Tilt	90	20

Constraints

Cell	Name	Cell value	Formula
C6	Tilt	20	C6 < =90
C6	Tilt	20	C6 > =10

It is worth mentioning that the Solver procedure requires a longer time to set up the problem than the time taken by iterations. The iterations required to reach a suitable solution are dependent on the precision of constraints, integer tolerance, variable scaling and the solution method. Readers may experiment with these settings to get a better grasp of the mechanics of this procedure.

References

ASHRAE (1993) *Handbook of Fundamentals*. American Society of Heating, Refrigerating and Air-conditioning Engineers. Atlanta, Georgia, USA.

CIBSE (1982) *CIBSE Guide*. Chartered Institution of Building Services Engineers, London.

Cole, R. and Sturrock, N. (1977) The convective heat exchange at the external surface of buildings. *Building and Environment* 12(4), 207–214.

Gronbeck, C. (1998) http://solstice.crest.org/software-central/html/forum.shtml

Hallberg, B., Kinkoph, S., Ray, B. and Nielsen, J. (1997) Special edition: *Using Microsoft Excel 97*. Que Corporation, Santa Rosa, California.

Hanley, H., McCarty, R. and Haynes, W. (1974) The viscosity and thermal conductivity coefficients for dense gases and liquid Argon, Krypton, Xenon, Nitrogen and Oxygen. *J. Phys. Chem.* 3, 979.

Harris, M. (1997) *Visual Basic for Applications 5*, 3rd edn. Sams Publishing, Indianapolis.

Ito, N., Kimura, K. and Oka, J. (1972) A field experiment study on the convective heat transfer coefficient on exterior surface of a building. Proc. ASHRAE Semi-annual meeting. New Orleans.

Liengme, B. V. (1997) *A Guide to Microsoft Excel for Scientists and Engineers.* Wiley, New York.

Loveday, D. L. and Taki, A. H. (1998) Outside surface resistance: Proposed new value for building design. *BSER&T* 19, 23–29.

McBride, P. K. (1997) *Introductory Visual Basic*, 2nd edn. Letts Educational, London.

Microsoft (1992) *Microsoft Excel User's Guide 2.* Microsoft Corporation, Seattle.

Microsoft (1995a) *Microsoft Excel/Visual Basic Programmer's Guide.* Microsoft Press, Redmond, Washington.

Microsoft (1995b) *Fortran Power Station Programmer's Guide.* Microsoft Corporation, Seattle.

Muneer, T. (1997) *Solar Radiation and Daylight Models for Energy Efficient Design of Buildings.* Butterworth-Heinemann, Oxford.

PE (1998) *Professional Engineering*, IMechE, London, 7 October 1998, 39–40.

Person, R. (1992) *Using Excel 4 for Windows.* Que Corporation, Santa Rosa, California.

Sharples, S. (1982) *Modelling the heat transfer through opaque building components for the detailed computation of thermal performance under varying climatic conditions.* Internal Report BS63. Department of Building Science, University of Sheffield.

3 THERMAL PROPERTIES OF WINDOWS

Recently greatly improved performance has been demanded of the building fabric in general and of the window in particular. Due to these requirements, window research has developed very rapidly over the last decade. Within the United Kingdom the Glass and Glazing Federation based in London, the Centre for Window and Cladding Technology in Bath, the Advanced Glazing Industry Club in Oxford, and the Building Research Establishment in Watford are all engaged in window research. In the USA the Lawrence Berkeley Laboratory at Berkley has undertaken pioneering research work related to window technology.

Over the last decade significant advances have been made in glazing technology and numerous new designs and new materials have been incorporated by the multiple glazing window industry. The most valuable advance in multiple glazed window technologies is the low-emissivity coated (low-e) glass and the use of heavier gases. For example, air (molecular mass, $M = 28.96$) is being replaced by argon ($M = 39.95$) in the UK, by krypton ($M = 83.8$) in the USA and Switzerland and by xenon ($M = 131.3$) in Germany. Table 3.0.1 shows the market share of gas-filled multiple-glazing windows in some European countries. The percentage market share of these inert gases has increased considerably in all the countries and it is over one quarter of the total sales within Belgium and Germany. The use of the above new technologies has dramatically changed the thermal performance of buildings and the way in which buildings utilise solar energy and daylight.

Table 3.0.1 Market share of gas filled multiple-glazed windows in Europe (Han, 1996) (%)

	1986	1987	1988
Sweden	10	12	14
Finland	10	12	14
Denmark	15	20	20
Great Britain	1	3	4
Belgium	20	25	25
Germany	20	25	25

3.1 Thermal comfort

Thermal comfort is often defined as that condition of mind that expresses satisfaction with the prevailing thermal environment (ASHRAE, 1985). This definition emphasises that comfort is a psychological phenomenon and not related just to physical environment or physiological state (Parsons, 1993). The feelings of thermal comfort or discomfort reported by humans are complex and are not completely understood. The human response to thermal environments is affected by four basic environmental parameters (air temperature, radiant temperature, humidity and air movement) and two personal parameters (the metabolic heat generated by human activity and clothing worn by a person). Humans respond to the interaction of these six parameters. Thermal comfort is often assessed in terms of air temperature alone but, in fact, it is not exclusively a function of air temperature as the other five parameters are also relevant. For example, thermal comfort in offices or vehicles may be greatly affected by solar radiation and specifying comfort limits in terms of air temperature alone will be inadequate (Parsons, 1993). When humans become thermally uncomfortable, health and productivity can be affected, morale can fall and workers may refuse to work in such an environment. For this reason, there has been interest in research into the conditions which produce thermal comfort.

Heat transfer into the body and generated within it must be balanced by heat outputs from the body in order to maintain the body's internal temperature at around 37°C. The heat balance equation for the human body can be represented in the following form (Fanger, 1973):

$$S = MET + W \pm RAD \pm C \pm K - E - RES \qquad (3.1.1)$$

where

C = rate of heat exchange by convection, W
E = rate of heat loss by evaporation, W
K = rate of heat exchange by conduction, W
MET = metabolic rate, W
RAD = rate of heat exchange by radiation, W
RES = rate of heat exchange by respiration, W
S = rate of heat storage, W
W = rate of external work, W

A heat balance is reached if the rate of heat storage $S = 0$. The above equation then suggests the way to establish equilibrium. A human has to adjust his/her clothing and activity and regulate his/her position with regard to heat sources (artificial or natural) in order to meet their requirements. In hot climates, consideration is generally given to how to cool indoor environments to provide thermal comfort. In cooler climates, consideration is given to how to heat environments.

A modern building is expected to provide a satisfactory thermal environment. Windows, as key elements of building construction, influence occupant thermal comfort by heat gain or heat loss through the glass, which either raises or lowers the room air temperature, and by radiation exchange between occupant and the glass and other surroundings.

For an occupant close to a window, the temperature of the internal glass surface influences thermal comfort as a result of heat loss produced by long wavelength radiation exchange between the occupant and the window (Button and Pye, 1993). In winter, the long wavelength radiation exchange between the cold surface of window glass and the occupant contributes to a sensation of cold discomfort. In summer, the situation is reversed, the internal surface of glass can be much hotter due to the absorption of solar radiation. The long wavelength radiation exchanged between the window glass and the occupant and also direct short wavelength solar radiation received by the body through the glass contribute to a sensation of hot discomfort. Traditionally, excessive window area with inappropriate or non-functioning solar control systems was to be avoided in order to improve thermal comfort and reduce heating plant capacity and running costs. Windows (of, say, up to 30% of main facade area) with simple, usable blinds and control devices were preferred (CIBSE, 1989).

The dry resultant temperature t_{res} is commonly used to describe the environmental conditions. It represents the temperature at any point in the room as influenced by the mean radiant temperature of the surrounding surfaces t_r, the air temperature t_{air} and the air velocity v (m/s). The dry resultant temperature can be calculated from the following formula

$$t_{res} = \frac{t_{air}\sqrt{10v + t_r}}{1 + \sqrt{10v}} \qquad (3.1.2)$$

where

t_{air} = air temperature, °C
v = air velocity, m/s
t_{res} = dry resultant temperature, °C
t_r = mean radiant temperature of the surrounding surfaces, °C

For indoor still air conditions a simpler formulation, $t_{res} = 0.5\,(t_{air} + t_r)$, is often used. During summer, the higher the window surface temperature, which arises from the absorption of solar radiation and higher temperature of the outside air, the higher the mean radiant temperature and the higher the dry resultant temperature and, consequently, the less comfortable the room.

Wray (1980) has presented a simple procedure for determining the comfort criteria in passive solar buildings and has shown that the optimum uniform comfort temperature for an office environment lies between 18 and 26°C. He also has established the following relationship:

$$t_{res} = 0.45t_r + 0.55t_{air} \qquad (3.1.3)$$

3.2 Thermal transmission of multiple-glazed windows

Double-glazed windows were recognised about a hundred years ago as an essential requirement for energy conservation and thermal comfort within buildings. All research so far undertaken on double-glazed windows has aimed to improve their thermal characteristics and hence reduce the overall heat loss from buildings. Thermal performance is the key issue of a multiple-glazed window. For example, a double-glazed window with a 20 mm air gap will reduce heat loss by up to about half compared with a single-glazed window. However, if the double-glazed window is also coated with one low-e coating and the air is replaced with argon, the heat loss can be reduced to a quarter of the single-glazed window (Muneer and Han, 1994). Thus through the use of new technologies, the indoor environment can be dramatically improved.

Heat exchange between buildings and their surroundings occurs in two ways. Firstly, heat transfers to or from a building due to the temperature difference between the building and its surroundings. This exchange can take place by conduction, convection or radiation, individually or in combination. Secondly, heat transfers to or from a building due to air exchange through the gaps in the fabric.

The steady-state heat transfer through the fabric of a building may be obtained through the analysis given below. In northern countries, winter conditions tend to govern building design. It is therefore usual to denote the rate of heat transfer from a building to the outside as positive, i.e.

$$q_F = U_F A_F \Delta T \qquad (3.2.1)$$

where

q_F = fabric heat loss rate, W
U_F = fabric thermal transmittance or U-value, W/m^{2}K
A_F = surface area of fabric, m^2
ΔT = temperature difference between the inside and outside air, K

The thermal transmittance, U_F, is given by

$$\frac{1}{U_F} = \frac{1}{h_{si}} + \Sigma R + \frac{1}{h_{so}} \qquad (3.2.2)$$

where

h_{si} = heat transfer coefficient for the fabric inside surface, W/m^2K
h_{so} = heat transfer coefficient for the fabric outside surface, W/m^2K
$\sum R$ = sum of the resistances of the individual layers of the fabric, m^2K/W

The thermal transmittances for a wide range of building components are given, for example, in CIBSE Guides (CIBSE, 1986, 1989).

In any building there is an infiltration and exfiltration of air due to unavoidable gaps in the construction. The rate of air movement into and out of any space within a building depends on the pressure differences, which in turn are affected by wind direction and speed around the building. In steady state, the mass flow rate of air into the space (kg/s), $\dot{m}$, can be calculated as

$$\dot{m} = \rho_i \dot{V}_i \qquad (3.2.3)$$

where ρ_i is the density of air entering the building space (kg/m³) and $\dot{V}_i$ is the volume flow rate of air entering the building space (m³/s).

The rate of energy transfer due to air movement, or the ventilation energy transfer rate (W), q_v, is

$$q_v = \dot{m}c_p(T_i - T_o) \qquad (3.2.4)$$

where c_p is the specific heat of air at constant pressure (J/kgK), T_i is the internal temperature (°C) and T_o is the external temperature (°C).

The term air change rate is frequently used in air movement calculations and is expressed as

$$n = 3600 \frac{\dot{V}_i}{V} \qquad (3.2.5)$$

where

n = air change rate per hour, $hour^{-1}$
V = volume of the space, m^3

A certain number of air changes are required to maintain fresh, comfortable conditions inside any occupied space. In winter the air from outside is heated as it enters the space and then leaves the space at the room temperature, so the net energy transfer rate is known as the ventilation loss, q_v. Combining Eqs (3.2.3) and (3.2.5) and substituting into Eq. (3.2.4) yields

$$q_v = \frac{1}{3600}\rho_i c_p n V(T_i - T_o) \qquad (3.2.6)$$

For atmospheric air over the normal inside temperature and humidity range, the mean value of the product $\rho_i c_p$ is approximately equal to 1200 J/m^{3}K. Hence as a good approximation for normal ventilation conditions, Eq. (3.2.6) can be written as:

$$q_v = \frac{1}{3} nV(T_i - T_o) \tag{3.2.7}$$

In accordance with Eqs (3.2.1) and (3.2.2), heat loss from windows is quantified by the thermal transmittance or U-value. The total thermal transmittance of windows, U_o, consists of three components arising from the glazing unit, frame, and the spacer between panes. These components can be measured or calculated separately.

Using area-weighted U-values for each contribution, the *ASHRAE Handbook of Fundamentals* (ASHRAE, 1993) provides Eq. (3.2.8) for the calculation of the overall U-value of a fenestration:

$$U_o = (UA_{cg} + U_{eg}A_{eg} + U_f A_f)/A_{pf} \tag{3.2.8}$$

where

A_{cg} = projected area of glazing, m^2
A_{eg} = projected area of edge-seal, m^2
A_f = projected area of frame, m^2
A_{pf} = projected area of the entire fenestration, m^2
U = centre-glass U-value, W/m^{2}K
U_{eg} = edge-of-glass U-value, W/m^{2}K
U_f = frame U-value, W/m^{2}K
U_o = overall U-value of the window, W/m^{2}K

3.2.1   Centre of glass thermal analysis

To understand the heat loss mechanism through glazing, it is worth while to start by analysing the heat loss through a single-glazed window. Since, in general, cold weather conditions govern the design of windows it is usual to assume that heat is transferred from the building to the outside atmosphere. In a single-glazed window, there are three identifiable regions associated with the heat loss through a window: these are conduction through the glass pane and combined convection and radiation on either side of the pane.

3.2.1.1   Heat transfer to the internal glass surface

Heat is lost from the room to the internal glass surface whenever the glass surface is at a lower temperature than the internal air temperature and the room surface temperature. This heat is transferred in two ways:

- By exchange of long wavelength radiation between the glass surface and the room surfaces.
- By convection and/or conduction from the room air moving over the surface of the glass.

The greater heat loss is usually that due to radiation exchange unless the glass surface has a low-emissivity coating.

3.2.1.2   Heat transfer through the glass

In this case heat transfer is by conduction. The resistance of glass to heat transfer is relatively low and this can be calculated as follows:

$$R_g = \frac{L_g}{k_g} \qquad\qquad (3.2.1.1)$$

where

R_g = glass thermal resistance, m^2K/W
L_g = glass thickness, m
k_g = glass thermal conductivity, normally taken as 1.0 W/mK

3.2.1.3   Heat transfer from the outer glass surface

As with the inner glass surface, heat transfer from the outer glass surface is by long wavelength radiation exchange to the outside surroundings and by convection and/or conduction to the air moving over the exterior surface of the glass. The heat transfer at this surface varies considerably and is climate dominated (Button and Bye, 1993). The long wavelength radiation exchange depends on the temperature of the surfaces of the outside surroundings and on the sky temperature. With clear skies, the sky temperature can be extremely low. This effect is demonstrated by the formation of dew and frost on surfaces exposed to clear skies due to their cooling below the ambient air temperature. The rate of heat transfer by convection/conduction is usually high due to the influence of wind, particularly on exposed sites. Wind-driven rain will further increase the heat loss due to contact cooling and evaporation.

An effective method for reducing window heat loss is to add a second pane of glass separated from the first pane by a sealed space. The gap and the additional pane increase the thermal resistance of the window. The sealed gap provides a significant thermal resistance due to the low thermal conductivity of the infill gas compared with glass. The additional pane also provides added thermal resistance to long wavelength radiation exchange. Figure 3.2.1 illustrates the mechanism for heat loss through double-glazed units.

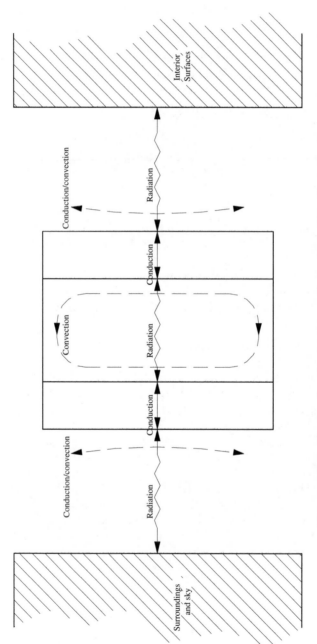

Figure 3.2.1 *Mechanism for heat loss through double-glazed units*

The thermal transmittance, U-value, for multiple-glazed windows can be calculated using the procedure outlined in BS 6993 (British Standards Institution, 1989). The U-value obtained can then be substituted into Eq. (3.2.1) to calculate the heat loss through the window. Present research work is targeted to the achievement of U-values of less than 0.4 W/m²K for windows of less than 30 mm total thickness. Such values are equivalent to those generally required by legislation for wall installation (Button and Bye, 1993).

3.2.1.4 U-value computation based on BS 6993

$$U = \frac{1}{\left[\frac{1}{h_{so}} + \frac{1}{h_t} + \frac{1}{h_{si}}\right]} \qquad (3.2.1.2)$$

where

h_t = conductance of multiple glazed unit, W/m²K

$$\frac{1}{h_t} = \sum_{s}^{N} \frac{1}{h_s} + L_g r_g \qquad (3.2.1.3)$$

where

h_s = cavity heat transfer coefficient, W/m²K
N = number of window cavities
L_g = total thickness of glass panes, m
r_g = thermal resistivity of glass, m K/W

$$h_s = h_c + h_r \qquad (3.2.1.4)$$

where

h_c = infill gas convection heat transfer coefficient, W/m²K
h_r = radiation heat transfer coefficient within the cavity, W/m²K

The infill gas convection heat transfer coefficient (h_c) will be discussed later in this chapter in more detail.

The radiation conductance (h_r) for each cavity is given as:

$$h_r = 4\sigma \left[\frac{1}{\varepsilon_o} + \frac{1}{\varepsilon_i} - 1\right]^{-1} T_f^3 \qquad (3.2.1.5)$$

where

σ = Stefan–Boltzmann constant, W/m²K⁴
ε_o = emissivity of the outer pane

ε_i = emissivity of the inner pane

T_f = absolute temperature corresponding to the average of the mean pane temperatures, K

The effective emissivities of the surfaces bounding each enclosed gas space are required in order to calculate h_r. The effective emissivity is 0.845 for un-coated glass surfaces (BS 6993) and range from 0.05 to 0.12 for low-emissivity coated glass surfaces. The latter values are frequently quoted by the respective manufacturers.

The external heat transfer coefficient, h_{so} is a function of mean wind speed. It also depends on wind direction as demonstrated experimentally by Sharples (1982) and Ito et al. (1972). Chapter 2 provides further information on models for obtaining h_{so}. Figure 3.2.2 shows the variation of surface convection coefficient against wind speed and direction. The external heat transfer coefficient, h_{so}, varies around 12.5, 16.7 and 33.3 W/m^{2}K corresponding respectively to the three conditions of exposure: sheltered, normal and severe. Sheltered condition corresponds to the third floor of buildings in urban centres. Normal condition is adopted for most suburban and rural buildings or the fourth to eighth floors of buildings in urban centres. Severe condition is applicable only for buildings on coastal or hill sites or above the fifth floor in suburban or rural areas or windows above the ninth floor in urban centres. Normally, the exterior heat transfer coefficient h_{so} is standardised to

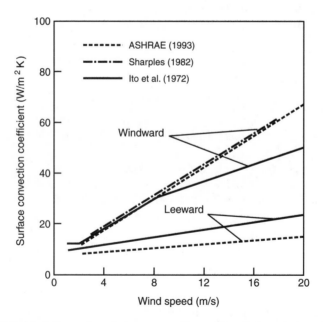

Figure 3.2.2 *Variation of surface convection with wind speed and direction*

16.7 W/m^{2}K for the purposes of comparison of glazing U-value for the vertical windows.

The internal heat transfer coefficient h_{si} is given by the expression

$$h_{si} = h_{ri} + h_{ci} \qquad\qquad (3.2.1.6)$$

where

h_{ri} = internal radiation heat transfer coefficient, W/m^{2}K
h_{ci} = internal convection heat transfer coefficient, W/m^{2}K

The radiation heat transfer coefficient for normal glass surfaces is 5.3 W/m^{2}K (BS 6993, 1989). If the interior surface of the glazing has a low hemispherical emissivity, the radiation coefficient h_{ri} is given by:

$$h_{ri} = 5.3 \times \frac{\varepsilon_h}{0.83} \qquad\qquad (3.2.1.7)$$

where ε_h = hemispherical emissivity of the coated surface.

The value of h_{ci} is 3.0 W/m^{2}K for natural convection at vertical surfaces. When a fan-blown heater is situated below or above a window, this value will be larger. Hence for ordinary glass surfaces and natural convection the value of $h_{si} = 8.3$ W/m^{2}K is usually assumed. Once again this is a standardised value for the purpose of comparing glazing U-values.

3.2.2   Edge of glass and frame thermal analysis

Any glazed aperture (fenestration) in a building envelope usually consists of glazing material, frame and shading system. The total rate of heat transfer through a fenestration system can be calculated knowing the separate heat transfer contributions of the centre-glass, edge-seal and frame. Thermally poor edge-seals and frames may increase the heat loss through the window and impair its overall U-value and, moreover, reduce the temperature in the vicinity of the edge-seal substantially, thus increasing the possibility of condensation occurrence on the inner pane.

As mentioned previously, the thermal performance of double-glazed windows has recently seen dramatic improvements. It is crucial that these improvements are accompanied by a parallel development in edge-seal (spacer) and frame technology.

The most widely used spacers in multiple-glazed units fall into one of the following classes:

- aluminium spacer
- steel spacer
- metal spacer with thermal break

- fibreglass/plastic spacer
- butyl spacer
- foam spacer

The products most commonly used in Europe are either hollow aluminium extrusions or roll-formed galvanised steel sections.

Spacers in multipane units greatly increase conductive heat transfer between the contacted inner and outer glazing. This phenomenon, called cold-bridging, degrades the thermal performance of the glazing unit locally. Laboratory measurements have shown that the conductive region of edge-seal is limited to a 65 mm wide band around the perimeter of the glazing unit (ASHRAE, 1993). The latter reference provides Eq. (3.2.2.1) for the calculation of the edge-of-glass *U*-value as a function of spacer type and centre-glass *U*-value:

$$U_{eg} = A + BU + CU^2 \tag{3.2.2.1}$$

where *A*, *B* and *C* are correlation coefficients. Table 3.2.1 gives values for *A*, *B* and *C* for metal, insulating (including wood) and fused glass spacers, and a combination of insulating and metal spacers.

The thermal conductivity of the aluminium spacer is much higher than that of a foam spacer. The *U*-value improvement for the foam spacer over the aluminium design is of the order of 0.1–0.2 W/m²K for most types of frames and glazing (Aschehoug and Baker, 1995). Using more insulative spacer helps in increasing edge zone temperatures on the inside, thus significantly reducing the risk of condensation.

Frame *U*-values for a variety of frame and spacer materials and glazing unit thickness are given in ASHRAE (1993). ASHRAE's procedure has been incorporated within the Calc3-01a.xls workbook. Example 3.3.1 below demonstrates the calculation of the centre-glazing, edge and frame heat loss.

Estimating the rate of heat transfer through the frame is complicated by:

- the variety of fenestration products and frame configurations
- the different combinations of the materials used for frames
- the different sizes available in residential and commercial applications
- the glazing unit width and spacer type

Table 3.2.1 Coefficients for edge-of-glass *U*-value (ASHRAE, 1993)

Spacer Type	A	B	C
Metal	1.266	0.842	−0.027
Insulating	0.681	0.682	0.043
Glass	0.897	0.774	0.010
Metal + insulating	0.769	0.706	0.033

Aschehoug and Baker (1995) measured the frame U-values for different window configurations. Such experimental results, shown in Table 3.2.2, demonstrate that the frame U-values are generally greater than the centre-glass U-values shown in Table 3.2.3.

The thermal conductivity of edge-seals as determined by Svendsen and Fritzel (1995) do not consider all modes of heat transfer involved within the window. Heat is transferred by radiation and also by convection of the surrounding air and of the infill gas within the window cavity. It can be concluded that better spacers help increase the temperature on the bottom edge of the inside pane and hence reduce the risk of condensation.

Frank and Wakili (1995) used a two-dimensional finite difference model to determine the linear thermal transmittance coefficient, ψ_g, for different frame and spacer bar types. They have proposed Eq. (3.2.2.2) to obtain U_o. Thus,

$$U_o = \frac{UA_{cg} + U_f A_f + \psi_g l_g}{A_{cg} + A_f} \tag{3.2.2.2}$$

Table 3.2.2 Typical frame U-values (W/m^{2}K) for conventional windows (Aschehoug and Baker, 1995)

Frame material	Spacer type	Frame type/number of panes Operable			Fixed		
		Single	Double	Triple	Single	Double	Triple
Aluminium	Aluminium	12.4	12.4	12.4	10.1	10.1	10.1
Aluminium	Aluminium	5.4	5.4	5.4	6.6	6.6	6.6
with thermal break	insulated	–	4.9	4.9	–	5.2	5.2
Aluminium clad wood,	Aluminium	3.9	3.6	3.3	3.2	3.0	2.8
reinforced vinyl	insulated	–	3.2	2.7	–	2.6	2.3
Wood, vinyl	Aluminium	3.1	2.9	2.7	2.9	2.8	2.7
	insulated	–	2.6	2.2	–	2.4	2.1
Fibreglass	Aluminium	2.7	2.5	2.3	2.6	2.3	2.0
	insulated	–	2.2	1.8	–	2.1	1.6

Table 3.2.3 Typical centre-glass U-values for conventional high-performance glazing (Aschehoug and Baker, 1995)

Glazing system	Centre-glass U-value (W/m^{2}K)
Double glazing, air filled	2.78
Double glazing, low-e, air filled	1.99
Double glazing, low-e, argon filled	1.70
Triple glazing, air filled	1.76
Triple glazing, low-e, air filled	1.36
Triple glazing, low-e, argon filled	1.19
Quadruple glazing, low-e, krypton filled	0.62

where

l_g = length of inner perimeter of window frame, m
ψ_g = linear thermal transmittance due to the combined thermal effects of the spacer, glazing and frame, W/mK

The frame and the centre-glass U-value are independent of each other and, therefore, can be measured or calculated separately. Table 3.2.4(a)–(c) shows the linear thermal transmittance ψ_g obtained by Frank and Wakili (1995) for the three different spacer bars.

Introducing new spacer materials such as silicon foam or thin stainless steel profiles can reduce ψ_g by up to 50% and therefore cause a rise of the surface temperatures of the glass edge which will reduce the risk of condensation (Frank and Wakili, 1995).

None of the above numerical methods for analysing frame and edge-seal heat loss, however, take account of infill gas convection and as such cannot be used to determine the minimum indoor pane temperature required to assess the condensation occurrence on a window. Local variations in surface temperature

Table 3.2.4(a) ψ_g values for aluminium spacer in W/mK (Frank and Wakili, 1995)

Glazing U-value W/m²K	Wood/PVC frame	Metal frame without thermal break	Metal frame with thermal break
DGW[*] > 2.7	0.04	0.06	0.00
DGW 2.2	0.05	0.07	0.01
DGW 1.6	0.06	0.08	0.02
DGW 1.0	0.07	0.09	0.03
TGW[**] > 2.1	0.04	0.06	0.00
TGW 1.6	0.05	0.07	0.01
TGW 1.0	0.06	0.08	0.02

[*] Double-glazed window
[**] Triple-glazed window

Table 3.2.4(b) ψ_g values for stainless steel spacer in W/mK (Frank and Wakili, 1995)

Glazing U-value W/m²K	Wood/PVC frame	Metal frame without thermal break	Metal frame with thermal break
DGW* > 2.6	0.03	0.04	0.00
DGW 2.0	0.04	0.05	0.01
DGW 1.4	0.05	0.06	0.02
TGW** > 2.0	0.03	0.04	0.00
TGW 1.4	0.04	0.05	0.01
TGW 0.7	0.05	0.06	0.02

[*] Double-glazed window
[**] Triple-glazed window

Table 3.2.4(c) ψ_g values for foam spacer in W/mK (Frank and Wakili, 1995)

Glazing U-value W/m²K	Wood/PVC frame	Metal frame without thermal break	Metal frame with thermal break
DGW* >2.2	0.02	0.03	0.00
DGW 1.3	0.03	0.04	0.01
TGW** >1.7	0.02	0.03	0.00
TGW 0.8	0.03	0.04	0.01

*Double-glazed window
**Triple-glazed window

can be found using very detailed numerical methods (Wright and Sullivan, 1995; Curcija and Goss, 1994) but this approach is very laborious. Any model attempting to quantify local heat transfer rates in the bottom region of a double-glazed window or any model intended to determine the temperature distribution across the face of the glazing must account for both the natural convection of the infill gas and conduction within the edge-seal, glass and frame components.

Wright and Sulivan (1995) provide a numerical, two-dimensional conduction analysis for the frame and edge-seal which can be extended to account for infill gas motion. Their method requires a computational fluid dynamics (CFD) procedure to determine the infill gas flow pattern.

Muneer et al. (1997) have developed numerical models for the heat transfer at the bottom edge of a double-glazed window. These models combine the effects of radiative energy exchange between the glass panes, natural convection due to circulating gas and conduction through the edge-seal and frame. This is in contrast to previous work that solely addressed the edge-seal conduction effects (Frank and Wakili, 1995; Svendsen and Fritzel, 1995). These models will be explained later in this chapter.

3.3   Free convection analysis for an enclosure

The free convection flow inside an enclosed space is a complex phenomenon. In heat transfer science this is known as the conjugate problem. Analytical, empirical and numerical solutions are usually required in dealing with such problems, e.g. multiple-glazed windows.

All multiple-glazed windows have one or more cavities. Each cavity contains a gas such as air, argon, krypton, xenon or sulphur hexafluoride. When the infill gas is subjected to a temperature difference across its boundaries, it starts to circulate within the cavity. The infill gas ascends along the hotter pane of glass and descends along the colder pane. Figure 3.3.1 shows a sectional view of a double-glazed window where a gas is contained between two vertical panes of glass separated by a distance, L. The two panes are maintained at different

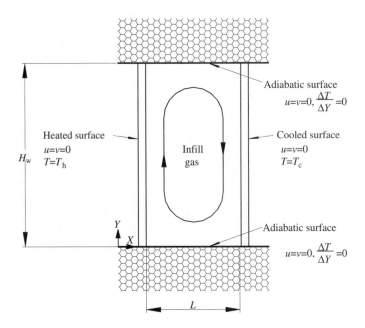

Figure 3.3.1 *The boundary conditions for the analysis of natural convection in an enclosed cavity*

temperatures ($T_h > T_c$), while the remaining walls are shown to be insulated from the surroundings.

3.3.1 Empirical correlations

The average free-convection heat transfer coefficient within the window cavity, h_c, is normally represented by the following formula:

$$h_c = \frac{Nu_L k}{L} \qquad (3.3.1.1)$$

where Nu_L is the Nusselt number based on the window cavity width (L) and k is the thermal conductivity of the infill gas. Note that at low Nusselt numbers heat transport takes place via effects of gas conduction and convection.

For free convection within an enclosure, the Nusselt number is generally obtained as follows:

$$Nu_L = cRa_L^n \qquad (3.3.1.2)$$

where c and n are constants and Ra_L is the Rayleigh number (based on the window cavity width, L) which is defined as

$$Ra_L = Gr_L Pr = \frac{g\beta(T_h - T_c)L^3}{\nu\alpha} \tag{3.3.1.3a}$$

$$Gr_L = \frac{g\beta(T_h - T_c)L^3}{\nu^2} \tag{3.3.1.3b}$$

$$Pr = \frac{\mu c_p}{k} \tag{3.3.1.3c}$$

$$\beta = \frac{1}{T_f} \tag{3.3.1.3d}$$

$$\alpha = \frac{k}{\rho c_p} \tag{3.3.1.3e}$$

$$\nu = \frac{\mu}{\rho} \tag{3.3.1.3f}$$

where

c_p = infill gas specific heat at constant pressure, J/kgK
g = gravitational acceleration, m/s^2
Gr_L = Grashof number (based on the characteristic length)
Pr = Prandtl number
T_c = cold pane temperature, K
T_h = hot pane temperature, K
ν = infill gas kinematic viscosity, m^2/s
α = infill gas thermal diffusivity, m^2/s
β = infill gas volumetric thermal expansion coefficient, K^{-1}
μ = infill gas dynamic viscosity, Ns/m^2
ρ = infill gas density, kg/m^3

All thermophysical properties of the infill gas are evaluated at the film temperature,

$$T_f = \frac{T_c + T_h}{2} \tag{3.3.1.4}$$

For small Rayleigh numbers, $Ra_L \leq 10^3$, the buoyancy-driven flow is weak and heat transfer is primarily by conduction across the infill gas. Practically speaking this limit is reached when the cavity width is 2–4 mm. The Nusselt number in this case is $Nu_L = 1$. With increasing Rayleigh number, the flow intensifies and becomes concentrated in thin boundary layers adjoining the two panes. The core becomes nearly stagnant, although additional cells can develop in the corners and side wall boundary layers eventually undergoing transition to turbulence (Bejan, 1984; Incropera and DeWitt, 1990).

Many correlations in the form of Eq. 3.3.1.2 have been developed to predict the heat transfer within a cavity. A few examples are given below.

- **MacGregor and Emery (1971)**

$$Nu_L = 0.046 Ra_L^{1/3} \qquad\qquad (3.3.1.5)$$

subject to $1 < A_r < 40$, $1 < Pr < 20$ and $10^6 < Ra_L < 10^9$

$$Nu_L = 0.42 Ra_L^{0.25} Pr^{0.012} A_r^{-0.3} \qquad\qquad (3.3.1.6)$$

subject to $10 < A_r < 40$, $1 < Pr < 2 \times 10^4$ and $10^4 < Ra_L < 10^7$

where A_r is the window aspect ratio, i.e. ratio of window height (H_w) to cavity width (L)

- **Raithby, Hollands and Unny (1977)**

$$Nu_L = \text{Max}[1, 0.75 C_i\{(\sin FRa_L)/A_r\}^{1/4}, 0.29 C_t(\sin FRa_L)^{1/3}] \qquad (3.3.1.7)$$

subject to $F > 70°$ and $3.5 \leq A_r \leq 110$ and where

$$C_i = 0.50/(1 + (0.49/Pr)^{9/16})^{4/9}, \quad C_t = \text{Min}[0.15, 0.14 Pr^{0.084}]$$

F is the angle of the enclosure cavity from the horizontal in degrees.

- **El-Sherbiny, Hollands and Raithby (1982)**

$$Nu_L = \text{Max}[1, 0.288(Ra_L/A_r)^{1/4}, 0.062 Ra_L^{1/3}] \qquad\qquad (3.3.1.8)$$

subject to $A_r \leq 110$

- **Inaba (1984)**

$$Nu_L = \text{Max}[1, 0.271 A_r^{-0.21}(Ra_L \sin F)^{0.25}] \qquad\qquad (3.3.1.9)$$

subject to $5 \times 10^3 \leq Ra_L \sin F \leq 1.2 \times 10^6$, and $5 \leq A_r \leq 83$

- **Wright (1990)**

$$Nu_L = \text{Max}[Nu_1, Nu_2] \qquad\qquad (3.3.1.10)$$

where

$$Nu_1 = 0.07 Ra_L^{1/3} \quad \text{subject to } 5 \times 10^4 < Ra_L < 10^6$$

$$Nu_1 = 0.03 Ra_L^{0.4134} \quad \text{subject to } 10^4 < Ra_L \leq 5 \times 10^4$$

$$Nu_1 = 1 + 1.76 \times 10^{-10} Ra_L^{2.298} \quad \text{subject to } Ra_L \leq 10^4$$

$$Nu_2 = 0.242 [Ra_L / A_r]^{0.272} \quad \text{subject to } A_r \leq 110$$

- **Muneer and Han (1996a)**

$$Nu_L = \text{Max}[1, \ 0.36(Gr_L Pr)^{0.245} A_r^{-0.28}] \tag{3.3.1.11}$$

The critical path of thermal network in a multiple-glazed window with low-e coated panes is h_c (Muneer and Han, 1996a). Thus the control of this parameter will yield beneficial savings in the energy consumption due to space heating load. Figure 3.3.2 provides design charts based on Eq. (3.3.1.11) and shows the relationship between h_c, temperature differential, cavity width and the window height.

3.3.2 CFD work

Convection in a sealed glazing unit is complicated as it is affected by many parameters, such as the width of the cavity, the height of the cavity, the temperatures of the hot and cold panes, the temperature differential and, most importantly, the properties of the infill gases. Traditionally, heat transfer characteristics of multiple-glazed windows were researched using experimental methods. Due to economic and efficiency advantages, computer modelling has, however, now gained favour.

The usefulness of CFD computer modelling in window research has been proven world-wide by several researchers (Curcija and Goss, 1994; Wright and Sullivan, 1995; Muneer and Han, 1995a), especially for two-dimensional modelling.

Heat transfer in a multiple-glazing system consists of fully coupled convective and radiation heat transfer in the cavity of the insulated glazing unit and conduction heat transfer in the solid parts. Furthermore, the exterior window surfaces are exposed to forced (outdoor) and natural (indoor) convective heat transfer. Convective heat transfer within a window cavity may be laminar, turbulent or in the transition regime between laminar and turbulent.

Most current models (Curcija and Goss, 1994; Wright and Sullivan, 1995) of heat transfer for a fenestration system are limited to two dimensions – along the height and depth of the enclosure cavity. This assumption reduces the number of variables that need to be considered and, at least qualitatively, gives all the features of the physical processes. Methods for improving the design of

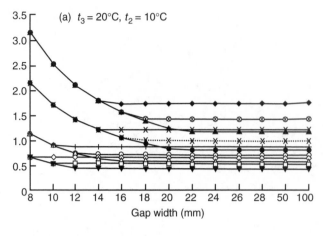

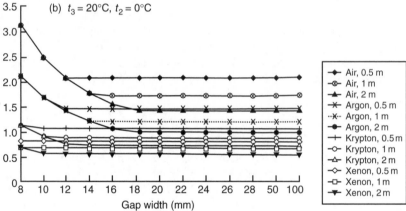

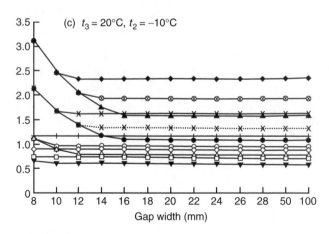

Figure 3.3.2 *Cavity convection heat transfer coefficient (W/m²K). The boxed text indicates the infill gas and the cavity height*

the window system can be developed by looking at the distribution of the local heat flux on the indoor and outdoor window surfaces and the motion of the flow to identify areas with high heat transfer rates.

The physical balances for laminar two-dimensional gas flow can be described mathematically by assuming that the fluid is Newtonian with compressibility and viscous dissipation effects neglected and the fluid properties treated as constant except in the formulation of the buoyancy term (Shaw, 1992; Kakac et al., 1985; Incropera and DeWitt, 1990). The partial differential equations which describe the conservation of energy, momentum and mass at any given point in the flow within a vertical cavity are:

$$\rho Cp \left\{ \frac{\partial T}{\partial t} + u \frac{\partial T}{\partial x} + v \frac{\partial T}{\partial y} \right\} = k \left\{ \frac{\partial^2 T}{\partial x^2} + \frac{\partial^2 T}{\partial y^2} \right\} \qquad (3.3.2.1)$$

$$\rho \left\{ \frac{\partial u}{\partial t} + u \frac{\partial u}{\partial x} + v \frac{\partial u}{\partial y} \right\} = \mu \left\{ \frac{\partial^2 u}{\partial x^2} + \frac{\partial^2 u}{\partial y^2} \right\} - \frac{\partial p}{\partial x} \qquad (3.3.2.2)$$

$$\rho \left\{ \frac{\partial v}{\partial t} + u \frac{\partial v}{\partial x} + v \frac{\partial v}{\partial y} \right\} = \mu \left\{ \frac{\partial^2 v}{\partial x^2} + \frac{\partial^2 v}{\partial y^2} \right\} - \frac{\partial p}{\partial y} + \rho g \beta (T - T_{\mathrm{f}}) \qquad (3.3.2.3)$$

$$\frac{\partial u}{\partial x} + \frac{\partial v}{\partial y} = 0 \qquad (3.3.2.4)$$

Figure 3.3.1 shows the boundary condition of Muneer and Han's (1996a) model. Zero heat transfer has been assumed through the edge-seal areas, the warm and cold sides are set as isothermal.

$T = T_{\mathrm{h}}$ at $x = 0$

$T = T_{\mathrm{c}}$ at $x = L$

$\frac{\partial T}{\partial y} = 0$ at $y = 0$ and $y = H_{\mathrm{w}}$ (zero heat flux)

$u = v = 0$ at $y = 0$ $y = H_{\mathrm{w}}$ $x = 0$ and $x = L$

where

$u =$ velocity in x (horizontal) direction
$v =$ velocity in y (vertical) direction

Table 3.3.1 gives the details of the CFD test conditions and the results for the double-glazing heat transfer analysis. Plate 3.1 (see colour plate section) shows

Table 3.3.1 CFD results for enclosure convection coefficient h_c, W/m²K (Han, 1996) (refer to Figure 3.3.6 for notation)

Enclosure gap, mm	4	8	12	16	20	24	28	50
Air, 0.6 m height, $t_3 = 20°C$, $t_2 = 0°C$	6.25	3.16	2.2	1.9	1.9	1.99	2.07	2.13
Argon, 0.6 m height, $t_3 = 20°C$, $t_2 = 0°C$	4.05	2.05	1.47	1.31	1.34	1.38	1.4	1.38
Krypton, 0.6 m height, $t_3 = 20°C$, $t_2 = 0°C$	2.15	1.14	0.96	1.00	1.03	1.04	1.03	1.01
Xenon, 0.6 m height, $t_3 = 20°C$, $t_2 = 0°C$	1.21	0.74	0.73	0.76	0.77	0.76	0.75	0.75
Air, 1 m height, $t_3 = 20°C$, $t_2 = 0°C$	6.25	3.14	2.16	1.76	1.64	1.67	1.75	1.8
Air, 1 m height, $t_3 = 20°C$, $t_2 = 5°C$	6.25	3.14	2.14	1.71	1.53	1.52	1.57	1.66
Air, 1 m height, $t_3 = 20°C$, $t_2 = -5°C$	6.15	3.1	2.15	1.79	1.73	1.79	1.84	1.85
Air, 1 m height, $t_3 = 25°C$, $t_2 = 5°C$	6.3	3.17	2.17	1.76	1.63	1.65	1.7	1.77
Air, 1 m height, $t_3 = 15°C$, $t_2 = -5°C$	6.15	3.11	2.12	1.74	1.64	1.68	1.73	1.75
Air, 2.4 m height, $t_3 = 20°C$, $t_2 = 0°C$	–	–	–	1.68	1.49	–	–	–
Air, 2.4 m height, $t_3 = 20°C$, $t_2 = -10°C$	–	–	–	–	1.57	–	–	–
Air, 2.4 m height, $t_3 = 30°C$, $t_2 = -10°C$	–	–	–	–	1.19	–	–	–
Air, 2.4 m height, $t_3 = 30°C$, $t_2 = -20°C$	–	–	–	–	0.94	–	–	–

temperature and velocity raster plots of the convective flow within two air-filled cavities. These plots were obtained by Han (1996) as part of a contractual work undertaken for Living Design, a Glasgow-based double-glazing manufacturer. The plots demonstrate the transition from a conduction-dominant to convection-dominant regime as the cavity increases from 8 mm to 20 mm width. Plate 3.2 (see colour plate section) which includes velocity raster plots for a range of cavity widths of reinforces this point. The flow structure seems to get more complicated, with a thickening of the inactive core, as the width increases. In effect at widths of 50 mm or over the flow within the enclosure becomes channel flow. Hence further increase in the cavity width will have negligible effect on h_c.

Using the data of Table 3.3.1, the ratio of the convective thermal resistance for each window cavity to the convective thermal resistance for a 4 mm cavity has been plotted against window cavity width as shown in Figure 3.3.3. Several interesting points may be noted here. The change from a conductive to a convective flow of heat through the cavity is noticeable as the contour of the line changes from linear to curvilinear. Following this logic it may be noted that for heavier gases the onset of convection occurs at narrower cavities. This point will be explained more fully later in this chapter. The attenuation effects of the cavity height may also be noted for air-filled cavities. Once again a theoretical discussion on this point is provided later. Figure 3.3.4 compares the results of Muneer and Han's work with measured results for eight window samples.

3.3.2.1 The effect of infill gases on convection heat transfer

The use of inert gases can dramatically reduce the convective heat transfer coefficient. The optimum width (corresponding to minimum h_c) decreases with

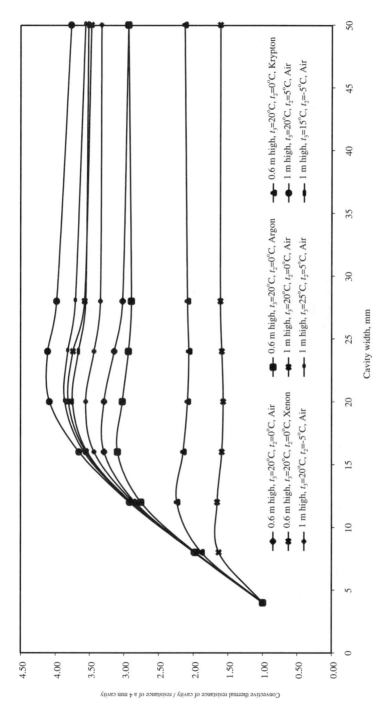

Figure 3.3.3 *Variation of the ratio of convective thermal resistance of window cavity to the resistance of a 4 mm cavity (see Figure 3.3.6)*

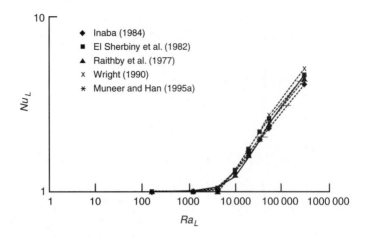

Figure 3.3.4 *Comparison of cavity convection models*

increasing molecular mass, M. For a given window height of 1 m the optimum width occurs at 8, 12, 16 and 20 mm for xenon, krypton, argon and air respectively (Muneer and Han, 1996a). This behaviour can be explained as follows. The buoyancy force, responsible for the ensuing convection, is proportional to the density differential between the cold and hot gas ($\rho_c - \rho_h$), in the immediate neighbourhood of the cold and hot sides of the enclosure. Using the ideal gas relationship Muneer and Han (1996b) have shown that

$$\rho_c - \rho_h = \frac{p}{\bar{R}}\left[\frac{1}{T_c} - \frac{1}{T_h}\right] M \qquad (3.3.2.5)$$

where

p = gas pressure, kPa
$\bar{R}$ = universal gas constant ($= 8.3144$ kJ/kmole K)
M = infill gas molecular mass, kg/kmole

For fixed p and T values, the above relationship shows that the driving buoyancy force is directly proportional to the molecular mass of the gas. With a heavier gas (larger buoyancy force) the onset of convection, as well as the point where h_c is minimum, occurs at reduced cavity width.

3.3.2.2   The effect of cavity width on convection heat transfer

Significant improvements in energy efficiency may be achieved by increasing the cavity width between two glazings. For small enclosure widths of say 4 mm, where almost all the energy is transported via conduction, the con-

ductive–convective coefficient drops sharply with increasing gap width. This is
due to conduction heat transfer resistance being directly proportional to the
thickness of the conducting material. Further increase in the gap width results
in a less rapid decrease in h_c and eventually h_c becomes almost constant.

3.3.2.3   The effect of window height on convection heat transfer

Figure 3.3.5 shows the effect of the increase in enclosure height on h_c. The
decrease in h_c with height has also been addressed by El-Sherbiny et al. (1982).
Experimental tests carried out by Rayment et al. (1992) shed further light on
this subject. Muneer and Han (1995b) have shown that for an air-filled window
of 20 mm cavity width under temperature conditions of 20°C on the warm side
and 0°C on the cold side, h_c for a 1 m high window cavity is 1.64 W/m²K and
for a 0.6 m high window $h_c = 1.90$ W/m²K. The decrease in h_c with height is
due to attenuation effects. The effect of window height, however, only applies
when convection dominates. In the conduction regime, there is practically no
effect.

3.3.2.4   The effect of temperature difference on convection heat transfer

By increasing the temperature difference, h_c increases. Muneer and Han
(1996a) have also illustrated this point graphically (Figure 3.3.2). The decrease
in the optimum gap occurs because when the temperature difference is in-

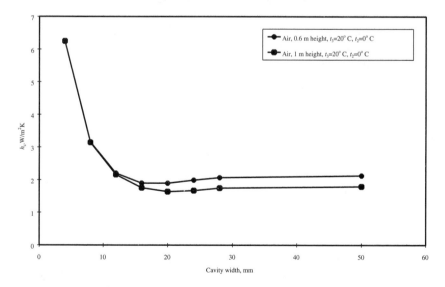

Figure 3.3.5 *Reduction of convection coefficient due to attenuation with
increased cavity height (see Figure 3.3.6)*

creased, the flow results in the motion of two increasingly independent boundary layers and this enables convection to dominate conduction effects at a smaller cavity width. This phenomenon has also been explained by Elder (1965) and Gill (1966). The temperature levels have no measurable impact on h_c as long as the temperature differential remains constant (Muneer and Han, 1996a).

3.3.2.5   The effect of low-emissivity coatings on glazing U-value

A low-emissivity (low-e) coating on the glass has the ability to reflect the longwave radiation. In air-filled cavities with uncoated surfaces, the longwave radiation exchange between glass surfaces is high, amounting to about 60% of the total heat exchange across the cavity. With one of the glass surfaces having a coating with emissivity less than 0.2 (compared with 0.88 for the uncoated glass surface), the radiation exchange is reduced by approximately 75% and consequently the *U*-value is reduced (Button and Pye, 1993).

3.3.3   Computer tools for obtaining window U-value

Excel workbooks Calc3-01 and Calc3-02 have been developed to respectively deal with analysis for double- and triple-glazing. Calc3-01a and Calc3-01b respectively provide approximate and precise solutions for double-glazed windows. The inputs are the internal and external ambient temperatures and the window specifications, e.g. window height, cavity width, infill gas type, pane thickness and emissivity of the coated surface.

If more accuracy is needed (see Calc3-01b.xls, one for each gas), the calculation is initiated by assuming a *U*-value for the glazing unit under consideration. An approximate *U*-value may be obtained from Calc3-01a. Next, the centre glazing temperature of the panes, t_1, t_2, t_3 and t_4 (see Figure 3.3.6), are calculated from the following equations:

$$t_1 = T_o + (1/h_{so})U[T_i - T_o] \tag{3.3.3.1}$$

$$t_2 = T_o + [R_{g1} + (1/h_{so})]U[T_i - T_o] \tag{3.3.3.2}$$

$$t_3 = T_i - [R_{g2} + (1/h_{si})]U[T_i - T_o] \tag{3.3.3.3}$$

$$t_4 = T_i - (1/h_{si})U[T_i - T_o] \tag{3.3.3.4}$$

The gas properties are determined at t_f using an average of t_2 and t_3.

The Nu_L and Gr_L numbers are then calculated using Eqs (3.3.1.11) and (3.3.1.3b) respectively. As mentioned previously, if the Nu_L number is less than unity, $Nu_L = 1$. Then h_r, h_c and h_t are calculated using the relevant equations in Section 3.2.1. h_{si} and h_{so} are given the standard values of 8.6 and 16.7 W/m^{2}K

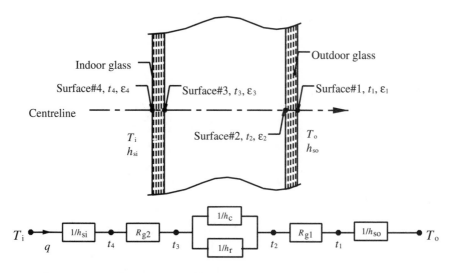

Figure 3.3.6 *Centreline thermal circuit for double-glazed windows*

respectively. Finally, the *U*-value is calculated from Eq. (3.2.1.2). The process is continued iteratively until convergence is achieved in the *U*-value.

Example 3.3.1

An argon-filled double-glazed window with a 12 mm cavity and 0.4 m height has one low-emissivity coating, $\varepsilon_2 = 0.12$ (see Figure 3.3.6). The internal and external ambient temperatures are 20°C and 0°C respectively. The thickness of each glass pane is 4 mm and the glass thermal conductivity is 1 W/mK. Compute the centre-glazing *U*-value using the approximate and precise methods.

The respective solutions are provided by workbooks Calc3-01a and Calc3-01bAr.xls. Launch workbook Calc3-01a and activate the sheet 'Ucg-Ar'. Insert the given data in cells C4:C14. The required centre-glazing *U*-value is 1.56 as shown in Cell E4. Note that Calc3-01a provides an approximate solution.

The Calc3-01a.xls workbook also enables calculation of the edge, frame and overall *U*-value. Activate the 'Ueg,Uf&Uo' sheet by clicking its tab. Provide the required input data in the cell range B3:B7. The requisite outputs are produced in the cell range B8:B14.

Launch the workbook Calc3-01bAr.xls. This workbook provides a precise solution. Activate the sheet 'Argon'. Insert the given data in cells C4:C18 as shown. The computed *U*-value is 1.54 (Cell E4).

Note that the results obtained by both methods are approximately the same. Thus, even an approximate solution would be adequate, at least at the preliminary design stage. The Calc3-01b family of workbooks also enables the investigation of the effect of wind speed on U-value. Within Calc3-01a the external wind resistance is set to the normal exposure conditions recommended by CIBSE (1986).

Example 3.3.2

Plot the temperature contours across the cavity for the following double-glazed windows. See Figure 3.3.6 to follow the notation. Note that a further visual aid is provided within Calc3-01b.xls.

Air filled, float glass ($\varepsilon_1 = 0.88$, $\varepsilon_2 = 0.88$, $\varepsilon_3 = 0.88$, $\varepsilon_4 = 0.88$)
Air filled, one low-e ($\varepsilon_1 = 0.88$, $\varepsilon_2 = 0.12$, $\varepsilon_3 = 0.88$, $\varepsilon_4 = 0.88$)
Argon filled, one low-e ($\varepsilon_1 = 0.12$, $\varepsilon_2 = 0.88$, $\varepsilon_3 = 0.88$, $\varepsilon_4 = 0.88$)
Argon filled, one low-e ($\varepsilon_1 = 0.88$, $\varepsilon_2 = 0.12$, $\varepsilon_3 = 0.88$, $\varepsilon_4 = 0.88$)
Argon filled, one low-e ($\varepsilon_1 = 0.88$, $\varepsilon_2 = 0.88$, $\varepsilon_3 = 0.12$, $\varepsilon_4 = 0.88$)
Argon filled, one low-e ($\varepsilon_1 = 0.88$, $\varepsilon_2 = 0.88$, $\varepsilon_3 = 0.88$, $\varepsilon_4 = 0.12$)
Krypton filled, one low-e ($\varepsilon_1 = 0.88$, $\varepsilon_2 = 0.05$, $\varepsilon_3 = 0.88$, $\varepsilon_4 = 0.88$)
Xenon filled, one low-e ($\varepsilon_1 = 0.88$, $\varepsilon_2 = 0.05$, $\varepsilon_3 = 0.88$, $\varepsilon_4 = 0.88$)

Note that manufacturers claim respective emissivities of 0.12 and 0.05 for SnO_2 and Ag coatings.

The solution has been obtained by using Calc3-01b for each of the above cases. Figure 3.3.7 shows the temperature contours for all cases. It may be

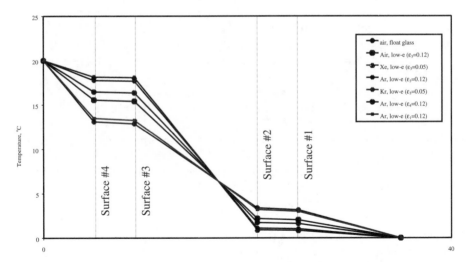

Figure 3.3.7 *Temperature variation along window depth (see Example 3.3.2 and Figure 3.3.6). Note that the bottom two cases in the box are presented by a common temperature profile*

noted that a significant improvement in the temperature of the inner glazing surface results with the use of low-e, inert gas-filled windows.

In cold climates, the low-e coating should be placed on surface number two of the double-glazed window (see Figure 3.3.6 for notation), so the energy absorbed by the low-e coating is conducted to the outer surface and removed away by the external air. In places where solar energy is not wanted, the low-e coating should not be placed on surface number three as it is easier for the energy absorbed by the coating to transfer into the room rather than across the cavity to the outside.

Example 3.3.3

A single bedroom in a detached house in Edinburgh, UK has a height of 2.3 m and a length of 3.4 m. The bedroom is 2.7 m wide. Along the width of the bedroom is an air-filled double-glazed window of 2.0 m width and 1.0 m height with a 12 mm cavity. Assume that the internal and external ambient temperatures are 15°C and 0°C respectively. The wind speed is assumed to be 3 m/s. Refer to the schematic drawing within sheet 'Air' of the workbook Calc3-01bAir.xls. The following data are provided: $L_{g12}=L_{g34}=4$ mm and $k_{g12}=k_{g34}=1.0$ W/mK. If the walls are assumed to be at the temperature of the internal air (t_s) find the dry resultant temperature, t_{res}, for the following cases:

Case 1: Air filled, float glass ($\varepsilon_1=0.88$, $\varepsilon_2=0.88$, $\varepsilon_3=0.88$, $\varepsilon_4=0.88$)
Case 2: Air filled, one low-e ($\varepsilon_1=0.12$, $\varepsilon_2=0.88$, $\varepsilon_3=0.88$, $\varepsilon_4=0.88$)
Case 3: Air filled, one low-e ($\varepsilon_1=0.88$, $\varepsilon_2=0.12$, $\varepsilon_3=0.88$, $\varepsilon_4=0.88$)
Case 4: Air filled, one low-e ($\varepsilon_1=0.88$, $\varepsilon_2=0.88$, $\varepsilon_3=0.12$, $\varepsilon_4=0.88$)
Case 5: Air filled, one low-e ($\varepsilon_1=0.88$, $\varepsilon_2=0.88$, $\varepsilon_3=0.88$, $\varepsilon_4=0.12$)

The workbook Calc3-01bAir.xls is required to obtain the centre-glazing temperature (t_4). Activate the sheet 'Air' and insert the given data for case 1 as shown in Example 3.3.1. Then activate the sheet 'CALC' and record the value of t_4 (cell O8). The values of t_4 for the above cases are respectively 9.9, 9.9, 11.8, 11.8 and 9.9°C. Next, the mean radiant temperature (t_r) is to be calculated for each case by using the formula,

$$t_r = \frac{A_s t_s + A_w t_4}{A_s + A_w}$$

where A_s is the wall area, A_w the window area, and t_s is the wall surface temperature. Finally, the dry resultant temperature, t_{res}, is to be calculated using Eq. (3.1.3). The calculated value of t_{res} for the third and fourth cases is 14.9°C while for the remaining cases it is 14.8°C. It is not surprising that t_{res} has not changed significantly due to the fact that the window area is much smaller compared to the area of the room walls. However, if the window area was much larger, there would be a noticeable difference in t_{res}.

In the above section it was demonstrated that two factors, i.e. convection within cavity and frame conduction as well as edge effects, contribute to a non-uniform temperature distribution. It is therefore logical to expect a non-uniform heat flux through any double-glazing. A sample of the flux measurements undertaken by Han (1996) is presented in Figure 3.3.8. The plot shows increased flux at the bottom end of the glazing which inevitably comes into contact with the cold air descending along the outer pane.

3.4   Temperature stratification in windows

It is customary to assume that the interior glass pane of a window is at a uniform temperature. The interior pane temperature is normally assumed to be equal to the centre-glazing temperature. This assumption, however, ignores the effect of infill gas convection within the window cavity and its impact on the temperature distribution of the glass pane. Muneer et al. (1996) and Abodahab and Muneer (1998) have shown the invalidity of this assumption and demonstrated the temperature stratification effect along the height of the inner pane. This stratification dictates that the lowest temperature of the interior pane would be experienced at its lower edge where condensation initiates.

Condensation prediction charts (Button and Pye, 1993), that are generally used to predict condensation occurrence, are produced under the simplified

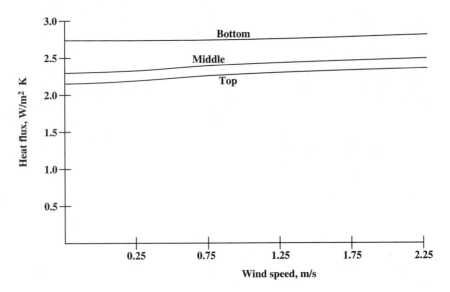

Figure 3.3.8 *Flux distribution over an air-filled double-glazing*

assumption of isothermal plate temperature. The charts use the following parameters to predict the condensation occurrence: inside air temperature, outside air temperature, indoor relative humidity, and U-value of the glazing.

As pointed out above the assumption of uniform pane temperature is invalid. This will be demonstrated via the following analysis.

3.4.1   Free convection along a vertical plate with a uniform heat flux

Consider the case of a vertical plate immersed in a quiescent fluid such as air. Assume the plate surface temperature, T_p, to be greater than air temperature, T_∞. The density of the air close to the plate is less than that which is further removed. Buoyancy forces, therefore, induce a free convection boundary layer in which the heated air rises vertically and is replaced by air from the quiescent region.

Bejan (1984) has shown that transition from laminar to turbulent flow within the boundary layer occurs when

$$Ra = \frac{g\beta(T_p - T_\infty)y^3}{\nu\alpha} \approx 10^9 \qquad (3.4.1.1)$$

where y is the critical height at which transition occurs. The Nusselt number and Rayleigh numbers are based on the height of the vertical plate H_w as the characteristic dimension.

For laminar flow,

$$Nu = 0.68 + \frac{0.670 Ra^{1/4}}{[1 + (0.492/Pr)^{9/16}]^{4/9}} \qquad (3.4.1.2)$$

In the case of a vertical plate with a uniform flux (q_p=constant) the temperature difference $\Delta T_y = T_p - T_\infty$) will vary with y, increasing from a value of zero at the leading edge. Churchill and Chu (1975) have shown that without loss of any serious accuracy the correlations obtained for the isothermal plate may be used for the case of constant heat flux. Then, if Nu and Ra are defined in terms of the temperature difference at the midpoint of the plate $\Delta T(H_w/2)$ and using the relationship

$$\bar{h} = \frac{q_p}{\Delta T(H_w/2)}$$

along with Eq. (3.4.1.2), the temperature at the midpoint of the plate $T_p(H_w/2)$ may be obtained in an iterative manner. The temperature difference at any point y may then be obtained by the following equation (Incropera and DeWitt, 1990):

Table 3.4.1 Window configurations (Abodahab and Muneer, 1998)

Window number	Trade name	Design details	U_{ref}*
1	4-Air12-4	4 mm float glass + 12 mm air gap + 4 mm float glass	2.86
2	4-Ar12-4	4 mm float glass + 12 mm argon gap + 4 mm float glass	2.72
3	4-Air12-E4	4 mm float glass + 12 mm air gap + 4 mm low-emissivity coated glass	1.83
4	4-Ar12-E4	4 mm float glass + 12 mm argon gap + 4 mm low-emissivity coated glass	1.53
5	4E-Kr12-E4	4 mm low-emissivity coated glass + 12 mm krypton gap + 4 mm low-emissivity coated glass	1.14
6	4E-Xe10-E4	4 mm low-emissivity coated glass + 10 mm xenon gap + 4 mm low-emissivity coated glass	0.91
7	4 + Air20-4	4 mm float glass + 20 mm air gap with 50 mm high baffle placed centrally on the bottom edge + 4 mm float glass	2.82

*U_{ref} : The reference U-value, calculated at the glazing centre with $T_i = 20°$ and $T_o = 0°C$ (W/m^2°C)

$$\Delta T_y = 1.15 \left(\frac{y}{H_w}\right)^{1/5} \Delta T_{H_w/2} \qquad (3.4.1.3)$$

Table 3.4.1 shows the specifications of the double-glazed windows that were tested by Abodahab and Muneer (1998) to investigate the temperature stratification along the height of the inner pane. The window edge spacers are usually made of aluminium. These may, however, be thermally broken to avoid excessive conduction heat transfer. A detailed cross-section of double-glazed window edge-seal is shown in Figure 3.4.1.

Abodahab and Muneer (1998) have shown that the temperature along the vertical centreline of the window inner pane increases as the height increases. They have also shown that there is a decrease in temperature at both the bottom and top edges of the window. Figure 3.4.2 shows the variation of the measured and computed temperatures against the window height for three window samples. It also shows the corresponding temperature of the glazing

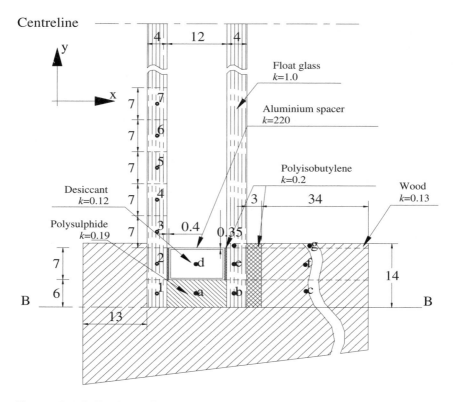

Figure 3.4.1 *Design schematic and nodal arrangement for window design considered by Muneer et al. (1997). Note: all dimensions are in mm and k values in W/mk*

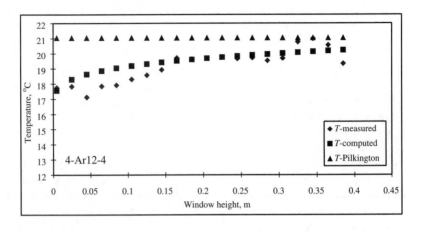

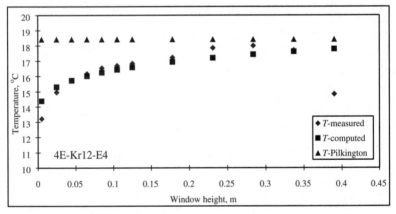

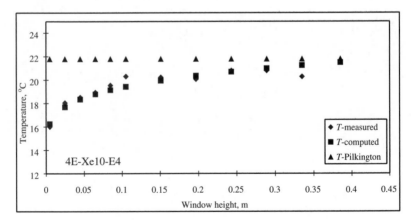

Figure 3.4.2 *Measured and computed temperature variations for three window configurations (Abodahab, 1998)*

bottom as obtained by Button and Pye (1993). Note that the latter work was carried out on behalf of Pilkington plc.

Figure 3.4.2 demonstrates the interplay of the two factors which determine the longitudinal temperature variation. These are:

- The circulation of the gas within the enclosure, alternating between the hot and cold sides. For most double-glazed designs this is the dominant factor and it is responsible for the rise in the temperature along the height. The infill gas in the sealed space flows upward along the indoor glazing and downward along the outdoor glazing. The descending gas becomes progressively colder. At the bottom of the cavity this cold gas turns its direction and comes into contact with the bottom edge of the indoor glazing. This effect has also been demonstrated by Frank and Wakili (1995) and Wright and Sullivan (1995).
- The conduction effect due to the metallic spacer which acts as a thermal bridge between the cold external environment and the warm internal environment. The cold bridging effect of the spacer is partly responsible for the temperature drop at the bottom and top edges of the glazing. Later in this chapter, a two-dimensional temperature model that involves cold bridging effects of the edge-seal will be presented.

In order to compare the temperature variation in diverse window configurations with disparate geometry, internal temperature and external weather conditions, two dimensionless parameters T^* and Y^* are introduced:

$$T^* = \frac{t_y - T_o}{T_i - T_o} \qquad\qquad (3.4.1.4)$$

$$Y^* = \frac{y}{H_w} \qquad\qquad (3.4.1.5)$$

where

T^* = dimensionless temperature
t_y = temperature of the inner glass pane at an arbitrary point, °C
y = height of the arbitrary point from the window bottom edge, m
Y^* = dimensionless height

Abodahab (1998) has shown that the temperature of the inner pane increases with the window height. For the respective indoor and outdoor conditions of 15.5 and 1°C it was shown via measurements that there is an average increase of 2.5°C between the highest and lowest longitudinal temperatures. Infrared photographs of ordinary double-glazed and superinsulated windows were taken at the Lawrence Berkeley Laboratory in California. Plate 3.3 (see colour plate section) compares those infrared images with a photograph of a double-glazed window in an experimental bedroom. The room was occupied with one adult person the night before the photograph was taken. The photograph shows water droplets forming at the bottom edge of the window. It can be seen that condensation occurred also on the side edges of the window due to cold bridging by the edge spacer. The infrared and photographic images of the double-glazed window clearly demonstrate the above-mentioned phenomenon of gas circulation and its effect of lowered temperature at the bottom edge of the cavity.

3.4.2   Physical model for longitudinal temperature profile of multiple-glazed windows

This work has been presented in an article by Abodahab and Muneer (1998). Only a précis of that publication is given below. The physical situation of a heated glass wall is neither isothermal nor constant heat flux. However, the latter condition is closer to reality for heat transfer through a double-glazing system. For gaseous fluids such as those used in window enclosures, Bejan (1984) has used scaling law analysis to show that

$$\delta_t \sim y[Ra_y^* Pr]^{-1/5} \tag{3.4.2.1}$$

where δ_t is the thickness of the thermal boundary layer and y is defined above. Also

$$\Delta T \sim [q/k]y[Ra_y^* Pr]^{-1/5} \tag{3.4.2.2}$$

where the expression for uniform heat flux Rayleigh number is

$$Ra_y^* = g\beta y^4 q/\alpha vk \tag{3.4.2.3}$$

All physical properties Pr, α, v, and k are evaluated at the enclosure film temperature T_f (see Eq. (3.3.1.4)).
   A generalised form of Eq. (3.4.2.2) was given by Abodahab and Muneer (1998):

$$\Delta T = c[q/k]y[Ra_y^* Pr]^m \tag{3.4.2.4}$$

where m is a constant and c is defined by Eq. (3.4.2.8).

$$\Delta T = t_Y - (T_f - 273.15) \tag{3.4.2.5}$$

A new parameter is introduced:

Napier Number, $Na = \Delta T k/(qy)$ (3.4.2.6)

Equation (3.4.2.4) then becomes

$$Na = c[Ra_y^* Pr]^m$$ (3.4.2.7)

where

$$c = c_0 + c_1 U_{ref}$$ (3.4.2.8)

m, c_0 and c_1 are given numerical values. These values are $c_0 = 1.1563$, $c_1 = -0.31$ and $m = -0.2$. A definition for U_{ref} is provided in Table 3.4.1.

Substituting Eqs (3.4.2.3), (3.4.2.5) and (3.4.2.8) into Eq. (3.4.2.4) and re-arranging the terms yields

$$t_y = t_f + (qy/k)(c_0 + c_1 U_{ref})([g \beta y^4 qPr]/[\alpha v k])^m$$ (3.4.2.9)

This equation represents the physical model which may be used to compute the longitudinal temperature variation of the inner glass pane of any multi-glazed window.

The following example shows the relevant calculation for a particular case.

Example 3.4.1

An air-filled double-glazed window of 2.0 m height has a U_{ref} of 2.86 W/m^{2}K. Compute the temperature stratification along the height of the inner pane. Assume that the internal and external ambient temperatures are 20°C and 0°C respectively. Refer to the schematic drawing in sheet 'Main' of the workbook Calc3-03.xls. Given data: $L_{g12} = L_{g34} = 4$ mm and $k_{g12} = k_{g34} = 1.0$ W/mK.

The solution is provided by the Calc3-03.xls workbook. Activate the sheet 'Main'. Insert the given data in the cell array C5:C12. The window height is divided into equal segments, e.g. 20 locations as shown in the cell array D6:D25. Because the above model is not applied for the bottom and top edges of the glazing, an average height of 25 mm has to be discarded from the bottom and from the top as shown in cells D6 and D25 respectively. The resultant temperature stratification is shown in the cell array F6:F25. The bottom and top temperatures are respectively 9.9 and 12.1°C, i.e. a temperature stratification of 2.2°C. Note that Calc3-03.xls provides a solution only for air-filled windows. For other gases the reader may wish to make suitable modifications in the 'Calc' sheet of the above workbook.

Abodahab and Muneer (1998) have shown that the semi-analytical model presented by Eq. (3.4.2.9) estimates the longitudinal temperature distribution for any multiple-glazed window with a mean bias error of 0.01°C and a root mean square error of 1.2°C.

3.4.3   Multimode thermal model

Modern double-glazed windows use hermetically sealed, insulative glazing units, which consist of two panes of glass separated by an edge-seal. The edge-seal isolates the space between the two glass panes and consequently creates an insulative cavity suitable for the use of low-emissivity coatings and/or low-conductivity infill gases, e.g. argon, krypton, or xenon.

It was shown above that the thermal transmittance of a complete double-glazed window depends on three components: the glazing unit, the edge-seal (spacer), and the frame. Double-glazed windows containing high-performance glass require a compatible high insulation in their edge spacer and frame. If this is not achieved, then the insulation benefits of the glass can be significantly diminished. While a conventional double-glazed window with low-e and argon infill gas achieves U-values between 1.3 and 1.8 W/m^2K, poorly insulated frames of wood, plastic, aluminium or steel may give U-values ranging from 2.8 to 7.0 W/m^2K (Button and Pye, 1993). The thermal effect of the edge-seal for different conditions of exposure, e.g. sheltered, normal, and severe, may be calculated from tables given in ISO 6946 (1983).

The edge-seal shown in Figure 3.4.1 consists of an aluminium spacer, desiccant, polyisobutylene, and polysulphide. The presence of the aluminium spacer creates a thermal short circuit at the window edge-seal. This increases the overall U-value of the window and lowers the local temperatures at the edge region.

A two-dimensional numerical technique was used by Muneer et al. (1997) to study the cold bridge effects of window edge-seal and frame on the temperature distribution along the height of the inner glazing. The above reference provides further details of the numerical model and its experimental validation.

Table 3.4.2 shows a comparison of the temperature difference between the centre glazing and the bottom node (node 3) for the two scenarios, i.e. an aluminium and a perfectly insulated spacer, respectively shown in columns 4 and 5. Note that the position of all nodes is shown in Figure 3.4.1. Column 4 shows an increasing trend for the above temperature differential. This has also been demonstrated by Frank and Wakili (1995). This phenomenon can be explained as follows. The indoor centre-glazing temperature t_3 increases and the outdoor pane temperature t_2 decreases with the decrease of U-value due to increased cavity thermal resistance. This conclusion can be verified by Eqs (3.3.3.2) and (3.3.3.3). As mentioned previously, the descending infill gas would approach the temperature of the cold outer glazing. Thus T_3, the bottom temperature of the inner pane, also decreases with a lowered U-value. Therefore, the temperature differential $(t_3 - T_3)$ will increase quite rapidly due to the combined effect of the elevated t_3 and lowered T_3. Reference is now made to column 5 of Table 3.4.2. Once again an increasing differential between t_3 and T_3 is noticeable between cases 1 and 2, and between cases 3 and 4. The above two comparisons demonstrate the effect of higher resistance to the heat flow due to convection. The temperature differential $(t_3 - T_3)$ also increases from

Table 3.4.2 Cold bridge effects demonstrated via the difference between centreline and bottom edge temperature (Muneer et al., 1997)

Case no.	Window type	U-value[A] (W/m^2K)	(t_3-T_3)[B] Conduction, convection, radiation[C]	(t_3-T_3) Convection, radiation[D] only
1	4 + Air12 + 4	2.86	3.3	2.7
2	4 + Arg12 + 4	2.72	3.4	2.9
3	4 + Air12 + E4	1.83	5.0	3.9
4	4 + Arg12 + E4	1.53	5.5	4.3
5	4E + Kr12 + E4	1.14	5.4	2.5
6	4E + Xe10 + E4	0.91	5.8	2.4

(A) Internal and external ambient temperatures are assumed 20°C, 0°C respectively.
(B) (t_3-T_3) is the temperature difference between centre-glazing and node 3.
(C) Temperature values calculated by the numerical model. All heat transfer modes are involved.
(D) Temperature values calculated by the numerical model. Cold bridge effects are excluded by replacing the aluminium spacer by an infinite resistance.

case 1 to 3 and from case 2 to 4 due to the increased radiative resistance between the respective cases. The situation in cases 5 and 6 is very involved. Several counteracting influences may be identified. Firstly, the descending colder gas gets cooler with decreasing U-value, thus tending to bring down T_3. Secondly, node 3 loses less heat by radiation and therefore tends to elevate T_3. Thirdly, (t_3-T_3) decreases due to increased thermal contact between these nodes for heavier, inert gases as shown by Muneer and Han (1996b). It should be borne in mind that even though (t_3-T_3) increases, T_3 may not be lowered, in absolute terms, for super-insulated windows. This is due to the fact that in the latter design t_3 will be higher by a wide margin.

For any given case, a comparison between columns 4 and 5 illustrates the effect of the conductivity of the edge-seal. Column 5 provides the values of (t_3-T_3) for a hypothetical situation wherein the aluminium spacer resistance is replaced with an infinite resistance. Cases 1 and 6 lie at the extreme ends of the comparative exercise. It is clear that for an air-filled window (case 1) the edge conductivity has a minor influence, e.g. its relative weighting is only 17%. However, for the low-emissivity xenon windows the spacer conduction is the major contributor in reducing the edge temperature. The relative weighting of the edge effect in this case is 60%.

Example 3.4.2

A double-glazed window with a 12 mm air gap, 0.4 m height and 1 m width uses an aluminium spacer. The centre-glazing U-value is 2.86 W/m²k. Assume that the internal and external ambient temperatures are 20°C and 0°C respectively. Refer to the sheet 'Main' of the workbook Calc3-03.xls wherein a schematic of the window structure is shown. Given $L_{g12} = L_{g34} = 4$ mm,

$k_{g12} = k_{g34} = 1.0$ W/mk and $\varepsilon_2 = \varepsilon_3 = 0.88$, find the temperature at the bottom edge of the glazing (node 3 of Figure 3.4.1) using sheet 'air' of workbook Calc3-04.xls.

The answer to this example can be obtained via the workbook Calc3-04.xls. Activate the sheet 'Air' and insert the given data in cell array B4:B16. The sheet 'CalcAir' contains the thermal resistance network related to Figure 3.4.1. The temperatures of all nodes, shown in Figure 3.4.1, have been iteratively calculated as shown in the cell range A33:U61. The iteration has been checked by performing an energy balance for each finite element as shown in the cell array B64:N68. The required temperature t_3 is given in cell D5 of the sheet entitled 'Air'. This temperature is 9.6°C.

3.5   Frequency of condensation occurrence on double-glazed windows

It is common experience that within dwellings condensation occurs on glazing surfaces during the early hours of the morning. It initiates at the coldest part of the glazing at window's bottom edge and then propagates upwards as the external temperature and/or the internal humidity increases. This phenomenon was demonstrated by Plate 3.3.

Condensation may occur on the outer pane of a window if its temperature goes below the outer dew-point temperature. This happens when there is a clear sky, and high relative humidity. Super-windows may also experience this phenomenon due to the fact that the temperature of the outer pane drops as a result of the low U-value.

3.5.1   Model for assessment of the potential of condensation occurrence

Condensation prediction charts (Button and Pye, 1993) are generally used to predict condensation occurrence. They are produced under the assumption of isothermal plate temperature as pointed out in Section 3.4.

To quantify the condensation problem encountered on windows, a simplified model for assessing the nocturnal temperature drop inside a building subjected to a daytime heating schedule has been provided by Muneer and Abodahab (1998). This approach assumes that the complete building is a single unit that loses heat to the external environment during the cooling-down period. The assumption is valid as the thermal resistance of the external film of air is high compared with the internal thermal resistances within the building.

From Newton's law of cooling it may be shown that

$$\ln(T_i - T_o) = -\left(\frac{hA_b}{\rho\,Vc}\right)\tau \qquad (3.5.1.1)$$

where

A_b = building surface area, m^2
c = building-specific heat, J/kg K
h = heat transfer coefficient from the building surface to external air, W/m^{2}K
ρ = building density, kg/m^3
T_i = building lumped temperature at a certain time, °C
τ = elapsed time, seconds
T_o = external air temperature at a certain time, °C

The term $(\rho Vc/hA_b)$ in Eq. (3.5.1.1) is called the time constant. A large time constant means that the building requires a longer time to cool down or heat up between specific temperatures.

During the unheated period, the building structure cools down due to the influence of the external environment. The temperature of the building structure, in general, can be affected by the external air temperature, T_o, the longwave radiation loss to the clear sky, wind speed, wind direction, infiltration and/or ventilation.

Figure 3.5.1 gives a relationship between T_i and T_o for the bedroom during the nocturnal cooling-down period, i.e. when there are no solar effects, the heating system is switched off and the house is cooled down by the external environment. The work of Webb and Concannon (1996) has shown similar behaviour. By knowing the external ambient temperature T_o, the internal ambient temperature T_i can be obtained using a regression of the form

$$T_i = aT_o + b \tag{3.5.1.2}$$

To determine the potential frequency of condensation occurrence on a building window the internal air temperature, T_i, and relative humidity, ϕ, should be known. These two properties enable the determination of the indoor dew-point temperature by using the principles of psychrometry.

Relative humidities within a single-occupancy bedroom were measured by Muneer and Abodahab (1998) for the above-mentioned experimental bedroom. It was thus shown that the relative humidity changes only slightly during the cooling-down period. This is due to the thermal capacity of the building structure that dampens the influence of the changing weather over a short period of time.

By comparing the internal air dew-point temperature, T_{dp}, with the bottom edge inner glazing temperature, t_3, an assessment of the occurrence of condensation may be made. Thus, if $t_3 \leq T_{dp}$ condensation will occur on the glazing edge.

The annual average of condensation occurrence for any given location decreases with a reduction in the U-value. Table 3.5.1 shows that the potential

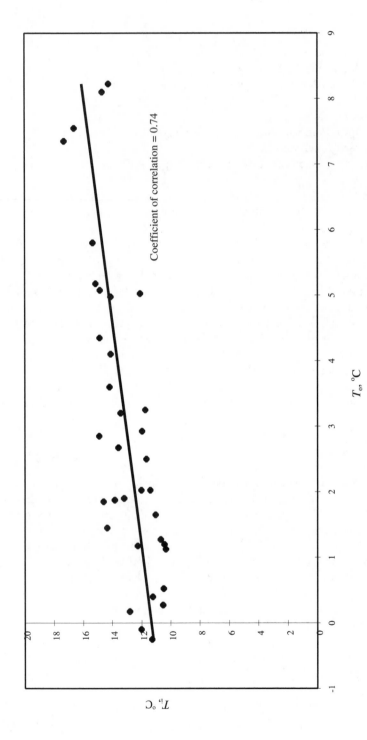

Coefficient of correlation = 0.74

T_o, °C

T_b, °C

Figure 3.5.1 *Nocturnal cooling performance of an occupied unheated bedroom (Abodahab, 1998)*

Table 3.5.1 Averaged annual potential of frequency of condensation occurrence (Abodahab and Muneer, 1998)

Year	Edinburgh	Manchester	London
Window no. 1	117	97	58
Window no. 2	106	88	50
Window no. 3	100	82	44
Window no. 4	90	70	38
Window no. 5	78	61	31
Window no. 6	71	55	28
Window no. 7	46	34	14

frequency of condensation occurrence will decrease by about 40–50% if less efficient glazing (e.g. window No. 1) are replaced by the most efficient ones (e.g. window No. 6). Of course these results apply for the bedroom under discussion but may be taken as indicative of the domestic scene in Northern Europe.

Example 3.5.1

For the window of Example 3.4.2, consider the early-morning condition of an occupied bedroom. The indoor and outdoor air temperatures are respectively 12°C and 0°C. The indoor relative humidity is 70%. Find the potential for condensation occurrence at the bottom edge of the window.

The solution is provided by workbooks Calc3-04.xls and Calc3-05.xls. The former workbook is used to obtain the temperature at the bottom edge of the glazing (t_3). t_3 was found to be 5.8°C, as shown in Example 3.4.2.

Because the workbook 'Calc3-05.xls' contains a macro entitled 'Prog72.dll', launch Excel, then open Calc3-05.xls within this environment. Insert the indoor air temperature (DBT = 12°C) and the relative humidity (RH = 70%) in cells C10 and D10 respectively. Initiate the calculations by running the macro thus: press 'Alt + F8' then click the 'Run' button in the Macro dialogue box.

The following psychrometric properties: humidity ratio (Wa, kg/kg of dry air), specific volume (v, m³/kg), specific enthalpy (h, kJ/kg), dew-point temperature (DPT, °C) and wet-bulb temperature (WBT, °C) are calculated in the cell array F10:J10. The required value for DPT is found to be equal to 6.7°C, as shown in cell I10.

Thus it may be concluded that condensation will occur on the glazing edge as t_3 is less than the dew-point temperature.

It is worth mentioning that the above DLL file provides a useful facility to compute the psychrometric properties for any number of input data, as shown in Calc3-05.xls.

Traditionally the potential for condensation occurrence on windows was based on the centre of glazing temperature (Carmody et al., 1996). Muneer and Abodahab (1998) have, however, shown that by using the work described in Section 3.4.3 a more realistic assessment of the potential of condensation occurrence can be made. Recall that the latter procedure takes into account the temperature stratification effects of the inner glass pane due to the circulation of infill gas and the cold bridging of the spacer. It therefore predicts the onset of condensation with a much higher accuracy.

3.5.2   Innovative developments

As mentioned previously, the circulating infill gas within the window enclosure is responsible for the lowered temperature of the bottom part of the inner pane. The identification of this phenomenon has led to an innovative development (Muneer et al., 1996). The innovation (window no. 7 of Table 3.4.1) uses a 50 mm high glass baffle, placed mid-way in the cavity on the bottom spacer. Table 3.5.1 shows that the window under discussion is least susceptible to condensation occurrence. The baffle plate constricts the descending cold air hugging the outer glass pane from hitting the bottom part of the inner glass. This helps in keeping the temperature at the bottom part of the inner pane at a higher value than would be otherwise.

Figure 3.5.2 shows the benefit achieved by the use of an in-cavity baffle. Provided the internal and external environments are maintained at 20°C and 0°C, an average increase of 2°C edge temperature is achieved by the above innovation.

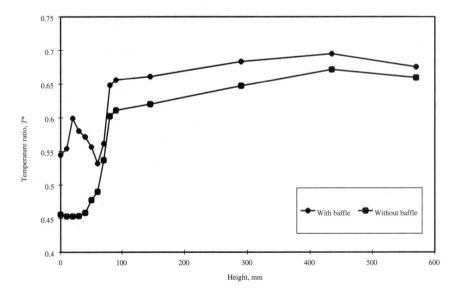

Figure 3.5.2 *Temperature distribution along the height of indoor pane of windows with and without a baffle plate (Han, 1996)*

References

Abodahab, N. (1998) *Temperature Distribution Models for Double-glazed Windows and their Use in Assessing Condensation Occurrence.* PhD thesis, Napier University, Edinburgh, UK.

Abodahab, N. and Muneer, T. (1998) Free convection analysis of a window cavity and its longitudinal temperature profile. *Energy Conversion and Management* 39, 257.

Aschehoug, O. and Baker, J. (1995) Frame and edge-seal technology – an international view. *Proceedings of the Window Innovations '95 conference,* Toronto, Canada.

ASHRAE (1985) *ASHRAE Handbook of Fundamentals.* American Society for Heating, Refrigeration and Air Conditioning Engineers, Atlanta, USA.

ASHRAE (1993) *ASHRAE Handbook of Fundamentals.* American Society for Heating, Refrigeration and Air Conditioning Engineers, Atlanta, USA.

Bejan, A. (1984) *Convection Heat Transfer.* Wiley, New York.

British Standards Institution (1989) BS 6993, Part I, London.

Button, D. and Pye, B. (1993) *Glass in building: A Guide to Modern Architectural Glass Performance.* Pilkington Glass Ltd, UK.

Carmody, J., Selkowitz, S. and Heschnog, L. (1996) *Residential Windows.* W. W. Norton & Company, New York.

Churchill, S. W. and Chu, H. (1975) Correlating equations for laminar and turbulent free convection from a vertical plate. *Int. J. Heat & Mass Transfer* 18, 1323.

CIBSE (1986) *CIBSE Guide to Current Practice Volume A.* London.

CIBSE (1989) *CIBSE Guide A3, Thermal properties of building structures.* London.

Curcija, D. and Goss, W. P. (1994) Two dimensional finite element model of heat transfer in complete fenestration systems. *ASHRAE Transactions* 100, 2.

Elder, J. W. (1965) Laminar free convection in a vertical slot. *Journal of Fluid Mechanics* 23, 99.

El-Sherbiny, S. M., Hollands, K. G. T. and Raithby, G. D. (1982) Heat transfer by natural convection across vertical and inclined layers. *Trans ASME J. Heat Transfer* 96.

Fanger, P. O. (1973) *Thermal Comfort.* McGraw-Hill, New York, p. 244.

Frank, T. and Wakili, K. (1995) Linear transmittance of different spacer bars. *Proceedings of the Window Innovations '95 Conference,* Toronto, p. 253.

Gill, A. E. (1966) The boundary layer regime for convection in a rectangular cavity. *Journal of Fluid Mechanics* 26, 515.

Han, B. (1996) *Investigation of Thermal Characteristics of Multiple Glazed Windows.* PhD thesis, Napier University, Edinburgh, UK.

Inaba, H. (1984) Experimental study of natural convection in an inclined layer. *Int. J. Heat Mass Transfer* 27, 1127.

Incropera, F. P. and DeWitt, D. P. (1990) *Fundamentals of Heat and Mass Transfer*. Wiley, New York, p. 542.

ISO (1983) Thermal insulation calculation methods, ISO 6946, Part 1 – Steady state thermal properties of building components and building elements.

Ito, N., Kimura, K. and Oka, J. (1972) A field study on the convective heat transfer coefficient on exterior surface of a building. *Proceedings ASHRAE, Semi-annual meeting*, New Orleans.

Kakac, S., Aung, W. and Viskanta, R. (1985) *Natural convection, fundamentals and applications*. Hemisphere, Washington, DC.

MacGregor, R. K. and Emery, A. F. (1971) Prandtl number effects on natural convection in an enclosed vertical layer. *J. Heat Transfer* May, 253.

Muneer, T. and Abodahab, N. (1998) Frequency of condensation occurrence on double glazings in the United Kingdom. *Energy Conversion and Management* 39, 717.

Muneer, T. and Han, B. (1994) Heat transmission characteristics of multiple glazed windows-measured and modelled results. *Proceedings Northsun '94 (Solar energy at high latitudes)*, eds: K. MacGregor and C. Porteous, Glasgow, UK.

Muneer, T. and Han, B. (1995a) Use of CFD for thermal analysis of double glazings. In *Computational Methods and Experimental Measurements VII*, eds G. M. Carlomagno and C. A. Brebbia, Computational Mechanics Publications, UK.

Muneer, T. and Han, B. (1995b) Environmental impact evaluation of high performance windows for sustainable buildings. *Proceeding International Workshop on Environmental Impact Evaluation of Buildings and Cities for Sustainability*, Florence, Italy.

Muneer, T. and Han, B. (1996a) Design charts for multiple glazed windows. *Building Services Engineering Research & Technology (BSER&T)* 17, 223.

Muneer, T. and Han, B. (1996b) Simplified analysis for free convection in enclosures – application to an industrial problem. *Energy Conversion & Management* 37, 1463.

Muneer, T., Abodahab, N. and Han, B. (1996) Gas flow in window enclosures and its effect on temperature distribution. *Proceedings of Advances in Fluid Mechanics (AFM '96) Conference*, New Orleans, USA, 11–13 June 1996, Computational Mechanics Publications, Southampton, UK, p. 233.

Muneer, T., Abodahab, N. and Gilchrist, A. (1997) Combined conduction, convection, and radiation heat transfer model for double glazed windows. *Building Services Engineering Research & Technology (BSER&T)* 18, 183.

Parsons, K. C. (1993) *Human Thermal Environments: The effects of hot, moderate and cold environments on human health, comfort and performance*. Taylor and Francis Ltd, London.

Raithby, G. D., Hollands, K. G. T. and Unny, T. E. (1977) Analysis of heat transfer by natural convection across vertical fluid layers. *Journal of Heat Transfer* 99, 287.

Rayment, R., Fishwick, P. J., Rose, P. M. and Seymour, M. J. (1992) A study of glazing heat losses and trickle ventilators. Building Research Establishment Occasional Paper, 38.

Sharples, S. (1982) Modelling the heat transfer through opaque building components for the detailed computation of thermal performance under varying climatic conditions. Internal Report BS63, Department of Building Science, University of Sheffield.

Shaw, C. T. (1992) *Using Computational Fluid Dynamics.* Prentice Hall International, Hemel Hempstead.

Svendsen, S. and Fritzel, P. (1995) Spacers for highly insulated windows. *Proceedings of the Window Innovations '95 Conference*, Toronto, 5 and 6 June, p. 90.

Webb, B. and Concannon, P. (1996) In the cool of the night. *Building Services Journal.* CIBSE, London.

Wray, W. O. (1980) A simple procedure for assessing thermal comfort in passive heated buildings. *Solar Energy* 25, 327.

Wright, J. L. (1990) *The Measurement and Computer Simulation of Heat Transfer in Glazing Systems.* PhD thesis, University of Waterloo, Canada.

Wright, J. L. and Sullivan, H. F. (1995) A 2-D numerical model for glazing system thermal analysis. *ASHRAE Transactions* 101.

4 WINDOWS AND SOLAR HEAT

4.1 Windows as solar energy providers

Within the United Kingdom, the European Union or the USA, more energy is used to maintain comfortable internal environments in buildings than for any other single purpose. The energy bill associated with the energy consumption due to heating of buildings is over 25% for the UK and 35% for the USA. Environmental conditioning in non-residential buildings accounts for about 15% of the UK energy consumption, nearly two thirds of which is used for space heating, one third for lighting, and about 5% for cooling.

Direct use of the sun's energy, through passive solar design in buildings, is one of the most economically attractive ways of utilising renewable energy. Passive solar design uses a building's form and fabric to capture, store and distribute solar energy received, thereby reducing the demand for heat and artificial light. In the northern hemisphere, it requires siting buildings so that large glazed areas can face south, free from overshadowing, minimising glazing on north-facing walls and incorporating complementary energy-efficiency features, such as adequate roof and wall insulation and automatic controls on heating systems. Without an added capital expenditure penalty, passive solar design enhances the internal environment of buildings. Passive solar concepts offer an ideal opportunity to reduce energy bills for industrial, commercial and domestic buildings. Moreover, this form of solar energy technology is both proven and economical. Studies such as the one undertaken by ETSU (1985) suggest that a significant part of the building heating energy requirement could be met by solar energy technologies.

4.1.1 Energy balance of a window

The role of windows in the exploitation of passive solar energy, for both space heating and daylighting, is unreservedly important. Most building regulations discriminate against windows in favour of ordinary opaque insulating materials. The result is that limiting window areas is recommended while prescribing minimum allowable U-values. The regulations make no allowance for the functions of the window, e.g. its transparency to solar heat and daylight. Owens (1982, 1984), CEN (1997) and Weir (1998) have presented the design requirements of any given window and have demonstrated the need for an objective energy balance. A synopsis of the former two references will be presented below.

Energy balance on any given window may be written in terms of its transmission characteristics, the incident solar radiation, and the internal and external temperatures. An expression for $(\tau\alpha)$, the glazing transmittance and room absorptance product, for windows in passive solar heated enclosures has been given by Duffie and Beckman (1991) as

$$(\tau\alpha) = \tau_G \alpha_R / [\alpha_R + (1 - \alpha_R)\tau_D A_W / A_R] \tag{4.1.1}$$

where τ_G and τ_D are respectively the transmittance of the window for global and diffuse solar irradiation, and α_R the diffuse absorptance for the room surface. A_W and A_R are the respective window and room surface areas. Techniques for obtaining the above-mentioned transmittances for any multi-glazed window will be presented in Section 4.3.

An important relationship which essentially represents the steady-state energy balance of any solar heat collector with an absorber area of A_W is the Hottel–Whillier–Bliss model, Eq. (4.1.2) (Duffie and Beckman, 1991). The equation enables calculation of useful energy gain (Q_u) as a function of the internal (T_i) and external (T_o) ambient temperatures:

$$Q_u = A_w F_R [I_W(\tau\alpha) - U(T_i - T_o)] \tag{4.1.2}$$

F_R and I_W are respectively the heat removal factor and irradiance on the given window (Duffie and Beckman, 1991).This equation can be rearranged by setting the heat collection Q_u to nil, to provide an expression for the critical irradiation threshold $(I_{critical})$. The latter may be defined as the minimum level of solar irradiance to sustain a net energy gain through any glazing system. Thus $I_{critical}$ may be obtained as

$$I_{critical} = U(T_i - T_o)/(\tau\alpha) \tag{4.1.3}$$

It was shown in Chapter 3 that the rapid development in superinsulated window technology has enabled the manufacture of glazing with an extremely low U-value, e.g. the German manufacturer Interpane's, triple-glazing with xenon has a U-value of 0.4 W/m^{2}K. Thus, with reference to Eq. (4.1.3) it may be shown that it is now feasible to collect solar energy for space heating even under overcast conditions. This is demonstrated by Example 4.1.1.

Table 4.1.1, based on the work of Muneer (1999), provides data for a number of commercially available windows. Muneer (1999) has presented the calculation procedure for $(\tau\alpha)$. Numerical values of this transmittance–absorptance product for an averaged-sized room with an average window size are included in Table 4.1.1. The critical threshold radiation is also included in this table. The low levels of $I_{critical}$ show that the newer windows are well placed for providing passive solar heating solutions.

Table 4.1.1 Design data for double-glazed windows (Muneer, 1999)

Window design	U-value W/m^{2}K	$(\tau\alpha)$	I_{critical} W/m^{2}K	I_G W/m^{2}K	Solution for Example 4.1.1 f-value[†] February	October
Float glass with air	2.8	0.65	65	130	45	55
Low-emissivity glass with air*	1.8	0.62	43	87	57	67
Low-emissivity glass with Argon*	1.5	0.62	36	72	63	74
Low-emissivity glass with Krypton**	1.0	0.56	27	54	66	79
Low-emissivity glass with Xenon**	0.9	0.56	24	48	68	81

*SnO$_2$ coating
**Ag coating
[†]fractional time (per cent of the month) when irradiance exceeds the critical value thus contributing towards space heating requirements

Note that the Calc3-01a.xls workbook may be used for obtaining the U-values.

Example 4.1.1

Figure 4.1.1 presents data for the frequency of occurrence of horizontal solar irradiation for the months of February and October for Bracknell, England (51.4°N). Plots such as these are easy to produce within Excel by invoking the histogram function. Using the I_{critical} data presented in Table 4.1.1 estimate the fraction of the time each of the given window design will provide a net contribution of solar energy towards space heating.

Note: It is possible to show that under overcast conditions the vertical slope irradiance for any window having an aspect of north-east to north-west including south is around half of the horizontal irradiance. In this respect the reader is referred to Muneer (1997a). Since the newer windows operate with quite low levels of I_{critical} it is reasonable to assume that the corresponding irradiance climate will be experienced under an overcast sky.

Using the above assumption the threshold of horizontal global irradiance for any given window will be twice that of I_{critical}. Table 4.1.1 includes the essential answers to the problem under discussion. It must be borne in mind that for any given window design the actual contribution towards space heating during the nine-month duration, i.e. February to October, will be in excess of the f-values provided in Table 4.1.1.

Owens (1982, 1984) has argued for the inclusion of solar heat transmission of any given window to determine its energy balance. The ordinary U-value characterises only the thermal losses without taking into account the solar gains. It is well known that solar radiation possesses temporal and spatial variability. Further, there are added difficulties in establishing how the building

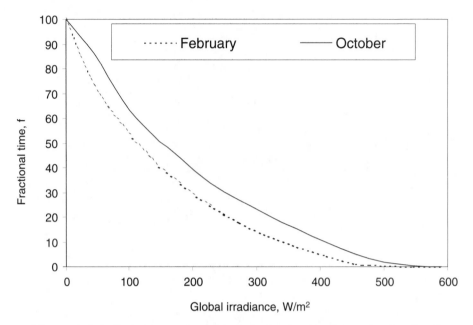

Figure 4.1.1 *Frequency of occurrence of solar irradiance for Bracknell, England*

and its use responds to this variable energy source. Using dynamic thermal analysis for a building of a given design, Owen has produced an equation to obtain an effective U-value of a window. This is defined as the U-value modified by the quantity of solar heat entering the window. As pointed out by Owens (1984) all simplified approaches are susceptible to limitations but, provided that the following approach is not used outside the context of conventional buildings, it is a useful means of establishing comparisons between various window designs.

The effective U-value may be obtained as

$$U_{\text{eff}} = U - [1000 f_u \tau F_d I_w / (24 HDD)] \tag{4.1.4}$$

where f_u is the utilisation factor, τ the window transmission, F_d the dirt or overshadowing factor and HDD is the degree-day value for the heating season. Owens (1984) has suggested that, typically, f_u and F_d may be assumed as having values of 0.6 and 0.8. Note that the term degree-day is increasingly being called 'Kelvin-day'.

Table A.1 of the CEN (1997) document provides data for I_w and HDD for a number of locations world-wide. An extract from the above reference is provided in Table 4.1.2. Note that a negative value of U_{eff} indicates a net flow of heat inwards into the building envelope.

Table 4.1.2 Effective U-value for selected sites (Owen, 1982)

Location	Heating season	Degree days	Solar irradiation, kWh/m^2			U_{eff}		
			North	East/west	South	North	East/west	South
Uccle, Belgium	Sept/May	2900	202	350	505	1.0	0.3	−0.3
Copenhagen, Denmark	Sept/May	3465	198	370	547	1.1	0.5	−0.1
Trappes, France	Sept/May	2625	230	410	590	0.7	−0.1	−0.9
Berlin, Germany	Sept/May	3335	203	358	518	1.1	0.5	−0.1
Rome, Italy	Nov/March	1401	110	239	442	0.9	−0.3	−2.0
London, England	Sept/May	2700	200	347	510	0.9	0.2	−0.5
Edinburgh, Scotland	Sept/May	2500	146	306	511	1.1	0.3	−0.7
Sapporo, Japan	Sept/June	3757	175	443	709	1.2	0.4	−0.5

Muneer (1989) has presented tables for monthly-mean slope irradiation for a number of UK locations. The European Union-funded *European Solar Radiation Atlas* provides these data for a large number of locations. Likewise, under the auspices of ASHRAE a large programme of work is under way to address the availability of such data for North American sites. Other world-wide web-based sources are presently identified for the acquisition of solar radiation data. By linking slope irradiation data with commonly available data for heating degree-days it is possible to obtain U_{eff} for any given location.

Table 4.1.2 contains solar radiation and heating degree-day data for a few world-wide locations. Using Eq. (4.1.4), U_{eff} for the given sites were obtained and these are included in the given table.

In the USA an 'energy rating index' (ERI) method is used to account for the impact of solar transmission through windows. A lower value of ERI indicates higher window efficiency. The ERI uses the following formula:

$$\mathrm{ERI} = 100[(0.87\mathrm{SCI_w}) - (T_i - T_o)U - (\text{air leakage})] \qquad (4.1.5)$$

where

$\quad$ ERI $\;=\;$ heating season energy rating (hundred Btu/hour-ft^2)
$\quad$ SC $\;=\;$ shading coefficient defined as the quotient of solar transmittance and 0.87
$\quad$ I_w $\;=\;$ 22.9 Btu/hour-ft^2 (average value)

Typical values of ERI for clear-single, clear-double and low-e coated double-glazing are respectively quoted as 329, −98 and −2376 (Pilkington, 1993).

Within the past decade there has been an explosion in the field of measurement, modelling and reporting of the available solar energy, particularly for use within buildings. In this respect information is available on the World Wide Web on the amount of transmitted solar radiation through multi-glazing for over 200 sites within the USA. This type of data is downloadable directly from the following website: http://rredc.nrel.gov/solar/. Other related websites are:

http://www.crest.org/renewables/solrad/
http://eosweb.larc.nasa.gov/DATDOCS/Surface_Solar_Energy.html

Other sources of information are the interactive *European Solar Radiation Atlas* produced by the European Union (Palz and Grief, 1996), the CIBSE Guide J for Weather and Solar Data, and the International Daylight Measurement Programme (IDMP) websites: http://www.cie.co.at/cie/home.html and http://idmp.entpe.fr/. New developments related to all aspects of window technology are available at: http://EETD.LBL.gov/CBS/NEWSLETTER/NL10/windows.html.

A most user-friendly and interactive tool is the sun angle calculator, available at: http://solstice.crest.org/staff/ceg/sunangle/index.html. Based on an algorithm developed by Dr Bernard Yallop, a well-known astronomer at the Royal Greenwich Observatory in England, the latter tool provides an accurate routine for obtaining the sun's position at any moment in time during the period 1980–2050.

This section has shown that during daylight hours, the energy balance of the window requires an assessment of the incident solar radiation. The following section provides an insight into the development of this science. A number of associated Excel workbooks are also provided to ease the necessary computations.

4.2   Solar radiation availability

While daylight is a building's form giver, solar radiation affects its thermal balance and thus has a significant influence on the building's internal environment. Thus it is important to understand the physics of solar radiation and daylight.

The terms solar radiation, irradiation, radiance, irradiance, luminance and illuminance are frequently encountered in the literature and a note on their use is perhaps appropriate at this stage. Solar radiation (W/m^2) or luminance (candela/m^2) refer to the energy emanating from the sun. Luminance is the energy contained within the visible part of the solar radiation spectrum (0.39 to 0.78 µm). The terms irradiation (Wh/m^2 or J/m^2) and illumination (lumen-hour/m^2) refer to the cumulative energy incident on a surface in a given period of time. Irradiance (W/m^2) and illuminance (lx) refer to the rate of incident energy.

The interception of solar radiation by arbitrary surfaces is a function of their geometry and a determinant of their microclimatic interaction, i.e. the energy exchange between the surface and its surroundings. Irradiation availability of arbitrary sloped surfaces is a prerequisite for determining a given window's thermal balance.

4.2.1 Solar radiation fundamentals

In the following paragraphs fundamentals of solar radiation are introduced. The object is to enable the user to perform computations related to solar radiation transmission through any given window.

4.2.1.1 Solar day

A solar day is defined to be the interval of time from the moment the sun crosses the local meridian to the next time it crosses the same meridian. Due to the fact that the earth rotates in a diurnal cycle as well as moves forward in its orbit, the time required for one full rotation of the earth is less than a solar day by about 4 minutes.

In many solar energy applications one needs to calculate the day number (DN) corresponding to a given date. In a given year, DN is defined as the number of days elapsed since the start of the year up to a given date.

4.2.1.2 Equation of time, EOT

The solar day defined above varies in length throughout the year due to:

(a) the tilt of the earth's axis with respect to the plane of the ecliptic containing the respective centres of sun and the earth, and
(b) the angle swept out by the earth–sun vector during any given period of time, which depends upon the earth's position in its orbit.

Thus, the standard time (as recorded by clocks running at a constant speed) differs from the solar time. The difference between the standard time and solar time is defined as the equation of time, EOT. EOT may be obtained as expressed by Woolf (1968):

$$\text{EOT} = 0.1236 \sin x - 0.0043 \cos x + 0.1538 \sin 2x + 0.608 \cos 2x \qquad (4.2.1)$$

where $x = 360 \, (\text{DN}-1)/365.242$, DN $= 1$ for 1 January in any given year. In any non-leap year, EOT is nil for 15 April, 13 June, 1 September and 25 December. A more precise model for EOT developed by Yallop (1992) will be presented later on in this section.

4.2.1.3 Apparent solar time, AST

Solar time is the time to be used in all solar geometry calculations. It is necessary to apply the corrections due to the difference between the longitude of the given locality (LONG) and the longitude of the standard time meridian (LSM). This correction is needed in addition to the equation of time. Thus,

$$\text{AST} = \text{standard time(local civil time)} + \text{EOT} \pm [(\text{LSM} - \text{LONG})/15]$$
$$(4.2.2)$$

In Eq. (4.2.2), EOT is expressed in hours. The algebraic sign preceding the longitudinal correction terms, contained in the squared brackets should be inserted as (+)ve for longitudes which lie east of LSM and vice versa. The LSM and LONG themselves have no sign associated with them.

4.2.1.4 Solar declination, DEC

The angle between the earth–sun vector and the equatorial plane is called the solar declination angle, DEC. As an adopted convention DEC is considered to be positive when the earth–sun vector lies northwards of the equatorial plane. Declination may also be defined as the angular position of the sun at noon (apparent solar time) with respect to the equatorial plane.

A simple formulation for DEC is provided in Kreider and Kreith (1981):

$$\text{DEC} = \sin^{-1}\{0.39795\cos[0.98563(\text{DN} - 1)]\} \qquad (4.2.3)$$

Yallop's (1992) algorithm given below enables a high-precision computation of EOT and DEC. The present routine is valid for the period 1980–2050 and has an accuracy of 3 seconds for the EOT and 1 minute of arc for DEC.

The following intermediate terms need to be obtained. For a given year (y), month (m), day (D), hour (h), minute (min) and second (s),

$$t = \{(\text{UT}/24) + \text{D} + [30.6\text{m} + 0.5] + [365.25(\text{y} - 1976)] - 8707.5\}/36525$$
$$(4.2.4)$$

where UT is the universal time $= h + (\text{min}/60) + (s/3600)$. In Eq. (4.2.4), if $m > 2$ then $y = y$ and $m = m - 3$, otherwise $y = y - 1$ and $m = m + 9$.

In the expression above for t, $[x]$ denotes the integer part of x.

$G = 357.528 + 35999.05t$
$C = 1.915 \sin G + 0.020 \sin 2G$
$L = 280.460 + 36000.770t + C$
$\alpha = L - 2.466 \sin 2L + 0.053 \sin 4L$
The Greenwich Hour Angle, $\text{GHA} = 15\text{UT} - 180 - C + L - \alpha$

If necessary add or subtract multiples of 360 degrees to G, L and GHA to set them in the range 0 to 360°.

The obliquity of the ecliptic, $\varepsilon = 23.4393 - 0.013t$
The solar declination angle, $\text{DEC} = \tan^{-1}(\tan \varepsilon \sin \alpha)$
The equation of time, $\text{EOT} = (L - C - \alpha)/15$

In this text all Visual Basic for Application (VBA) routines for EOT and DEC are based on Yallop's algorithm. These routines are, of course, part of the various workbooks provided in the accompanying compact disc. The electronic data file Data4-01.xls contains a complete four-year (leap) cycle, daily values of EOT and DEC computed for noon GMT. Where high computing speed is required this file may be used with the users' own routines or workbooks. These data were provided by the Royal Greenwich Observatory for Muneer's earlier book (Muneer, 1997a) and the accuracy of the EOT and DEC values are far higher than those obtainable via Yallop's algorithm presented above.

4.2.1.5 Solar geometry

Refer to Figure 4.2.1. The sun's position in the sky can be described in terms of two angles, solar altitude (SOLALT), the elevation angle above the horizon, and solar azimuth (SOLAZM), the azimuth from north of the sun's beam projection on the horizontal plane (clockwise = +ve). These co-ordinates which describe the sun's position are dependent on the apparent solar time (AST), the latitude (LAT) and longitude (LONG) of the location, and DEC. The solar geometry may be obtained as follows:

$$\sin(\text{SOLALT}) = \sin \text{LAT} \sin \text{DEC} + \cos \text{LAT} \cos \text{DEC} \cos \text{SHA} \qquad (4.2.5)$$

$$\cos(\text{SOLAZM}) = \frac{\cos \text{DEC}(\cos \text{LAT} \tan \text{DEC} - \sin \text{LAT} \cos \text{SHA})}{\cos(\text{SOLALT})} \qquad (4.2.6)$$

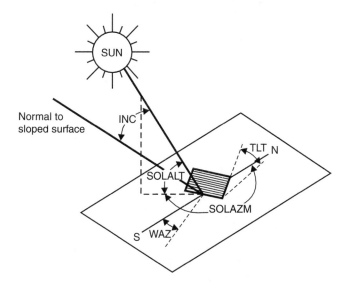

Figure 4.2.1 *Solar geometry for a sloping surface (Muneer, 1997a)*

The solar hour angle, SHA, is the angular displacement of the sun from the local meridian at 15° per hour.

The angle of incidence, INC, that the sun's beam strikes a sloped surface of any given tilt can then be calculated from the solar altitude, azimuth and the orientation of the surface as expressed by its wall azimuth angle (WAZ). The sign convention adopted for WAZ is the same as that used for SOLAZM, i.e. clockwise from North is considered positive.

$$INC = \cos^{-1}[\cos SOLALT \cos(SOLAZM - WAZ) \sin TLT \\ + \cos TLT \sin SOLALT] \tag{4.2.7}$$

Figure 4.2.1 shows the angles relevant to the determination of sun's position and the geometry for a tilted surface.

An interactive sun position calculator based on Yallop's algorithm is available via the World Wide Web. See Section 4.1.1 for further details.

4.2.1.6 Sunrise and sunset

Astronomers define sunrise and sunset as the moment at which the centre of the solar disk is along the horizon of the earth. Using Eqs (4.2.5) and (4.2.2) (in that order), the sunrise/sunset instance may be computed by setting SOLALT $=0$. The actual sunrise and sunset, however, do not occur at the time when the sun's elevation is zero. This is due to the refraction of light by the terrestrial atmosphere. A ray of light travelling in vacuum from the sun which is actually below the earth's horizon is bent towards the earth by the heavier medium, air. Hence actual sunrise appears slightly before astronomical sunrise and actual sunset occurs after astronomical sunset. Further, for locations which are higher than the sea level, the sun will appear in the morning slightly earlier. Corrections have therefore to be made for the above refraction and altitude effects. Eq. (4.2.8) for SOLALT (degree) refers to the instance of actual sunrise or sunset:

$$SOLALT = -0.8333 - 0.0347H^{0.5} \tag{4.2.8}$$

H in the above equation is the station height in metres above sea level.

Muneer (1997a) has presented an exhaustive account of models and electronic tools, on a compact disc, for precisely obtaining solar geometry. Using the latter reference a number of Excel workbooks have been developed. These workbooks enable solar radiation computations to be performed with much more ease within the spreadsheet environment. Examples extracted from the above reference are given below. These may be used as illustrations for the computational routines discussed above.

Example 4.2.1

Calculate the EOT, DEC, AST, solar altitude and sun's azimuth for Edinburgh, UK [LAT = 55.95°N, LONG = 3.20°W and LSM = 0] at 12 noon LCT on 21 March 1997. Find the angle of incidence of the sun's beam on a surface with a given tilt of 45° and orientation 15° west of south. Also, find the time for sunrise and sunset for the given date (assume $H = 0$). Note that the required input value of the wall azimuth angle, WAZ, is 195° (= 180 + 15).

Using Excel workbooks Calc4-01 (for EOT and DEC), Calc4-02 (for AST), Calc4-03 (for sunrise and sunset times) and Calc4-04a (for solar geometry) the following are obtained:

EOT = −0.12 h (7 minutes and 10 seconds)
DEC = 0.40° (0° 21′)
AST = 11.67 h
Sunrise time = 0611 hours GMT
Sunset time = 1828 hours GMT
SOLALT = 34.3°
SOLAZM = 174°
INC = 19.3°

Note that a supplementary workbook, Calc4-04b, is also available on the compact disc. This workbook provides mid-hour (based on solar time) sun geometry for the 24-hour cycle, taking into account the sunrise and sunset events. For the hours neighbouring these events the geometry is computed in the following manner. For the sunrise event the geometry is computed at mid-point between the sunrise and the integer hour immediately following sunrise, and likewise, at mid-point between the integer hour preceding the sunset and sunset event itself. For example, if for a given date and location, the sunrise and sunset events were respectively to occur at 0540 and 1820 hours AST, the geometry would respectively be computed at 0550 and 1810 hours AST.

The choice of AST in Calc4-04b is justified on the grounds that most meteorological office data are available in solar time.

4.2.2 Hourly horizontal irradiation

The frequency at which solar radiation data are required depends on the application. With the advent of cheap yet powerful desktop computers it is now possible to perform energy-system simulations using hourly or sub-hourly data. Such simulations, however, require reliable estimates of slope irradiation and illuminance, computed from the corresponding horizontal global and diffuse energy data. Note that global refers to total amount of irradiation and diffuse to the irradiation received from the sky and that reflected from the ground, if any. Under an overcast sky the diffuse and global irradiation become equal.

Table 4.2.1 Monthly-averaged horizontal daily global and diffuse irradiation (kWh/m^2) – UK sites (Muneer, 1999)

Month	1	2	3	4	5	6	7	8	9	10	11	12
Lerwick 60.133°N, 1.183°W												
Global	0.21	0.79	1.76	3.28	3.94	4.81	4.16	3.35	2.06	1.03	0.37	0.14
Diffuse	0.18	0.51	1.11	1.98	2.46	2.72	2.75	2.11	1.35	0.69	0.28	0.12
Aberdeen 57.15°N, 2.1°W												
Global	0.42	1.02	1.83	3.19	3.96	4.32	3.83	3.15	2.26	1.26	0.55	0.32
Diffuse	0.27	0.6	1.09	1.73	2.23	2.46	2.29	1.88	1.31	0.74	0.35	0.21
Dundee 56.483°N, 3.0°W												
Global	0.45	1.07	1.82	3.2	3.96	4.26	3.91	3.19	2.29	1.27	0.6	0.34
Diffuse	0.29	0.63	1.1	1.75	2.23	2.45	2.31	1.89	1.33	0.76	0.37	0.22
Edinburgh 55.95°N, 3.2°W												
Global	0.43	1.0	1.82	3.21	4.1	4.5	4.09	3.34	2.35	1.3	0.57	0.33
Diffuse	0.29	0.62	1.11	1.76	2.25	2.48	2.34	1.93	1.35	0.78	0.37	0.23
Glasgow 55.867°N, 4.233°W												
Global	0.4	0.95	1.77	3.19	4.22	4.49	3.96	3.28	2.18	1.18	0.54	0.3
Diffuse	0.28	0.61	1.1	1.76	2.26	2.48	2.32	1.92	1.32	0.75	0.37	0.22
Eskdalemuir 55.317°N, 3.200°W												
Global	0.38	1.12	2.01	3.25	3.9	4.67	4.06	3.42	2.31	1.29	0.65	0.34
Diffuse	0.28	0.68	1.25	1.94	2.4	2.72	2.51	2.16	1.45	0.81	0.41	0.23
Newcastle 54.983°N, 1.583°W												
Global	0.47	1.03	1.9	3.28	4.06	4.51	4.08	3.36	2.41	1.37	0.61	0.37
Diffuse	0.32	0.65	1.15	1.78	2.26	2.49	2.35	1.94	1.38	0.82	0.4	0.25
Aldergrove 54.650°N, 6.217°W												
Global	0.48	1.15	2.18	3.63	4.34	5.24	4.37	3.59	2.65	1.38	0.73	0.39
Diffuse	0.33	0.73	1.31	2.08	2.61	2.86	2.76	2.34	1.59	0.89	0.46	0.28
Belfast 54.583°N, 5.917°W												
Global	0.49	1.06	1.92	3.35	4.38	4.44	3.67	3.26	2.23	1.26	0.65	0.36
Diffuse	0.34	0.67	1.16	1.8	2.29	2.48	2.27	1.93	1.36	0.8	0.42	0.26
Manchester 53.5°N, 2.25°W												
Global	0.51	1.06	2.05	3.27	4.32	4.75	3.99	3.52	2.47	1.44	0.65	0.42
Diffuse	0.36	0.69	1.21	1.81	2.3	2.51	2.34	1.99	1.42	0.87	0.44	0.29
Liverpool 53.417°N, 2.917°W												
Global	0.53	1.08	2.06	3.31	4.32	4.85	4.12	3.54	2.44	1.39	0.67	0.43
Diffuse	0.37	0.7	1.21	1.82	2.3	2.51	2.36	1.99	1.42	0.86	0.45	0.3
Sheffield 53.383°N, 1.5°W												
Global	0.51	1.0	1.87	3.07	4.01	4.63	4.06	3.39	2.38	1.37	0.62	0.41
Diffuse	0.36	0.67	1.17	1.79	2.27	2.5	2.35	1.97	1.41	0.85	0.43	0.29
Leicester 52.633°N, 1.083°W												
Global	0.55	1.12	2.0	3.26	4.28	4.71	4.22	3.59	2.52	1.47	0.7	0.45
Diffuse	0.39	0.72	1.22	1.83	2.3	2.51	2.38	2.01	1.45	0.89	0.47	0.32
Birmingham 52.5°N, 1.833°W												
Global	0.57	1.07	1.97	3.65	4.15	4.68	4.16	3.55	2.5	1.45	0.69	0.47
Diffuse	0.39	0.71	1.22	1.86	2.29	2.51	2.37	2.0	1.45	0.89	0.47	0.33
Cambridge 52.217°N, 0.1°E												
Global	0.61	1.28	2.35	3.28	4.56	5.14	4.65	3.59	2.86	1.66	0.93	0.49
Diffuse	0.45	0.83	1.38	2.0	2.66	2.92	2.76	2.19	1.63	1.0	0.58	0.36
Aberporth 52.133°N, 4.567°W												
Global	0.63	1.36	2.58	3.99	4.88	5.54	5.1	4.08	3.07	1.71	0.83	0.53
Diffuse	0.48	0.86	1.43	2.16	2.56	2.76	2.81	2.34	1.69	1.03	0.59	0.39

Table 4.2.1 (Continued)

Month	1	2	3	4	5	6	7	8	9	10	11	12
London 51.517°N, 0.017°W												
Global	0.56	1.14	2.06	3.12	4.1	5.03	4.46	3.58	2.69	1.59	0.81	0.48
Diffuse	0.4	0.73	1.22	1.89	2.4	2.55	2.55	2.07	1.5	0.92	0.53	0.33
Cardiff 51.483°N, 3.217°W												
Global	0.65	1.28	2.32	3.65	4.61	5.1	4.6	4.01	2.75	1.64	0.82	0.55
Diffuse	0.44	0.79	1.3	1.88	2.33	2.52	2.42	2.05	1.51	0.95	0.53	0.37
Bristol 51.43°N, 2.58°W												
Global	0.62	1.17	2.17	3.53	4.52	5.04	4.58	3.89	2.7	1.56	0.78	0.53
Diffuse	0.43	0.76	1.28	1.87	2.32	2.53	2.42	2.05	1.5	0.94	0.52	0.36
Easthampstead 51.383°N, 0.783°W												
Global	0.62	1.24	2.32	3.32	4.41	5.22	4.7	3.9	2.92	1.7	0.91	0.53
Diffuse	0.45	0.83	1.36	2.01	2.64	2.76	2.75	2.26	1.69	1.02	0.58	0.38
Plymouth 50.383°N, 4.167°W												
Global	0.75	1.4	2.48	3.99	5.0	5.32	4.84	4.21	3.01	1.8	0.93	0.64
Diffuse	0.49	0.84	1.35	1.9	2.33	2.52	2.43	2.07	1.55	1.0	0.58	0.42
Jersey 49.183°N, 2.183°W												
Global	0.8	1.59	2.86	4.27	5.3	5.96	5.56	4.53	3.36	2.12	0.98	0.64
Diffuse	0.57	0.95	1.46	2.15	2.59	2.68	2.68	2.32	1.68	1.1	0.64	0.44

The UK radiation measurement network is one of the best in Europe, yet long-term hourly data for the latter quantities are available for only a limited number of sites. Therefore, methods are required for estimations to be carried out from long-term records of daily irradiation or other meteorological parameters such as humidity, pressure, sunshine and cloud-cover. In this section models are presented which enable computation of horizontal irradiance and illuminance.

It will be shown in this section that provided monthly-averaged horizontal daily irradiation data for the global and diffuse components are available, the electronic tools presented herein will enable:

(a) the decomposition of daily into hourly values, and
(b) the horizontal, hourly irradiation can then be used to obtain slope irradiation.

Table 4.2.1 presents monthly averaged horizontal daily irradiation data for a number of UK locations. There is extensive activity to produce an atlas of the solar energy resource. Examples in this respect are the work of Mani (1981) for India, Palz and Grief (1996) for Europe and Duffie and Beckman (1991) for the USA.

4.2.2.1 Hourly horizontal global irradiation

It will be shown in the following section that Liu and Jordan (1960) models may be used to obtain hourly irradiation data from long-term records of monthly-averaged daily values. Building simulation programs, however, need detailed hour-by-hour data. In the absence of measurements, reliable computational methods based on other meteorological data may be used. Such models estimate the beam transmission through the terrestrial atmosphere and its attenuation due to the presence of clouds and mixed gases (such as oxygen, nitrogen and carbon dioxide), water vapour, ozone and aerosols. The amount of cloud is a measure of the proportion of the sky-cover while the duration of bright sunshine determines the frequency of cloud-cover.

Models based on sunshine are considered to be more reliable as the input variable is properly registered by a sunshine recorder in contrast to a single spot reading of the cloud amount based on a visual estimate. According to Bennett (1969) 70–85% of solar radiation variance is explained by sunshine duration in contrast to the figure of 50% quoted against cloud amount.

Research teams at Napier University in Scotland, Sheffield University in England and Waterloo University in Canada have been engaged in separate projects to develop solar radiation models, based on variables routinely recorded by meteorological networks, for the generation of world-wide data tables. The so-called meteorological radiation model (MRM) is based on sunshine fraction and temperature data. In the present text the MRM has been renamed SRM (sunshine radiation model). The cloud-cover radiation model (CRM) uses information regarding the amount of sky covered with clouds. When evaluated, these models have been found to confirm the findings of Bennett (1969). A new approach developed by Page (1997), called the 'PRM' for (Page radiation model) is based on a combination of sunshine and cloud-cover data to calculate solar radiation.

The SRM, the CRM and Page's combined approach using data from UK sites: London (51.6°N, 0.2°W), Bracknell (51.3°N, 0.5°W)/Heathrow (51.3°N, 0.3°W), Finningley (53.0°N, 1.0°W), Aughton (53.3°N, 2.5°W)/Ringway (53.2°N, 2.1°W) and Stornoway (58.2°N, 6.4°W) will be discussed later in this chapter. Page's model has been found to perform effectively under overcast conditions, with a slightly poorer performance compared with the SRM and CRM under intermediate and clear sky conditions. Readers will be able to perform their own computations using a number of relevant workbooks and sample data files provided on the accompanying compact disc. Data4-02.xls provides simultaneous meteorological and irradiation (horizontal and slope) data and these may be used for undertaking independent evaluations of the above procedures.

4.2.2.2 The cloud radiation model (CRM)

Cloud data are extensively used for estimating global and diffuse irradiance. Kasten and Czeplak (1979) have shown that for any given cloud amount, the ratio of global irradiance to global irradiance under a corresponding cloudless sky is independent of solar elevation. In order to determine global irradiance I_G under a cloud amount of N, the irradiance under a cloudless sky $I_{G,0}$ must be known first. $I_{G,0}$ depends on solar altitude, SOLALT, and may be obtained thus:

$$I_{G,0} = (A \sin(\text{SOLALT}) - B) \qquad (4.2.9\text{a})$$

N is usually expressed in oktas of the sky obscured by clouds where an okta is a one-eighth portion of the hemisphere. The ratio of global irradiance I_G for a given cloud amount N to $I_{G,0}$ has been shown to be independent of the solar altitude:

$$I_G/I_{G,0} = 1 - C(N/8)^D \qquad (4.2.9\text{b})$$

The diffuse component is calculated as follows:

$$I_D/I_G = 0.3 + 0.7(N/8)^2 \qquad (4.2.9\text{c})$$

The values of the A, B, C and D coefficients are provided in Table 4.2.2. An improvement in performance results from the use of locally fitted coefficients. However, even with the coefficients originally presented by Kasten and Czeplak (1979) the CRM performs quite satisfactorily.

The Calc4-05.xls workbook provides an easy means of generating solar irradiance data based on the CRM procedure.

4.2.2.3 Solar radiation transmission through a terrestrial atmosphere

Most broadband solar radiation sensors work in the 300 nm to 3 μm band since this region covers 98% of the energy radiated by the sun. The distribution of the solar spectral irradiance is not uniform in the range of 250 nm to 25 μm, i.e. that part of the electromagnetic spectrum which starts with ultraviolet (UV) radiation and ends in the near-infrared (NIR) region. The summation of all energy received at individual wavelengths in the solar spectrum equals the solar constant, I_{SC} ($=1367$ W/m^2). This is the rate of the energy received on a surface normal to the sun's rays at the top of the earth's atmosphere and at a sun–earth distance equal to 1 AU (1 Astronomical Unit, $AU = 1.496 \times 10^{11}$ m), occurring at the vernal and autumnal equinoxes. The energy of the solar

Table 4.2.2 Coefficients for CRM (Eq. (4.2.9a–c) refers) (Gul et al., 1998)

	Latitude, N	A	B	C	D
Hamburg	58.3	910	30	0.75	3.4
Stornoway	58.2	979	45	0.73	3.4
Aldergrove	54.6	956	34	0.70	3.1
Finningley	53.0	902	36	0.71	3.7
London	51.5	948	49	0.71	3.4

spectrum is approximately distributed as follows: UV (8%), visible-band (46%) and NIR (46%).

The atmosphere extends to an altitude of 100 km or a pressure of 0.0005 mbar. The naturally occurring gases, O_2, N_2 and CO_2 (mixed gases), O_3, H_2O and aerosols, play a significant role in the absorption of solar radiation. When solar radiation enters the earth's atmosphere a part of the incident energy is lost by the mechanisms of scattering and absorption. The scattered radiation is called diffuse radiation, while that part which arrives at the earth's surface directly from the sun is called direct or beam radiation. According to the Bouguer–Lambert law, the attenuation of light through a medium is proportional to the distance traversed in the medium and the local flux of radiation. Thus,

$$I_B = I_E \exp(-km) \tag{4.2.10}$$

k and m are respectively known as the total attenuation coefficient and air mass. Defining the transmission coefficient as $\tau = \exp(km)$, Eq. (4.2.10) may be written as $I_B = I_E \tau$, where I_B and I_E are respectively the beam and extra-terrestrial irradiance on a horizontal surface. I_E may be computed from

$$I_E = 1367[1 + 0.033\cos(0.0172024DN)]\sin(\text{SOLALT}) \tag{4.2.11}$$

When an electromagnetic wave strikes a particle, part of the incident energy is scattered in all directions. If the particle size is smaller than the wavelength, the phenomenon is called Rayleigh scattering. However, if the particle is of the order of the wavelength the process is known as Mie scattering. Usually air molecules cause Rayleigh and aerosols Mie scattering. Therefore if τ_r and τ_α are the respective transmittances for the Rayleigh and Mie scattering and τ_g, τ_o, and τ_w the mixed-gases, ozone and water vapour transmittances, Eq. (4.2.10) becomes

$$I_B = I_E \tau_r \tau_\alpha \tau_g \tau_o \tau_w \tag{4.2.12}$$

4.2.2.4   The sunshine radiation model (SRM)

Sunshine radiation model estimates the horizontal beam and diffuse components from only ground-based meteorological data – air temperature, relative humidity (or wet-bulb temperature) and sunshine duration. Such data are readily available world-wide. The SRM is therefore a useful tool and can provide reliable estimates of horizontal diffuse, beam and global irradiance.

The SRM for non-overcast conditions consists of regression between the hourly diffuse to beam ratio (DBR $= I_D/I_B$) and the beam clearness index ($k_B = I_B/I_E$). Thus,

$$\text{DBR} = 0.285 k_B^{-1.00648} \tag{4.2.13}$$

The beam irradiance, attenuated with the hourly sunshine fraction (SF) for non-overcast conditions, is defined as

$$I_B = (SF)I_E \tau_r \tau_\alpha \tau_g \tau_o \tau_w \qquad (4.2.14)$$

For a given value of SF, i.e. the duration of bright sunshine within the hour, the SRM respectively computes I_B and I_D using Eqs (4.2.14) and (4.2.13). Global irradiance for a non-overcast sky is then obtained as the sum of diffuse and beam irradiance. In the case of overcast skies the direct radiation reaching the earth is nil, hence there is no beam component. In this case the diffuse irradiance is modelled as

$$I_G = I_D = I_E \tau_{\alpha\alpha} \tau_g \tau_o \tau_w \left[\frac{0.5(1 - \tau_r)}{1 - m + m^{1.02}} + \frac{0.84(1 - \tau_{\alpha s})}{1 - m + m^{1.02}} \right] \qquad (4.2.15)$$

where $\tau_{\alpha\alpha}$ and $\tau_{\alpha s}$ are functions of m and τ_α. Further details are available in Muneer (1997a).

The model enables hour-by-hour computation of beam, diffuse and global irradiance. Its accuracy is most precise for clear sky conditions and worst during overcast periods. Gul et al. (1998) have provided a detailed account of the development of SRM.

The Calc4-06.xls workbook provides an easy means of generating solar irradiance data based on the SRM procedure.

4.2.2.5 Page radiation model (PRM)

The radiation model developed by John Page of Sheffield University was based on the work undertaken for the development of the *European Solar Radiation Atlas*. The cloudless sky model estimates the global irradiation from the sum of the estimated beam and diffuse irradiation falling on a horizontal surface. The overcast model determines the hourly values of overcast day irradiances from the daily models as a function of solar altitude using a sine-based second-order polynomial. A condensed version of the procedure is presented here. The procedure is quite involved, but it nevertheless produces good estimates of irradiation once the hourly sunshine and cloud cover are provided. In particular, the PRM procedure returns more precise values of overcast irradiation which will be of use in daylight design. Readers may, however, if they so wish, remain 'transparent' to the rather elaborate procedure by the use of workbooks presently available on the accompanying compact disc. The workbooks were built to generate all-sky and clear-sky irradiance.

4.2.2.6 Page clear sky radiation model

This clear sky irradiation model was originally developed by Page as a key component needed in the development of the *European Solar Radiation Atlas*

(Page, 1997). The cloudless sky model predicts the irradiance on the horizontal surfaces as a function of solar altitude and air mass 2 Linke turbidity factor, after incorporating the standard corrections to the mean solar distance, and air mass adjustment for station height. Global irradiation is estimated from the sum of estimated beam and diffuse irradiation falling on a horizontal surface. Note that a definition of some of the parameters presently under discussion is beyond the scope of this book. In this respect, the reader is referred to the work of Page (1997).

The solar beam irradiation normal to the beam depends on the solar altitude and the Linke turbidity factor is obtained first:

$$I_{Bn} = 1367 K_d \exp(-0.8662 m T_{LK} \delta_r(m)) \qquad (4.2.16)$$

K_d is the correction factor to allow for the varying solar distance and T_{LK} is the air mass 2 Linke turbidity factor. The air mass, m, is obtained by

$$m = 1/\{\sin \text{SOLALT} + 0.50572(\text{SOLALT} + 6.07995)^{-1.6364}\} \qquad (4.2.17)$$

$\delta_r(m)$ is the Rayleigh optical depth at air mass m and is calculated using the work of Louche et al. (1986).

In this model the diffuse irradiation of the cloudless sky depends on the solar altitude and air mass 2 Linke turbidity factor. As the sky becomes more turbid the diffuse irradiance increases while the beam irradiance decreases.

The diffuse modelling is carried out in two stages. First the value of diffuse transmittance is established. This is the theoretical diffuse irradiance on a horizontal surface with the sun vertically overhead for the air mass 2 Linke turbidity factor, T_{LK}, selected. The cloudless sky diffuse irradiance is then obtained as the product of K_d, the diffuse transmittance and a solar altitude dependent function.

Total global irradiation under clear sky conditions, I_{Gc}, is then calculated as the sum of beam and diffuse components. Further details may be obtained from Kinghorn and Muneer (1998).

4.2.2.7   Page extreme clarity clear sky model

In order to establish credible upper limits over the wide range of air mass 2 Linke turbidity factors that may occur in practice, a second beam irradiance calculation is performed. The Linke turbidity factor is set to its lowest possible value. The model provides control values of the maximum acceptable values of hourly global irradiance using the cloudless sky model described above.

4.2.2.8   Page overcast sky radiation model

The key initial input into the daily overcast sky model is the daily transmittance for the overcast conditions. This is the ratio of the overcast day daily irradiation, on a horizontal plane to the extraterrestrial daily irradiation. For hours with cloud = 8 oktas, the daily transmittance for overcast conditions in the UK is estimated using the work of Cowley (1978). For hours with cloud = 7 oktas, the daily transmittance for overcast conditions is set as being equal to 0.30 for all months.

4.2.2.9 Conversion from daily global irradiation to hourly diffuse irradiance

The daily global radiation information has next to be linked with the overcast sky diffuse irradiance model. This associated hourly overcast radiation model is based on the estimation of the overcast sky transmittance with the sun directly overhead combined with the application of an overcast sky solar elevation function to estimate the overcast day global irradiance value at any solar elevation. If the hourly transmittance were constant, the correction would be equal to the sine of the solar altitude. As this is not so, a second-order sine polynomial is used to calculate the overcast day solar elevation function. The formula used to calculate the overcast day irradiation is of the form

$$I_{Do} = K_d Tr_d[A(0) + A(1)\sin \text{SOLALT} + A(2)\sin^2 \text{SOLALT}] \qquad (4.2.18)$$

I_{Do} is the overcast day irradiation and Tr_d the corresponding transmittance for a solar elevation of $90°$ and $A(0)$, $A(1)$ and $A(2)$ are constants dependent on sky type. Global irradiance is then obtained as

$$I_G = (I_{Gc} - I_{Do})\text{SF} + I_{Do} \qquad (4.2.19)$$

The DLL-based workbooks Calc4-07a.xls and Calc4-07b respectively provide easy means of generating solar irradiance data for all-sky and clear-sky conditions based on the PRM procedure.

Example 4.2.2

Table 4.2.3 provides measured hourly weather data for Bracknell, west London. Using the CRM, SRM and PRM models, obtain the respective hourly horizontal global and diffuse irradiation values.

Calc4-05.xls, Calc4-06.xls and Calc4-07a.xls workbooks may be used to generate the output shown in Table 4.2.3. Note that Calc4-07a.xls is a DLL-based workbook. The text box provided below should be referred to for the execution of all such files. It may be seen that for the non-overcast conditions, the CRM and SRM provide global irradiation estimates which are better than the corresponding PRM values. On the other hand, the PRM produces better irradiation estimates under overcast conditions as has been shown by Kinghorn and Muneer (1998). Table 4.2.4, based on the material presented in this reference, provides a more detailed evaluation of the above three procedures for obtaining irradiation on a horizontal plane.

Table 4.2.3 Comparison of radiation models for Bracknell, England (August 1990)*

Date	Hour ending	Measured	Solar irradiation, W/m^2 CRM	SRM	PRM
19	5	0	6	6	6
19	6	12	31	31	31
19	7	29	50	124	45
19	8	44	85	225	76
19	9	55	116	321	106
19	10	107	142	404	132
19	11	167	160	463	151
19	12	198	169	491	161
19	13	294	169	489	161
19	14	340	334	375	443
19	15	253	296	399	282
19	16	105	243	319	227
19	17	65	177	223	162
19	18	66	104	123	96
19	19	17	30	30	30
19	20	1	6	6	6
20	5	1	6	6	6
20	6	45	29	29	29
20	7	161	103	163	161
20	8	329	176	313	335
20	9	441	242	456	491
20	10	548	295	577	625
20	11	616	456	661	721
20	12	591	571	705	770
20	13	428	483	704	770
20	14	643	456	658	720
20	15	523	404	538	589
20	16	303	390	381	411
20	17	253	175	286	299
20	18	65	102	113	110
20	19	37	28	28	28
20	20	1	6	6	6

*Data4-02.xls refers

For all DLL-based workbooks the following procedure **MUST** be used:
- Launch Excel software
- Open the DLL-based workbook
- Enter data in the relevant worksheet(s)
- Simultaneously press ALT + F8 keys
- Select the relevant macro from the dialog box
- Either click the Run button, or simultaneously press ALT + R keys

Table 4.2.4 Comparison of hourly global irradiation models

Location	Latitude N	MBE* (W/m^2)			RMSE** (W/m^2)		
		CRM	MRM	PRM	CRM	MRM	PRM
(a) Overcast skies, K_t < 0.2							
London	51.5	33	53	6	54	65	34
Bracknell	51.4	38	53	−1	63	67	43
Finningley	53.0	33	51	2	57	63	47
Aughton	53.3	55	55	5	83	74	131
Stornoway	58.2	37	51	−2	57	64	66
(b) Intermediate skies, 0.2 < K_t < 0.6							
London	51.5	2	18	21	69	66	64
Bracknell	51.4	−6	5	20	81	80	99
Finningley	53.0	−1	0	22	71	68	113
Aughton	53.3	−2	−3	17	87	92	130
Stornoway	58.2	1	4	13	72	82	98
(c) Clear skies, K_t > 0.6							
London	51.5	−56	−11	88	95	38	122
Bracknell	51.4	−86	−40	93	129	71	153
Finningley	53.0	−55	−22	96	91	49	178
Aughton	53.3	−101	−75	95	142	122	213
Stornoway	58.2	−95	−77	81	122	108	149

K_t Hourly clearness index
MBE*   Mean Bias Error
RMSE**   Root Mean Square Error

4.2.2.10   Page clear-sky radiation model (PCSRM)

It will be demonstrated here that the Page clear-sky radiation model provides an accurate means of obtaining global irradiation for worldwide locations. As a matter of fact this procedure was adopted in the production of CIBSE Guide J. The only parameter required is the turbidity factor. An average value of 3.5 for the air mass 2 Linke turbidity was found to produce reasonably good estimates for world-wide locations. The following example demonstrates the use of the PCSRM.

Example 4.2.3

In many instances it is important to obtain estimates of clear-sky irradiation so that the effect of large glazed facades on the cooling load of a building may be investigated. The PCSRM originally developed as part of the new *European Solar Radiation Atlas* is a powerful and useful facility for such an exercise. The PCSRM was also used in the production of clear-day tables for world-wide locations within the CIBSE Guide J for Weather and Solar data. The PCSRM has been validated by Page (1997) using clear-sky data from Indian locations and shows consistency with an optimum value of 3.5 for the Linke turbidity factor. Use the Calc4-07b.xls workbook to evaluate the PCSRM against clear-sky data for Jodhpur (India) data provided in Table 4.2.5. Calc4-07b.xls is a DLL-based workbook. The text box provided above should be referred to for the execution of all such files.

The computed values of I_G and I_D are included in Table 4.2.5. Table 4.2.6 shows the performance of the PCSRM on a monthly-averaged basis.

The CRM, SRM and PRM are good tools when missing records of measured irradiance are to be filled-in to create complete (and unbroken) time series. Such time-series are required for serious simulation work on building energy performance.

Table 4.2.5 Evaluation of Page clear sky radiation model (PCSRM) for Jodhpur, India
Latitude = 26.3°N, Longitude = 73°E, LSM = 82.5°E
Date: 26 October 1971

			Measured data*		Computed data	
Hour	DBT	WBT	I_G W/m^2	I_D W/m^2	I_G W/m^2	I_D W/m^2
1	24.9	17.0	0	0	0	0
2	24.2	16.8	0	0	0	0
3	23.5	16.7	0	0	0	0
4	23.0	16.6	0	0	0	0
5	22.4	16.4	0	0	0	0
6	21.8	16.2	0	0	0	0
7	21.4	16.2	38	10	20	20
8	22.2	16.4	243	51	192	68
9	25.1	17.9	465	71	415	101
10	28.2	19.0	640	80	613	120
11	31.0	19.9	752	81	756	129
12	33.0	20.1	826	88	830	132
13	34.1	19.8	820	87	830	132
14	34.7	19.5	740	88	755	129
15	34.8	19.2	600	78	612	120
16	34.5	18.9	405	66	414	101
17	33.9	18.6	185	45	191	68
18	32.4	18.6	13	6	20	20
19	30.3	17.9	0	0	0	0
20	28.8	17.7	0	0	0	0
21	27.6	17.4	0	0	0	0
22	26.8	17.4	0	0	0	0
23	26.1	17.2	0	0	0	0
24	25.3	16.7	0	0	0	0

DBT	Dry-bulb temperature, °C
WBT	Wet-bulb temperature, °C
I_G	Hourly global irradiance, W/m^2
I_D	Hourly diffuse irradiance, W/m^2

*Mani (1981).

Table 4.2.6 Evaluation of PCSRM for Jodhpur, India (data averaged over a 10-year period)
Latitude = 26.3°N, Longitude = 73°E, LSM = 82.5°E

Month	Hour	SF	Measured* I_G	Computed I_G	% error	Measured I_D	Computed I_D	% error
February	10	1	607	604	−1	143	120	−16
	11	1	740	747	1	159	129	−19
	12	1	802	822	2	166	132	−20
	13	1	803	822	2	168	102	−40
	14	1	729	748	3	164	96	−42
April	9	1	577	625	8	194	121	−37
	10	1	754	830	10	227	132	−42
	11	1	883	976	11	243	135	−44
	12	1	944	1051	11	254	135	−47
	13	1	942	1051	12	256	102	−60
	14	1	865	976	13	260	96	−63
May	9	1	603	685	14	231	125	−46
	10	1	771	882	14	259	134	−48
	11	1	892	1022	15	274	135	−51
	12	1	953	1094	15	278	135	−51
	13	1	951	1094	15	281	135	−52
	14	1	884	1022	16	276	135	−51
	15	1	751	882	17	269	134	−50
October	11	1	758	807	6	132	131	−1
	12	1	824	882	7	141	133	−5
	13	1	823	882	7	147	102	−31
November	9	1	363	343	−5	85	88	3
	10	1	541	532	−2	100	110	10
	11	1	663	670	1	108	122	13
	12	1	727	742	2	115	126	10
	13	1	723	742	3	116	126	9
	14	1	654	669	2	116	121	5
	15	1	526	531	1	102	110	8

*Mani (1981).

4.2.2.11 Hourly horizontal diffuse irradiation

Following the approach of Liu and Jordan (1960), Orgill and Hollands (1977) have presented a case to correlate hourly diffuse ratio (I_D/I_G) and hourly clearness index (K_t). Erbs et al. (1982) followed their procedure to develop a regression model for the USA. Spencer (1982) and Muneer et al. (1984) have respectively presented models for Australian and Indian locations. Muneer and Saluja (1986) have provided Eq. (4.2.20), fitted for the mean global data and this may be used to estimate the horizontal diffuse irradiance in the absence of a regression model for any given location. If, however, models for specific locations are available they may indeed be used instead for achieving higher accuracy:

$$I_D/I_G = 1.006 - 0.371K_t + 3.1241K_t^2 - 12.7616K_t^3 + 9.7166K_t^4 \qquad (4.2.20)$$

Muneer (1997a) has provided an extensive survey of the relevant diffuse radiation models for locations world-wide.

Example 4.2.4

Hourly global irradiance values are provided for Bracknell in the electronic workbook Data4-02.xls contained in the compact disc. Use Eq. (4.2.20) to obtain the corresponding diffuse irradiance estimates. Evaluate these estimates against the measured values reported in the above workbook.

Calc4-08.xls may be used to obtain the above estimates for I_D. The estimated and measured diffuse radiation values are respectively given in columns J and L of the workbook. It is evident that using the given regression provides reasonable estimates of the desired quantity.

4.2.2.12 *Monthly-averaged hourly horizontal global irradiation*

Often a window designer needs to perform abbreviated analysis using monthly-averaged hourly irradiation and temperature data. For this purpose one needs to obtain hourly data from records of monthly-averaged daily data sets, which are readily available in the meteorological archives. The following section presents models for these tasks.

The original work in this field is attributed to Whillier (1956). Liu and Jordan (1960) and Collares-Pereira and Rabl (1979) extended that work to develop a relationship which takes into account the effect of the displacement of the hour from solar noon (ω) and the day-length (ω_s), on the ratio of hourly to daily global irradiation (r_G):

$$r_G = \frac{\pi}{24}(a' + b' \cos \omega) \frac{\cos \omega - \cos \omega_s}{\cos \omega_s - \omega_s \cos \omega_s} \qquad (4.2.21)$$

$a' = 0.409 + 0.5016 \sin(\omega_s - 1.047)$ and $b' = 0.6609 - 0.4767 \sin(\omega_s - 1.047)$.

4.2.2.13 *Monthly averaged hourly horizontal diffuse irradiation*

Long-term averages of hourly diffuse irradiation can be computed from monthly-average values of daily diffuse irradiation if the ratio of hourly to daily diffuse irradiation, r_D, is known. Liu and Jordan (1960) have presented such a model:

$$r_D = \frac{\pi}{24} \frac{\cos \omega - \cos \omega_s}{\cos \omega_s - \omega_s \cos \omega_s} \qquad (4.2.22)$$

Example 4.2.5

Table 4.2.7 provides the monthly averaged daily irradiation for Eskdalemuir, Scotland. Using Eqs (4.2.21) and (4.2.22) obtain hourly estimates of irradiation.

Calc4-09.xls enables such computations. Note that Calc4-09.xls is a DLL-based workbook. The text box provided below Example 4.2.2 should be referred to for the execution of all such files.

Table 4.2.7 includes measured and computed hourly irradiation data. It is evident that except the sunrise/sunset period the procedure under discussion provides reasonable estimates of averaged-hourly irradiation.

Using Eqs (4.2.21) and (4.2.22) or Calc4-09.xls the monthly-averaged daily irradiation data presented in Table 4.2.1 may easily be decomposed into hourly values. For any given window design these data may then be used for undertaking the critical threshold analysis presented in Section 4.1.

Table 4.2.7 Monthly averaged hourly horizontal irradiation for Eskdalemuir (55.3°N, 3.2°W) (Muneer, 1997a)

Month	Time, h	6.5	7.5	8.5	9.5	10.5	11.5	12.5	13.5	14.5	15.5	16.5	17.5	Totals Wh/m^2
Measured values														
Jan.	I_G	0	0	8	36	64	83	81	67	36	8	0	0	381
	I_D	0	0	8	28	47	56	56	47	28	8	0	0	281
Feb.	I_G	3	14	61	125	172	197	194	164	117	58	14	0	1119
	I_D	3	11	42	75	103	117	114	100	72	42	11	0	683
March	I_G	19	81	153	219	267	286	289	258	208	147	75	19	2014
	I_D	17	53	97	133	164	172	169	156	128	94	53	17	1250
April	I_G	92	178	269	333	369	400	403	361	308	244	164	86	3247
	I_D	61	108	156	189	217	233	233	211	181	147	103	61	1936
May	I_G	147	231	297	358	411	422	428	397	358	303	225	144	3900
	I_D	94	142	178	214	242	261	258	244	217	183	139	94	2397
June	I_G	186	281	361	406	458	486	500	464	414	347	269	186	4669
	I_D	114	156	203	236	267	281	281	267	233	197	156	114	2717
Computed values														
Jan.	I_G	0	0	0	35	68	87	87	68	35	0	0	0	380
	I_D	0	0	0	29	50	60	60	50	29	0	0	0	278
Feb.	I_G	0	12	66	121	167	192	192	167	121	66	12	0	1116
	I_D	0	10	47	77	99	110	110	99	77	47	10	0	686
March	I_G	11	73	144	211	265	294	294	265	211	144	73	11	1996
	I_D	10	57	99	133	157	170	170	157	133	99	57	10	1252
April	I_G	88	165	246	319	376	406	406	376	319	246	165	88	3200
	I_D	66	112	153	187	211	223	223	211	187	153	112	66	1904
May	I_G	142	218	295	363	415	442	442	415	363	295	218	142	3750
	I_D	101	144	184	215	238	250	250	238	215	184	144	101	2264
June	I_G	191	270	348	416	467	494	494	467	416	348	270	191	4372
	I_D	123	164	201	231	252	263	263	252	231	201	164	123	2468

4.2.2.14   Hourly slope irradiation

The task of computing beam (direct) energy is a matter purely related to solar geometry. Hourly beam irradiance on a surface of slope TLT ($I_{B,TLT}$) is obtained by

$$I_{B,TLT} = I_B r_B \qquad (4.2.23a)$$

$$r_B = \max[0, \cos(\text{INC})/\sin(\text{SOLALT})] \qquad (4.2.23b)$$

where I_B is the difference between horizontal global (I_G) and diffuse irradiance (I_D).

Computation of the diffuse component on a surface of given orientation and tilt, however, is not as simple. Historically, the development of sky-diffuse models began with the work of Moon and Spencer (1942) who used measured data from Kiel in Germany, Chicago and Washington DC to demonstrate the anisotropic nature of the luminance distribution of overcast skies.

Many anisotropic sky-diffuse models use one form or another of a sky clarity index to describe the prevailing condition. Under non-overcast conditions the constituent components of sky-diffuse irradiance are circumsolar (sun's aureole) and background diffuse irradiance. The sky clarity indices are used to 'mix' the above-mentioned components. The most common of all the sky clarity indices is the 'clearness function' of solar irradiation, F_{IR}:

$$F_{IR} = (I_G - I_D)/I_E \qquad (4.2.24)$$

A lower value of F_{IR} indicates higher turbidity.

With the exception of clear skies, very often the sky-diffuse irradiance is the dominant component. Precise estimation of this is therefore important for all solar energy-related work. The simplest of all slope irradiance models assumes an isotropic sky,

$$I_{D,TLT} = I_D \cos^2(\text{TLT}/2) \qquad (4.2.25)$$

However, diffuse irradiation is not isotropic in nature and is an angular function of the solar altitude and azimuth. More recent slope irradiance models therefore treat the sky-diffuse component as anisotropic. Most models under this category decompose non-overcast irradiance as the sum of two components, i.e. circumsolar and background sky-diffuse irradiance.

Muneer's model (Muneer, 1987, 1990a,b, 1995) and Saluja and Muneer (1987) treat the shaded and sunlit surfaces separately and further distinguish between overcast and non-overcast conditions of the sunlit surface. In this model the slope diffuse irradiation for surfaces in shade and sunlit surfaces under overcast sky is computed as

Plate 3.1 CFD plot of a double-glazing of 8 mm (left) and 20 mm (right) width. Temperature rasters on left, velocity rasters on right.

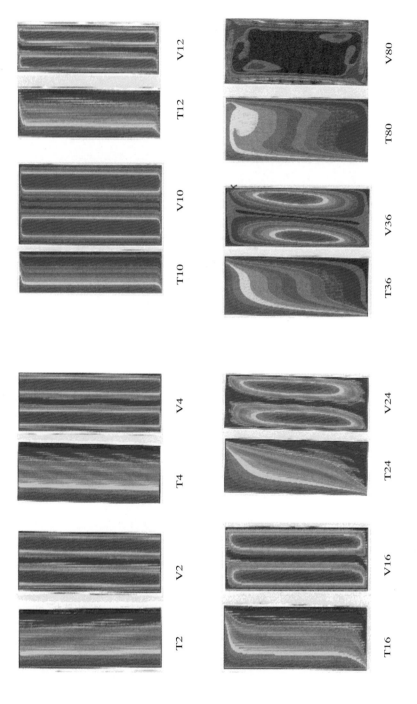

Plate 3.2 CFD temperature (T) and velocity (V) raster plot for varying cavity widths. Numbers indicate cavity width in mm

Plate 3.3 Infrared thermographs of ordinary double-glazed (top left) and super-insulated (bottom left) window. Condensation pattern on a double-glazed window (right)

Plate 5.1 RADIANCE output for daylight visualization in buildings

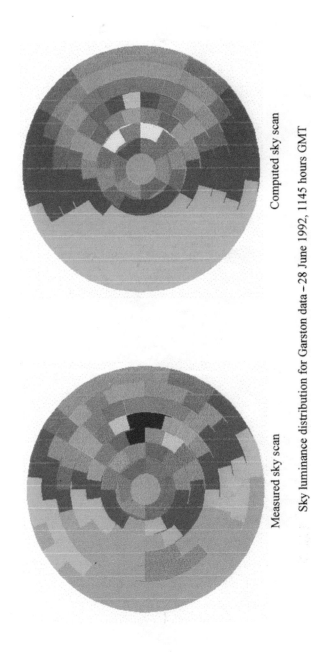

Measured sky scan

Computed sky scan

Sky luminance distribution for Garston data – 28 June 1992, 1145 hours GMT

Plate 5.2 Luminance distribution plot for Garston, UK – clear sky

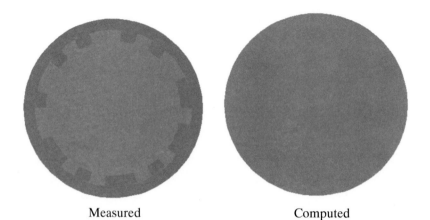

Measured   Computed

Heavy overcast sky 15 January 1992, 1105 hours

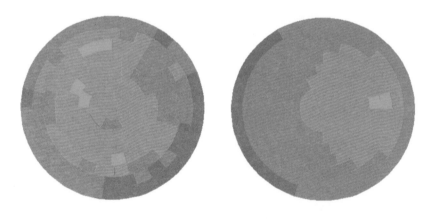

Measured   Computed

Thin overcast sky 17 March 1992, 1340 hours

Sky luminance distribution plots for Garston, UK

Plate 5.3 Luminance distribution plot for Garston, UK – overcast sky

$$I_{D,TLT} = I_D[TF] \tag{4.2.26}$$

where TF is the surface tilt factor. A sunlit surface under a non-overcast sky is modelled as

$$I_{D,TLT} = I_D[TF(1 - F_{IR}) + F_{IR}r_B] \tag{4.2.27}$$

$$TF = \cos^2(TLT/2) + 2b\{\pi(3 + 2b)\}^{-1}[\sin TLT - TLT \cos TLT \\ - \pi \sin^2(TLT/2)] \tag{4.2.28}$$

TF is obtained using a value of b, which corresponds to the appropriate sky and azimuthal condition. For the European climate a shaded surface is modelled with $b = 5.73$, while $b = 1.68$ for sun-facing surfaces under an overcast sky. Non-overcast skies, on the other hand, exhibit a continuously decreasing behaviour of b and therefore the following equations, obtained via data from 14 world-wide locations (Muneer, 1990a, 1995), are recommended:

$$2b\{\pi(3 + 2b)\}^{-1} = 0.003\,33 - 0.415\,F - 0.698\,7\,F^2 \text{[for Northern Europe]} \tag{4.2.29a}$$

$$2b\{\pi(3 + 2b)\}^{-1} = 0.002\,63 - 0.712\,F - 0.688\,3\,F^2 \text{[for Southern Europe]} \tag{4.2.29b}$$

$$2b\{\pi(3 + 2b)\}^{-1} = 0.080\,00 - 1.050\,F - 2.840\,0\,F^2 \text{[for Japan]} \tag{4.2.29c}$$

$$2b\{\pi(3 + 2b)\}^{-1} = 0.040\,00 - 0.820\,F - 2.026\,0\,F^2 \text{[for the world]} \tag{4.2.29d}$$

Example 4.2.6

Table 4.2.8 provides hourly horizontal and vertical irradiance for Edinburgh, UK. Estimates of slope irradiance using the isotropic and Muneer models, based on Calc4-10.xls, are included. The analysis suggests that the accuracy of predictions improves significantly when the isotropic model is replaced with the anisotropic model.

A considerable amount of data on solar radiation and daylight is available via the World Wide Web. See Section 4.1.1 and the Appendix for further details.

4.2.2.15 *Frequency distribution of irradiation*

Prediction of solar energy system performance can be achieved via detailed computer simulations using hourly or sub-hourly weather data or by simpler

Table 4.2.8 Measured and computed vertical irradiation for Edinburgh (55.95°N) (Muneer, 1997a)
Date: 12 August 1993. Units: W/m^2

Hour	I_G	I_D	North	Isotropic	Muneer	East	Isotropic	Muneer	South	Isotropic	Muneer
6	38	31	30	37	29	83	80	69	13	16	11
7	96	80	55	47	41	170	104	103	44	40	28
8	269	102	55	51	36	542	454	455	131	96	112
9	329	172	72	86	61	414	336	342	202	176	190
10	391	223	81	112	79	332	288	283	271	235	251
11	581	204	84	102	73	376	339	299	467	411	445
12	542	284	98	142	101	210	212	161	400	364	393
13	594	269	97	135	96	137	135	96	464	418	449
14	340	215	77	108	77	91	108	77	250	214	222
15	763	280	104	140	100	106	140	100	524	523	553
16	507	187	69	94	67	76	94	67	322	312	308
17	422	121	62	61	43	55	61	43	209	205	171
18	221	122	77	61	63	44	61	43	73	68	43
19	132	64	117	101	180	29	32	23	34	32	23
20	32	22	73	101	12	8	11	14	9	11	12

methods based on statistical analysis of long-term measurements. In this respect the daily clearness index, K_T, is widely used as a categorising parameter. Figures 4.2.2 – 4.2.4 show the K_T distributions, respectively, for the USA,

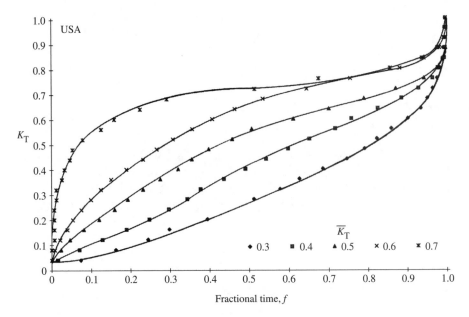

Figure 4.2.2 *Generalised curves for frequency of solar radiation – USA (Muneer, 1997a)*

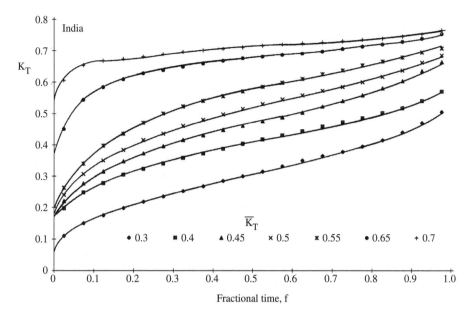

Figure 4.2.3 *Generalised curves for frequency of solar radiation – India (Muneer, 1997a)*

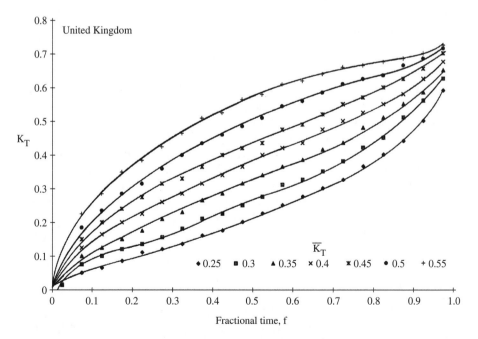

Figure 4.2.4 *Generalised curves for frequency of solar radiation – UK (Muneer, 1997a)*

India and the UK. The respective plots are based on the works of Liu and Jordan (1963), Hawas and Muneer (1984) and Lloyd (1982). The above curves, also known as generalised K_T-curves, present the insolation character for the respective regions. These frequency curves enable analysis of the availability of solar energy above a given threshold.

4.3　Solar radiation transmission

Passive solar architecture involves the design of buildings to collect the appropriate amount of energy to be used for the provision of heating and lighting needs. Almost all buildings collect, as well as reject, some solar energy. By selecting a suitable glazing system the designer may optimise the admitted solar energy so that the maximum amount of fossil fuel is conserved and yet the building does not overheat during the summer months.

Selection of the above-mentioned 'optimum' glazing system requires a detailed hour-by-hour thermal simulation of the building and, as an intermediate step, the transmission characteristics of the candidate glazing systems. Johnson (1991) has provided an interesting discussion on this item.

The transmission properties are most precisely obtained via experimentation. This is particularly the case for heat-absorbing glazing systems as pointed out by Jones (1980). This is due to the fact that such glazing systems may only approximately be modelled on the basis of Fresnel reflection properties. However, glazing manufacturers are somewhat 'coy' about providing the transmission models or characteristics. Often the transmission properties usually made available are those for normal incidence. Table 4.3.1 provides transmission data for single- and double-glazing systems. Some of these data were provided by Pilkington plc of Merseyside, England. A small number of missing data were filled in using fitting routines.

In the absence of readily available, incidence angle-dependent, transmission data one has to resort to fundamental physical principles for derivation of these. Jones (1980) has provided an excellent summary of glazing transmission properties and the relevant physics. Jones' work includes derivation of solar heat gain factors and is the basis of the sections on 'Estimation of plant capacity' (Section A9) and 'Thermal response of buildings' (Section A5) within CIBSE Guide A (CIBSE, 1986). The work of Jones (1980) is summarised in Sections 4.3.1–4.3.4.

4.3.1　Transmission, absorption and reflection characteristics of glazing systems

The angular variations in transmittance (τ), absorptance (α) and reflectance (ρ) of most glass-based glazing systems are determined by the 'KL' value and the refractive index, μ of glass. KL is the product of the absorption coefficient K of glass and its thickness L. Glass may be specified by its normal incidence solar

Table 4.3.1 Glazing daylight and solar radiation transmission (indicative values),* %

Glass (type/thickness)	Light Direct	Light Diffuse	Solar radiant heat Direct	Total	Shading Coefficient
Single					
Sheet/3	89	82	82	84	97
2**	91	84	88	90	103
3	90	83	85	88	101
4	89	82	82	86	98
5	88	81	80	84	97
6	87	80	78	83	95
8	85	78	74	80	92
10	84	77	70	78	89
12	82	75	67	76	87
15	81	74	62	73	84
19	78	71	56	69	79
25	74	67	49	64	74
Clear coated/3	80	73	49	64	79
Clear coated/4	79	72	62	64	74
Clear coated/6	77	70	56	59	68
Antisun float/6 – bronze	50	46	46	62	72
Suncool float/6 – bronze	10	9	6	24	27
Double					
Clear float + clear float	80	70	67	75	87
Clear float + clear coated	75	69	60	72	83
Clear coated + clear coated	67	65	54	66	76
Clear float + suncool float/6	9	8	5	16	18
Triple					
Triple clear float	79	66	56	67	77
Two clear coated + one clear/1	72	60	45	59	71

*Unless stated the thickness of glass = 4 mm
**Clear float thickness

transmittance, T_o and its refractive index μ. The respective angles of refraction (θ_r) and incidence (θ_i) are related by the well-known Snell's Law,

$$\sin \theta_i = \mu \sin \theta_r \qquad (4.3.1)$$

4.3.2 Characteristics for single-glazing

The procedure to obtain the angular dependence of the properties under discussion starts with obtaining the ratios of intensities of the reflected beam to the incident beam radiation for polarised parallel (Eq. (4.3.2)) and perpendicular (Eq. (4.3.3)) components thus:

$$R_\parallel = \tan^2(\theta_i - \theta_r)/\tan^2(\theta_i + \theta_r) \tag{4.3.2}$$

$$R_\perp = \sin^2(\theta_i - \theta_r)/\sin^2(\theta_i + \theta_r) \tag{4.3.3}$$

For any given angle of incidence the fraction of energy absorbed is

$$F_\alpha = (1 - R_p)[(1 - \exp(-KL/\cos\theta_r)] \tag{4.3.4}$$

where R_p represents any one of the above two components (parallel or perpendicular). The transmittance, absorptance and reflectance may then be obtained as

$$\tau = [(1 - R_p)^2(1 - F_\alpha)]/[1 - R_p^2(1 - F_\alpha)^2] \tag{4.3.5}$$

$$\alpha = [F_\alpha(1 - R_p)(1 + R_p(1 - F_\alpha))]/[1 - R_p^2(1 - F_\alpha)^2] \tag{4.3.6}$$

$$\rho = R_p + [R_p(1 - R_p)^2(1 - F_\alpha)^2]/[1 - R_p^2(1 - F_\alpha)^2] \tag{4.3.7}$$

The glazing properties τ, α and ρ are calculated for each of the two components of polarised light, i.e. perpendicular and parallel components, and then averaged values obtained for each one of the three properties. For beam (direct) radiation, τ_B would be taken as the average of τ_B calculated for the perpendicular and parallel components.

In the case of diffuse radiation the transmission (τ_d) and absorption (α_d) values are averaged over angles of incidence varying from 0 to 90°. Thus,

$$\tau_d = \int_0^{\pi/2} \tau_B(\theta) \sin 2\theta \, d\theta \tag{4.3.8}$$

and

$$\alpha_d = \int_0^{\pi/2} \alpha_B(\theta) \sin 2\theta \, d\theta \tag{4.3.9}$$

Jones (1980) has recommended that the above numerical integration be carried out between incidence angles of 2.5 to 87.5°, at 5° intervals. An Excel spreadsheet, which undertakes the computations and integrations, highlighted in Eqs (4.3.1)–(4.3.9), was originally developed by Weir (1998). Figure 4.3.1 presents solar transmission characteristics for five glazing configurations. Transmission functions for other glazing combinations may be developed from first principles if basic data related to refractive indices and normal incidence transmissivity are available. The relevant physical analysis and computer tools

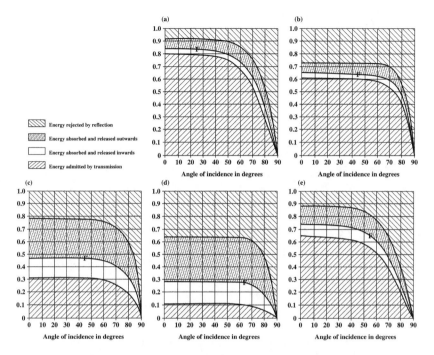

Figure 4.3.1 *Glazing solar transmission characteristics (Pilkington, 1969). (a) Float glass, (b) coated clear glass, (c) coated heat-absorbing glass, (d) Solarshield glass, (e) float glass + float glass. F represents the solar factor*

are introduced in the following paragraphs. Workbook Calc4-11.xls, presently included in the compact disc, builds upon the work of Weir and enables easy numerical manipulation. This workbook will be more appropriately introduced later in this section.

4.3.3   Characteristics for double-glazing

The characteristics of double-, triple- or indeed quadruple-glazing systems may be obtained by the extension of the procedure laid out above for single-glazing. The analysis is presented below. Here the numerals 1, 2 and 3 refer to the system elements, 1 being for the outermost element of the system and so on. τ', α_n' respectively denote the proportion of the incident radiation transmitted by the entire system and the fraction of the energy absorbed in the nth element. The following assumptions are made for the interaction of shortwave energy with glass. The irradiation is assumed to be unpolarised and the parallel and perpendicular components of irradiation are assumed to be equal. The transmissivity and absorptance are calculated for the above components and then an average value adopted.

For direct radiation,

$$\tau'_B = \tau_{1B}\tau_{2B}/(1 - \rho_{1B}\rho_{2B}) \qquad (4.3.10)$$

$$\alpha'_{1B} = \alpha_{1B} + \alpha_{1B}\tau_{1B}\rho_{2B}/(1 - \rho_{1B}\rho_{2B}) \qquad (4.3.11)$$

$$\alpha'_{2B} = \alpha_{2B}\tau_{1B}/(1 - \rho_{1B}\rho_{2B}) \qquad (4.3.12)$$

The characteristics for sky-diffuse and ground-reflected radiation are obtained likewise by replacing the subscript B with that for the respective case.

4.3.4 Characteristics for triple-glazing

For triple-glazing systems the expressions for transmittance and absorptance become quite involved. For ease of presentation a dummy variable Z is introduced which represents either one of the terms in any given expression or the entire denominator,

$$Z = (1 - \rho_{1B}\rho_{2B})(1 - \rho_{2B}\rho_{3B}) - \tau_{2B}^2\rho_{1B}\rho_{3B} \qquad (4.3.13)$$

Thus,

$$\tau'_B = \tau_{1B}\tau_{2B}\tau_{3B}/Z \qquad (4.3.14)$$

$$\alpha'_{1B} = \alpha_{1B} + [\alpha_{1B}\tau_{1B}\rho_{2B}/(1 - \rho_{1B}\rho_{2B})] + [\alpha_{1B}\tau_{1B}\tau_{2B}^2\rho_{3B}/\{Z(1 - \rho_{1B}\rho_{2B})\}] \qquad (4.3.15)$$

$$\alpha'_{2B} = \alpha_{2B}\tau_{1B}(1 - \rho_{2B}\rho_{3B} + \tau_{2B}\rho_{3B})/Z \qquad (4.3.16)$$

$$\alpha'_{3B} = \alpha_{3B}\tau_{1B}\tau_{2B}/Z \qquad (4.3.17)$$

It has to be mentioned once again that the characteristics for sky-diffuse and ground-reflected radiation are obtained by replacing the subscript B with that for the respective case. Note that Eqs (4.3.2)–(4.3.17) have been extracted from the work of Jones (1980).

Calc4-11.xls enables the determination of the angular dependence of direct solar and daylight transmission through multi-glazed windows.

4.3.5 Computer-aided tools for obtaining window solar transmission characteristics

An Excel workbook, which comprehensively produces the solar transmission characteristics for single-, double- and triple-glazed windows, with any combination of uncoated and low-emissivity coated glass, is included. This workbook, Calc4-11.xls, includes 10 worksheets and a description of each of these worksheets is provided below.

The worksheet called 'KL', located on the extreme left-hand end, contains the basic property data for the normal incidence solar transmission (T_0 value) for the commonly used glass (Table KL2 within 'KL'). The coated glass transmission data refers to Pilkington-K type material with a low-e coating of tinoxide. Data for other types of glass of varying thicknesses and more innovative coatings such as silver, as used by the German glazing company Interpane, may be inserted within Table KL1 by the user. This table enables the selection of the glass combination for the multi-glazed window by keying in the type /position of each element of the glazing system in cells B3:D5. The default glazing combination is provided as 4e (enter 0.72 in cell B4) for a single-, 4e-4 (enter 0.86 in cell C4) for a double-, and 4e-4-4e (enter 0.72 in cell D4) for a triple-glazed window. If any other glazing material is used then the user may key-in the relevant data as discussed above. Note that μ (cell A5) stands for refractive index.

The computational chain provided in the suite of Eqs (4.3.2)–(4.3.17) is carried out within the worksheets TR1D through to T3d. The former type of worksheet provides the necessary transmissivity for the direct, and the latter sheet the transmissivity for diffuse component of solar radiation. These data are then respectively collated in the 'single' (row 5), 'double' (row 8) and 'triple' (row 13) worksheets. Whereas direct radiation transmissivities are presented in each of the above-mentioned worksheets as a function of the incidence angle, the diffuse radiation transmissivity is provided as a single value (refer to (Eq. 4.3.8)). Note that data for the direct component of daylight transmission are also provided in a graphical format within each of the above-named sheets.

There is an ever-growing demand for window transmission data from architects and the building services engineering community. In this respect glass manufacturers are continually publishing new material. One such compendium, which provides normal incidence solar transmission data for a large number of glass types, is Pilkington (1998). Using such normal incidence data in conjunction with the Calc4-11.xls workbook, the user may easily obtain the angular transmission characteristics for multi-glazed windows.

Most users would be content with the numerical output of the angular transmission data available for each of the respective glazing worksheet, i.e. row 5 for 'single', row 8 for 'double' and row 13 for 'triple'. However, transmission models in the form of polynomial equations relating the direct tranmissivity to the angle of incidence are often desired. Microsoft Excel does provide a facility to fit polynomial functions if x (independent variable), y (dependent variable) data are provided in a column-wise manner. However, the accuracy of such a fit is far from satisfactory. It is possible to use Excel's Solver tool to fit polynomial functions, or indeed non-linear models, with a high degree of accuracy. The object is to minimise the objective function, i.e. the sum of squares of errors, by varying a given set of 'seed' coefficients. A demonstration of the use of the Solver tool is provided in Example 2.2.7.

4.3.6   Total solar transmission, F

For any given set of glazing the radiation that is neither reflected nor transmitted is absorbed and therefore raises the temperature of the glass. The work undertaken by Pilkington (1969) covers an analysis of the total heat contribution of multi-glazed windows (solar factor) under steady-state conditions. The fraction, f, of the solar energy absorbed by single-glazing that is released inwards has been shown to be

$$f = \frac{h_{si}}{h_{si} + h_{so}} \tag{4.3.18}$$

where h_{si} and h_{so} are respectively the internal and external surface conductance.

The total solar transmission is also known as the solar factor. For a single-glazing it is defined as

$$F = \tau + f\alpha \tag{4.3.19}$$

It is possible to extend this analysis to double- (Eq. (4.3.20)) and triple-glazing (Eq. (4.3.21)) as

$$F = \tau_1 F_2 \tag{4.3.20}$$

$$F = \tau_1 \tau_2 F_3 \tag{4.3.21}$$

where τ_i and F_i respectively refer to the solar radiant transmission and solar factor for the nth pane of a multi-glazing, n being the number of the innermost pane.

For building surfaces, CIBSE (1986) defines sheltered, normal and severe conditions as being those which are respectively exposed under wind regimes of 3, 8 and 24 km/h. For a double-clear glazing the F factors corresponding to the above conditions are 0.4, 0.3 and 0.2.

Figure 4.3.1(a)–(e) presents the angular transmission characteristics of single- (plots (a)–(d)) and double-glazing (plot (e)). The symbol 'F' identifies the curve for total solar transmission under the above-mentioned normal condition of exposure. These plots have been extracted from information contained in Pilkington (1969, 1993, 1998).

Baker et al. (1993) have provided a very simple yet robust model for obtaining angle dependent transmittance (τ) of multiple-glazing systems. It may be used with almost equal effectiveness for obtaining direct or total angular transmittance provided the normal incidence transmittance (τ_n) is known:

$$\tau = 1.018\tau_n[\cos\theta + \sin^3\theta\cos\theta] \tag{4.3.22}$$

4.3.6.1 Shading coefficient

Solar radiant properties are often compared by their shading coefficient which is derived by comparing them against the total transmittance of a clear glass of thickness between 3 and 4 mm. The latter has a total transmittance of 0.87. Sometimes the long- and short-wavelength components are given separately so that their individual effects can be examined. The most commonly reported property is, however, the total shading coefficient.

Shading coefficients are calculated for radiation at normal incidence. For other angles of incidence the glass is compared with clear glass in a likewise condition. The shading coefficients are therefore fairly constant for almost all angles of incidence. Pilkington (1998) is a useful source to obtain the long- and short-wavelength shading coefficients for a number of glazing combinations.

Window 4.1 is another useful tool for obtaining the radiation transmission characteristics of multi-glazing (LBL, 1994). The program was developed at the Lawrence Berkeley Laboratory and its main features are its ability to compute U-value, solar heat gain coefficients, shading coefficient and visible transmittance. The program contains optical spectral data files for glass manufactured by ten major manufacturers. The program with a companion manual is available without cost from its producers as well as being downloadable via the internet from the following website: http://windows.lbl.gov/materials/materials.html.

4.3.6.2 Heat capacitance effects in multi-glazed windows

To date, all glass manufacturers have reported values of F under the assumption of steady-state conditions. Strictly speaking under the varying conditions of solar radiation experienced under European and North American climates, the above analysis becomes somewhat redundant, in particular for the newer designs of superinsulated windows. It will be shown in this section that with the development of superinsulated windows, the above assumption is not valid for proper load estimations.

The thermal time-constant, τ_{ttc}, of any body is

$$\tau_{ttc} = \frac{\text{mass} \times \text{specific heat capacity } (c)}{\text{total heat transfer coefficient } (h) \times \text{surface area } (A)}$$

The time constant represents the time taken by any given solid to change its temperature to 37% of its initial value. For further discussion on this item reference is made to Suryanarayana (1995).

For any glazing,

$$\tau_{ttc} = \frac{\rho L_g c}{h}$$

Table 4.3.2 Time constant for inner glazing

Glazing	Infill gas	h_{se} or cavity conductance (W/m^2K)	h_{si} (W/m^2K)	Σh (W/m^2K)	τ (minutes)
Single – 3 mm	n/a	16.7	8.3	25.0	3.75
Single – 4 mm	n/a	16.7	8.3	25.0	5.0
Double, float – 4 mm	air	5.8	8.3	14.1	8.9
Double, 1 low-e – 4 mm	Krypton	1.16	8.3	9.46	13.2
Double, 1 low-e – 4 mm	Xenon	0.92	8.3	9.22	13.6

where ρ (2500 kg/m^3) and δ (nominal value, 4 mm) are respectively the density and thickness of the glass. $c = 750$ J/kgK. Σh is the sum of the inner and outer heat transfer coefficients.

Table 4.3.2 shows the time-constants for single- and double-glazing while Figure 4.3.2 shows the irradiance plot for Edinburgh for a frequency of interval of one minute. A comparison of these makes it clear that the assumption of steady-state transfer of thermal energy is not valid. This is due to the fact that the time-constant for a low-e coated super-window is four times that of a single glazing. This implies that the heating and cooling-down periods of the modern glazing systems are considerable and this warrants a dynamic solar energy transmission analysis.

Historically, the steady-state conditions for single- and low-tech double-glazing were valid due to their short thermal memories. However, with the advent of superinsulated windows the time-constant has quadrupled to nearly quarter of an hour. The assumption of steady-state transfer of solar heat is thus no longer valid bearing in mind the large irradiance fluctuations under European and North American climates.

4.4 Passive solar buildings

Combined with the appropriate energy efficiency measures, passive solar design makes use of sunlight to heat and light buildings, with little or no mechanical assistance. The adoption of passive solar techniques can substantially reduce the amount of energy needed to operate a building. Incidental heat gains and daylight already make a contribution to the energy needs of most buildings. Passive solar design seeks to optimise that contribution (ETSU, 1988).

In the early 1980s over 100 solar houses built at Milton Keynes in the UK were closely monitored (ETSU, 1985). The energy consumption of these houses was then compared with similar houses without passive solar features. It was found that, like with like, passive solar measures reduced heating bills by 40%. Figure 4.4.1 summarises the performance of one such house.

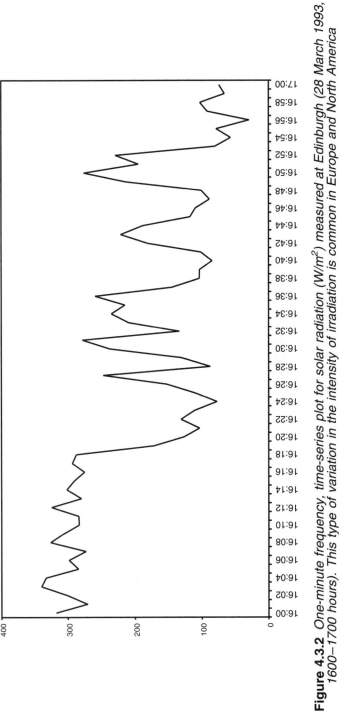

Figure 4.3.2 One-minute frequency, time-series plot for solar radiation (W/m^2) measured at Edinburgh (28 March 1993, 1600–1700 hours). This type of variation in the intensity of irradiation is common in Europe and North America

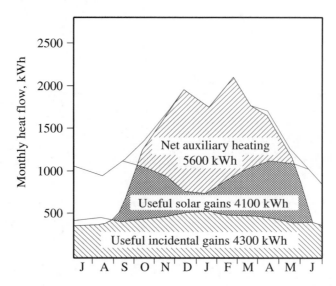

Figure 4.4.1 *Energy flows for a solar house, July to June (Muneer, 1999)*

Worthwhile improvements in the energy performance of buildings can be achieved by arranging windows and skylights to allow solar energy into areas that need to be heated. Such direct gain passive designs, which can be constructed at little or no extra cost, typically have large windows on the south side and smaller glazed areas facing north. Another method of capturing solar energy is to add an extra highly glazed unheated room – a sun-space or conservatory – to the south side of the house. Solar gains always make sun-spaces warmer than the outside air, and this reduces heat losses from the house and warms any ventilation air which passes through the sun-space. When solar gains are enough to raise the sun-space above house temperature the heat collected can be let into the house by opening communicating doors and windows, or with thermostatically controlled fans. Overheating can be avoided by providing thermal mass, vents at floor and roof level and reflective blinds. As well as thermal benefits, sun-spaces provide pleasant extensions to the home for up to three quarters of the year: typically conditions within them are like outside conditions three months nearer summer. In the UK, around 50 000 house extensions are built annually, and many of these are highly glazed.

Sun-spaces open up a different range of design possibilities and unlike direct gain features, they can readily be added to many existing houses. With good design and proper use, their thermal performance can be similar to or even better than direct gain designs. Design studies in the UK show that sun-spaces can be equally effective in large and small houses and can make passive design possible even in high-density urban housing.

One of the more complex passive solar design is what is known as the 'Trombe wall' – a glazed heat collector, which collects heat during daylight hours and releases it to the building interior via conduction and convection. A Trombe wall can be thought of as a shallow sun-space designed solely for solar heat gain and cooling. User-operated vents at the top of the wall allow warm air to flow into the house. The wall itself is massive, dark coloured externally to maximise heat absorption, and uninsulated; it conducts heat slowly from outside to inside over 6–12 hours, so that solar heat collected during the day radiates into the living spaces overnight. Trombe walls work well in some climates where there is a regular alternative of sunny days and cold nights, but less well in more unpredictable climates. Other design approaches insulate the mass wall and use blown air to transfer heat into the house, or replace the masonry wall with a water wall. Figure 4.4.2 shows the design schematic of the above-mentioned passive solar heating systems.

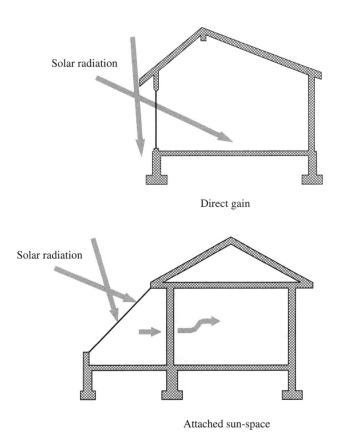

Figure 4.4.2 *Design schematic for a passive solar design (Muneer, 1999)*

4.4.1   *Simulation of passive solar heated buildings*

CIBSE has identified the pros and cons of a number of sophisticated design tools. These require long-term, hourly data sets of solar radiation and other weather parameters. The forthcoming CIBSE Guide J addresses the present lack of availability of such quality-controlled data.

An hourly simulation design study was undertaken by Muneer (1990b) to determine the performance of solar-heated and daylit office buildings under the climate of the United Kingdom. The simulation study used data from three years which consisted of hourly horizontal global and diffuse irradiation, ambient temperature and wind speed for four sites. The building design involved a southern facade of double-glazed, argon-filled 'Kappafloat' windows and a medium-weight concrete floor. These windows offer a high daylight and a moderate solar radiant heat transmittance. The sites considered were Easthampstead (England), Aberporth (Wales), Eskdalemuir (Scotland) and Aldergrove (Northern Ireland). The simulation procedure was based on precise models for slope irradiation, daylight penetration, wind-conductance, comfort and energy-exchange.

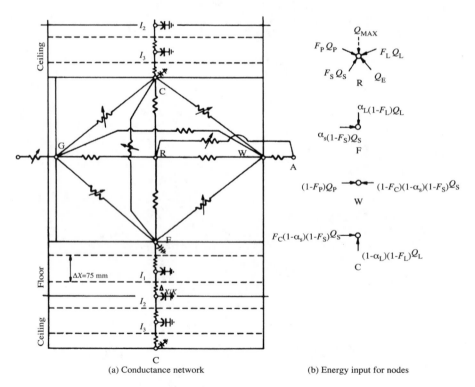

(a) Conductance network   (b) Energy input for nodes

Figure 4.4.3 *Thermal model for a direct-gain solar-heated office building (Muneer, 1990b)*

Figure 4.4.3 shows the thermal model for the type of building considered by Muneer (1990b). The conductance network takes into account the convective heat exchanges between room air and ceiling, floor, walls and inside glazing and infrared radiation exchanges between the ceiling, glazing, walls, and floor. The dynamic thermal model has five capacitative nodes: ceiling, floor and three inner nodes I_1, I_2 and I_3. The other three nodes for wall, glass and room air were considered to be non-capacitative due to their small thermal mass and consequently small time-constants. The energy inputs to the various nodes shown in Figure 4.4.3(b) are as follows. A fraction F_P of the total sensible heat emitted by the occupants, Q_p, isconvective and hence is added to the room convective node, R. Likewise the convective proportions of the solar gains, F_sQ_s, and lighting gains, F_LQ_L are added to node R. Q_E represents the convective heat input due to office equipment.

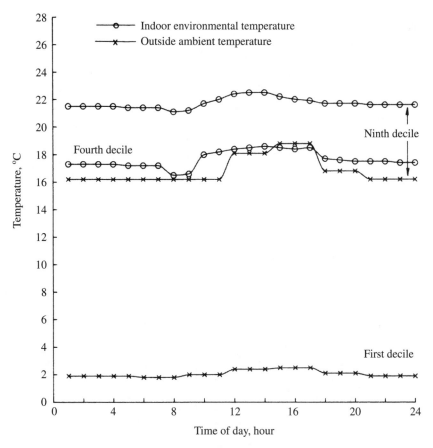

Figure 4.4.4 *Free temperature swings for a solar-heated office building in west London (Muneer, 1990b)*

One way of evaluating the free (uncontrolled) temperature swings of solar heated buildings is to plot percentiles or deciles of hourly temperatures. Figure 4.4.4 shows the fourth to ninth decile bandwidth for the indoor temperature and the first to ninth decile bandwidth outdoor temperature. The study showed that 50–60% savings might be achieved in the primary electrical consumption by exploiting daylight potential. The solar gains in conjunction with the occupancy and equipment gains were found to be adequate for most of the space heating requirements. Figure 4.4.5 shows the breakdown of the above-mentioned energy quantities.

Solar-heated buildings require special treatment of thermal comfort evaluation. An environment in which the mean radiant temperature (T_R) and air temperatures (T_a) are equal is termed as thermally uniform. In passive solar buildings the above is rarely the case. For an office environment Wray (1980) has shown that the optimum comfort temperature is about 22°C with a comfort range of about 4°C. Thus the comfort temperature lies in the interval of 18–26°C.

4.4.2 Examples of solar-heated buildings

The object of this section is to report brief performance results of a few solar-heated buildings in the UK. The aim is to demonstrate the possibility of the satisfactory functioning of such buildings under the influence of local climate.

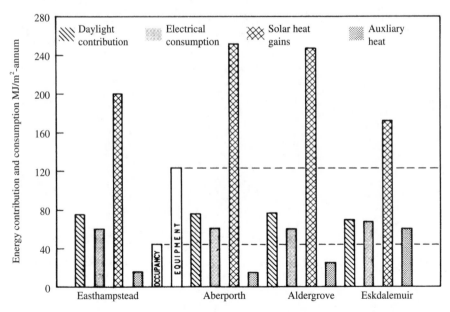

Figure 4.4.5 *Contribution of solar energy to heating and lighting of an office building in the UK (Muneer, 1990b)*

The first example is the extension of St George's School (now St Mary's College), Wallasey, near Liverpool. Opened in 1962, the building is heated by solar radiation and the heat from the lighting and the occupants. No conventional heating is used. Facing almost due south the two blocks of extension to the existing building contain an assembly hall, a gymnasium and classrooms. Almost half of the south elevation is a direct gain system with two skins of glass with a 62 cm cavity in between. In an observational study (Davies, 1976) carried out between 1 January 1969 and 28 July 1970, only 40 days out of 494 were noted in which the classroom temperature was below 16°C. Throughout the monitored period the temperatures were found to be higher than in the older building which was heated by conventional means. During the summer the mean daily temperature exceeded 23°C on 34 out of 494 days. The maximum temperature noted was 24.5°C.

Another example of effectively utilising solar gains for space heating is the 'Berm House' in Caer Llan near Monmouth, South Wales. The building faces 30° west of south and is built on the bank of the river Usk. About half of the outer wall area is covered with double-glazed windows, which is followed by a solar corridor and another wall with single-glazed windows. The building contains 10 main rooms, 8 of which are accommodation units. The main part of the building is covered with 1.5 m of soil with a garden at the top. Figure 4.4.6 presents the monitored winter performance of the Berm House as reported by Muneer (1990b).

The third example is the Napier solar 'sauna' (Muneer, 1997b). The heating season in Scotland typically lasts up to 10 months in the year. The project's aim was to investigate the feasibility of using superinsulated windows in a light-weight, direct gain system for maximising the temperature boost. Thus, in 1995, with the collaboration of Nordan window manufacturers, an experimental test unit was developed in Edinburgh. The unit has been successful in producing sauna-like conditions. At the heart of the 'sauna' design are high-performance triple-glazed windows, which act as thermal diodes. The windows cover the entire southern facade of the cube-shaped test room, with the other sides and door being heavily insulated. Two window designs have been tested, each for a period of one year. Argon- and xenon-filled glazing have been evaluated for their U-value performance and their contribution to solar energy gains. The respective measured U-values have been found to be 0.73 and 0.4 W/m^{2}K. Hourly records of temperature and incident solar radiation have been maintained. Figures 4.4.7 and 4.4.8 respectively show the performance of the test room on a long-term and short-term (an average winter day) basis. It may be seen that both designs have been successful in producing extremely warm conditions indoors. It was noted that, except those days in which heavy overcast occurred, the temperature for at least 4 to 5 hours around mid-day remained in the warm to unpleasant end of the comfort band. With a more realistic thermal mass it would be possible to stabilise the temperature and bring it down to fall within the comfort band. In a medium- to heavy-weight design the temperature would also remain within the comfort band for longer periods.

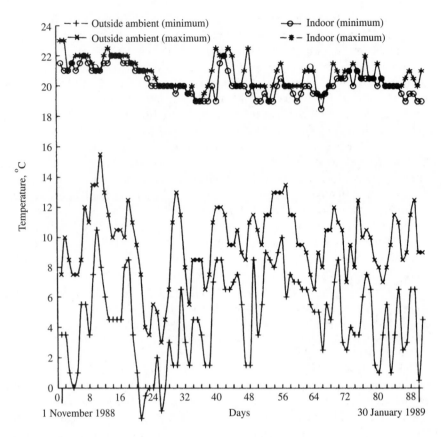

Figure 4.4.6 *Winter heating performance of the 'Berm House', South Wales (Muneer, 1990b)*

An abbreviated way of analysing the potential for the use of solar energy is to plot the annual receipt of vertical surface radiation (supply) against heating degree-days (demand). Figure 4.4.9 presents a supply and demand scenario for various British locations. Muneer's experiments have shown that even under the cold and dull climate of the east of Scotland the superinsulated windows have a good potential to provide comfort conditions within unheated conservatories. Records have indicated that either of the above two windows, i.e. argon- and xenon-filled triple-glazing, maintain the temperature of the conservatory above 20°C for over three-quarters of the time. This measured performance for Edinburgh may now be used to investigate the potential of duplicating such an application for other locations. Figure 4.4.9 shows data for seven UK locations. It may be noted that Edinburgh presents the severest test, e.g. highest heating demand and lowest level of supply of the solar energy resource. The performance for many other European and North American

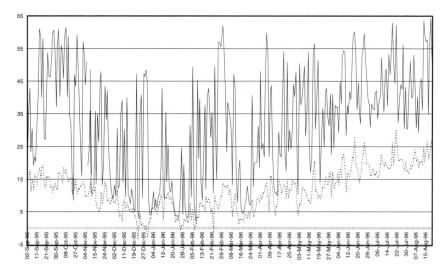

Maximum daily temperatures (Celsius) for the solar sauna with argon windows.
Solid line (sun-space temperature), dashed line (outside ambient temperature)

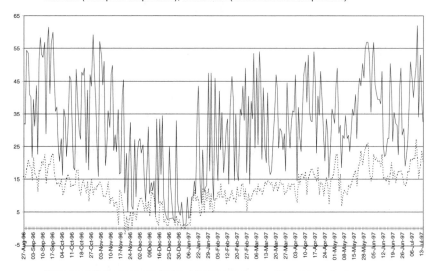

Maximum daily temperatures (Celsius) for the solar sauna with xenon windows.
Solid line (sun-space temperature), dashed line (outside ambient temperature)

Figure 4.4.7 *Thermal performance of the Napier solar 'sauna' (Muneer, 1997b)*

locations may thus be extrapolated and indeed it would be reasonable to expect a better thermal performance.

It was shown above that a larger supply of insolation and reduced demand for heat may provide an overall better thermal performance for passive solar

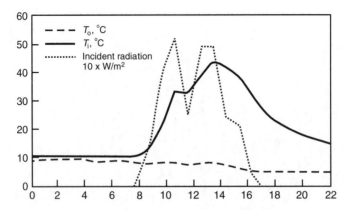

Figure 4.4.8 *Hourly temperatures and incident radiation for the Napier solar 'sauna', 16 February 1996 (Muneer, 1997b)*

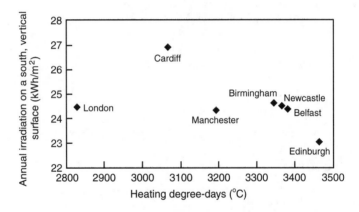

Figure 4.4.9 *Solar irradiation (resource) versus heating degree-days (demand) diagram for UK locations (Muneer, 1997b)*

heating using the now commonly available super-insulated windows. However, the situation may alter when economics is brought into the picture. This will be discussed in the following section.

4.4.3 Economics of solar heating

The primary function of a well-designed solar space heating system is to op-timise the reduction of the auxiliary energy consumption in such a way that the minimum overall cost solution is obtained. For maximum exploitation of solar energy for space heating applications there must be a sufficient heating de-mand. With an abundance of available insolation but little or no demand for heating, the laws of economics would work against the use of solar energy. Based on the above argument MacGregor (1981) has postulated the idea that the northern (or high-latitude) locations are the ones which are most suited for an economical application of solar energy. MacGregor analysed insolation and other weather data from 25 world-wide locations to obtain the energy quantities on the two sides of the equation – solar irradiation on a vertical surface (supply) and heating load on a candidate building (demand). Table 4.4.1 provides a summary of the results for a given solar-heated building.

The last column of Table 4.4.1 provides an indication of the annual solar contribution towards saving of conventional fuel. It is apparent that the maximum exploitation of solar energy concurs with higher-latitude locations. This point is further amplified by Figure 4.4.10 which compares the solar fuel savings for Lerwick (60°N) against De Bilt (52°N). The lack of uptake of deliverable solar energy for De Bilt for almost a third of the year is noticeable (nil heating load during summer).

Table 4.4.1 Annual irradiation on south-facing vertical surface, heating demand and solar energy contribution to space heating (MacGregor, 1981)

Location	Latitude °N	Irradiation kWh/m^2	Heating demand kWh	Solar contribution kWh
Bethel	60.78	930	14 020	5 690
Lerwick	60.15	670	7 400	4 240
Copenhagen	55.67	770	6 800	3 270
Eskdalemuir	55.32	670	7 750	4 250
Hamburg	53.63	690	6 430	3 070
Berlin	52.38	790	6 540	3 230
Abepporth	52.13	780	5 540	3 810
De Bilt	52.10	660	5 760	2 780
Valentia	51.93	760	1 550	3 470
London	51.47	640	4 920	2 670
Brussels	50.80	660	5 410	2 620
Winnipeg	49.90	1 050	11 320	5 040
Wurzburg	49.80	770	5 970	3 090
Paris	48.82	700	4 610	2 570
Tours	47.42	820	4 720	3 110
Bolzano	46.47	680	4 560	2 500
Limoges	45.82	760	5 100	3 290
Turin	45.18	710	1 550	2 660
Nice	43.67	1 000	2 450	2 410
Madison	43.13	890	7 230	3 790
Ajaccio	41.92	910	2 640	2 530
Rome	41.80	810	2 300	2 210
New York	40.77	830	4 650	3 160
Messina	38.20	590	1 090	1 090
Albuquerque	35.05	1 160	3 540	3 510

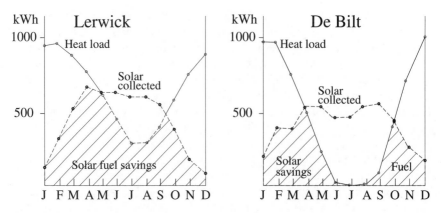

Figure 4.4.10 *Solar energy supply and heating demand for two European locations, January–December (MacGregor, 1981)*

4.4.4   Designing buildings against overheat

During the 1990s a large number of buildings have been built which use large glass facades and yet effectively rely on natural means of ventilating/cooling. It is not possible to enumerate here the very many fine examples which clearly demolish the dictum that a large glass facade results in summer overheating. One example of avoiding overheating of such buildings is that of Oxford Instruments headquarters (Bunn, 1998). The building is located in Abingdon Business Park in Oxfordshire. The 4800 m^2 building which accommodates 110 people uses 50% glazing for the north and south facades, the latter protected by a fixed brise soleil. The shades comprise fins bolted at an angle of 45°. A nominal value of 1.9 W/m^{2}K has been quoted for the low-e coated double-glazing. The passive solar architecture sets out to thermally condition the space using the building fabric. Solar gains and daylight are fully exploited with high levels of insulation and the right choice of thermal properties for the building structure. Most ambient lighting is switched off by timers.

The windows are all operable by hand levers. Occupants tend to open these when additional ventilation is required, although night cooling is carried out using an air handling plant. The atrium roof has glazed smoke vents which act as ventilators when the internal temperature rises above 21.5°C and the external ambient is above 15°C. The design brief for this building was to maintain comfort conditions without introducing mechanical cooling. Specific strategies for environmental control against overheat are shown in Figure 4.4.11. Simulations have indicated that the temperature may rise above 25°C for only 5% of the occupied period per year.

The Tokyo Electric Power Company's new R&D Centre is another good example of a building which is designed against overheat, yet using passive solar energy during winter. Refer to Figure 4.4.12. By automatically controlling the

Summer day

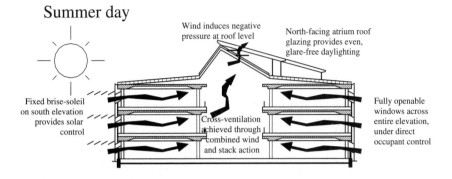

Summer night

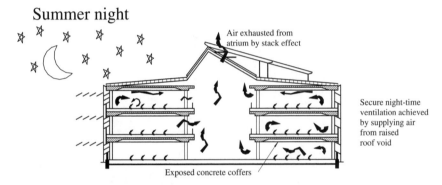

Figure 4.4.11 *Natural ventilation for Oxford Instruments building in Oxfordshire, UK (Bunn, 1998)*

angle of the slats, the blind prevents direct solar radiation from entering the room beyond a certain distance. This action prevents excessive building cooling loads. Studies have indicated that the blinds system shown in Figure 4.4.12 reduced the cooling load to a fifth that of interior blinds with the same solar shading characteristics. If there is a low level of sunlight, however, the slats are raised to admit beneficial energy from the sun. Further information on this building project is provided in the CADDET Newsletter (CADDET, 1998).

4.4.5   Windcatcher system

Figure 4.4.13 shows another innovative natural ventilation technique developed by Monodraught Limited, England (Monodraught, 1998). This technique provides controlled ventilation within buildings by exploiting roof-level wind admittance. With reference shown to the 'wind chimney' shown in Figure 4.4.13, the system ensures that irrespective of the direction of the wind there will always be one side that will be subject to wind pressure.

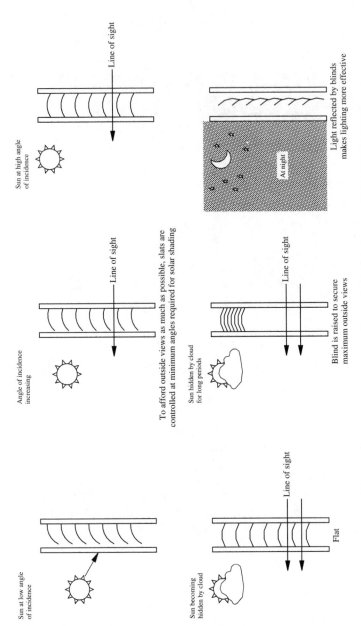

Figure 4.4.12 *Blind control for overheating avoidance (CADDET, 1998)*

SUMMER DAYTIME OPERATION

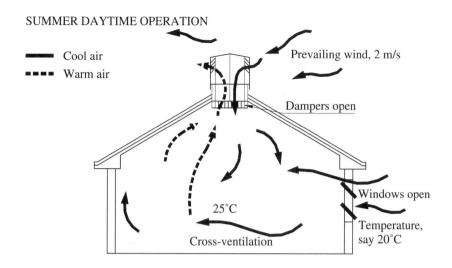

NIGHT-TIME OPERATION

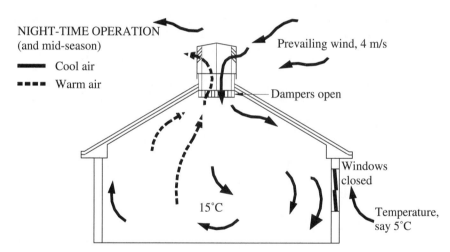

Figure 4.4.13 *Schematic of the operation of the Monodraught 'Windcatcher' natural ventilation system (Monodraught, 1998)*

In summer months doors and windows are more likely to be opened and this aids cross-ventilation, with fresh air coming in through windows on the windward side of the building and being exhausted through the passive stack. Warm air rises to ceiling level and is carried out through the passive stack element. The advantage of this type of ventilation system is that it is not dependent on openable windows or vents in the side of the building. In midseason or during daytimes or weekends when the building may not be in use the system continues to ventilate naturally. The volume control dampers at the base of the system at ceiling level will control the amount of the airflow through the system depending on the internal temperature levels and external weather conditions.

The Building Research Establishment, UK, has undertaken a series of tests to evaluate the effectiveness of the above Windcatcher system. In a study undertaken at the University of Hertfordshire two lecture theatres were monitored during the summer of 1998. Both, day- and night-time cooling strategies were monitored. Ventilation rates, flow visualisation and the cooling effect of the naturally ventilated air were investigated. It was noted that in August 1998, with temperatures ranging up to 30°C, the system achieved a ventilation rate of five air changes per hour corresponding to a wind speed of 4.5 m/s. With the wind speed dropping to 1.5 m/s the ventilation rate dropped to 1.5–2 air changes. Overnight cooling resulted in a 2°C drop in temperature of the building.

4.4.6   Night-time cooling

Night-time cooling or 'free cooling' is considered to be one of the most important aspects of natural ventilation strategies. The volume control dampers can be programmed to open fully at night to encapsulate the cool night air. Any prevailing wind carries this air down into the building below. Since the building may be otherwise closed at night, the prevailing wind pressure pushes air throughout the passive stack. This leaves the building interior fresh without security being compromised. The dampers are programmed to close again at set times in the morning and a temperature limit can be introduced to ensure that the building is not over-cooled.

References

Baker, N., Fanchiotti, A. and Steemers, K. (1993) *Daylighting in Architecture*. James and James Ltd, London.

Bennett, I. (1969) Correlation of daily insolation with daily total sky cover, opaque sky cover and percentage of possible sunshine. *Solar Energy* 12, 391–393.

Bunn, R. (1998) Precise services. *Building Services Journal* 20–24, November.

CADDET (1998) Energy efficient windows. Centre for the Analysis and Dissemination of Demonstrated Energy Technologies, Newsletter, No. 4, December, 1998.

CEN (1997) Glass in building – Determination of energy balance value – Calculation method. Comité Européen de Normalisation. DOC. CEN/TC 129/WG9 N. 19 Rev. 2, January 1997. Secretariat UNI, Via Battistotti Sassi 11B, 20133 Milano, Italy.

CIBSE (1986) *CIBSE Guide A*. Chartered Institute of Building Services Engineers, London.

Collares-Pereira, M. and Rabl, A. (1979) The average distribution of solar radiation – correlations between diffuse and hemispherical and between daily and hourly insolation values. *Solar Energy* 22, 155.

Cowley, J.P. (1978) The distribution over Great Britain of global solar radiation on a horizontal surface. *Meteorological Magazine* 107, 357.

Davies, M.G. (1976) The contribution of solar gain to space heating. *Solar Energy* 18, 6, 361.

Duffie, J.A. and Beckman, W.A. (1991) *Solar Engineering of Thermal Processes*. Wiley, New York.

Erbs, D.G., Klein, S.A. and Duffie, J.A. (1982) Estimation of the diffuse fraction of hourly, daily and monthly average global radiation. *Solar Energy* 28(6), 293–302

ETSU (1985) *Passive solar design*. Energy Technology Support Unit, DTI, London.

ETSU (1988) *Using energy from the sun*. Energy Technology Support Unit, DTI, London.

Gul, M.S., Muneer, T. and Kambezidis, H. (1998) Solar radiation models based on meteorological data. *Solar Energy* 64, 99–108

Hawas, M. and Muneer, T. (1984) Generalized monthly K_T-curves for India. *Energy Conv. & Mgmt* 24, 185.

Johnson, T.E. (1991) *Low-e Glazing Design Guide*. Butterworth-Heinemann, Boston.

Jones, R.H.L. (1980) Solar radiation through windows – theory and equations. *BSER&T* 1, 2, 83–91.

Kasten, F. and Czeplak, G. (1979) Solar and terrestrial radiation dependent on the amount and type of cloud. *Solar Energy* 24, 177–189.

Kinghorn, D. and Muneer, T. (1998) Daylight illuminance frequency distribution: Review of computational techniques and new data for UK locations. *LR&T* 30, 139.

Kreider, J.F. and Kreith, F. (1981) *Solar Energy Handbook*. McGraw-Hill, New York.

LBL (1994) *Window 4.1 – A PC Program, LBL-35298*. Lawrence Berkeley Laboratory, Berkeley, CA, USA (March 1994).

Liu, B.Y.H. and Jordan, R.C. (1960) The inter-relationship and characteristic distribution of direct, diffuse and total solar radiation. *Solar Energy* 4, 1.

Liu, B.Y.H. and Jordan, R.C. (1963) The long-term average performance of flat plate solar energy collectors. *Solar Energy* 7, 53.

Lloyd, P.B. (1982) A study of some empirical relations described by Liu and Jordan. Report No. 333, Solar Energy Unit, University College, Cardiff, July 1982.

Louche, A., Peri, G. and Iqbal, M. (1986) An analysis of Linke turbidity factor. *Solar Energy* 37, 393.

MacGregor, A.W.K. (1981) A comparison of climatic suitability of various locations in the European community for solar space heating. *Proc. Solar World Forum*, Brighton.

Mani, A. (1981) *Handbook of Solar Radiation Data for India*. Allied Publishers, New Delhi.

Monodraught (1998) Windcatcher natural ventilation system (brochure). Monodraught Ltd, High Wycombe, England.

Moon, P. and Spencer, D.E. (1942) Illumination from a non-uniform sky. *Trans. Illum. Eng. Soc., London* 37, 707.

Muneer, T. (1987) *Solar Radiation Modelling for the United Kingdom*. PhD thesis. CNAA, London.

Muneer, T. (1989) Monthly mean solar irradiation availability for the United Kingdom. *BSER&T* 10, 75.

Muneer, T. (1990a) Solar radiation model for Europe. *BSER&T* 11, 153.

Muneer, T. (1990b) Solar heated and daylit offices: Design study. *BSER&T* 11, 4, 141.

Muneer, T. (1995) Solar irradiance and illuminance models for Japan. I: Sloped surfaces. *LR&T* 27, 209.

Muneer, T. (1997a) *Solar Radiation and Daylight Models for Energy Efficient Design of Buildings*. Architectural Press, Oxford.

Muneer, T. (1997b) A solar powered sauna. *Proc. Green Enertopia Conf.*, Cheju, Korea, 1–3 September 1997.

Muneer, T. (1999) Solar energy. In *Kempe's Engineers Year Book*, Miller-Freeman UK Ltd, Tonbridge, Kent.

Muneer, T. and Saluja, G.S. (1986) Correlation between hourly diffuse and global solar radiation for the UK. *BSER&T* 7, 37.

Muneer, T. Hawas, M. M. and Sahili, K. (1984) Correlation between hourly diffuse and global radiation for New Delhi. *Energy Conv. & Mgmt* 24, 265.

Orgill, J.F. and Hollands, K.G.T. (1977) Correlation equation for hourly diffuse radiation on a horizontal surface. *Solar Energy* 19, 357.

Owens, P.G.T. (1982) Effective *U*-value, *BSER&T* 3, 4, 189–192.

Owens, P.G.T. (1984) Heat reflective coatings on glass, *BSER&T* 5, 2, 81–85.

Page, J.K. (1997) Proposed quality control procedures for the Meteorological office data tapes relating to global solar radiation, diffuse solar radiation, sunshine and cloud in the UK. Report presented to CIBSE Solar Data Task Group, October 1997.

Palz, W. and Grief, J. (1996) *European Solar Radiation Atlas*, Springer-Verlag, Berlin.

Pilkington (1969) *Windows and Environment*. Pilkington Glass Ltd, St Helens, England.

Pilkington (1993) *Glass in Building: A guide to modern architectural glass performance*, eds: D. Button and B. Pye. Pilkington Glass Ltd, St Helens, England.

Pilkington (1998) *Glass*. Pilkington Glass Ltd, St Helens, England.

Saluja, G.S. and Muneer, T. (1987) An anisotropic model for inclined surface solar irradiation. *Proc. Inst. Mech. Engrs* 201, C1, 11.

Spencer, J.W. (1982) Correlation equation for hourly diffuse radiation on a horizontal surface. *Solar Energy* 29, 19.

Suryanarayana, N.V. (1995) *Engineering Heat Transfer*. West Publishing Company, New York.

Weir, G. (1998) *Life Cycle Assessment of Multi-glazed Windows*. PhD thesis, Napier University, Edinburgh, UK.

Whillier, A. (1956) The determination of hourly values of total radiation from daily summations. *Arch. Met. Geoph. Biokl. Series B* 7, 197.

Woolf, H.M. (1968) Report NASA TM-X-1646. NASA, Moffet Field, CA, USA

Wray, W.O. (1980) A simple procedure for assessing thermal comfort in passive solar heated buildings. *Solar Energy* 25, 6, 327.

Yallop, B.D. (1992) A simple model for solar declination (unpublished report). Royal Greenwich Observatory, Cambridge, England.

5 WINDOWS AND DAYLIGHT

The famous architect Louis Kahn has been very aptly quoted as having said 'A room is not a room without natural light. Natural light gives the time of day and the mood of seasons to enter' (Ander, 1995). The design of non-residential, passive solar buildings usually starts with consideration of daylighting. Electric lights generate more heat than light but daylight does not. This is due to the fact that the luminous efficacy of daylight is much higher. So good lighting design reduces cooling needs as well as direct electricity consumption. Daylight is, however, a greatly under-utilised energy resource. In the newer offices lighting accounts for some 50% of the electrical load. For commercial offices it has been reported that a saving of 30–70% by exploitation of daylight results in a payback period of 2 to 3 years.

Daylight is a crucial and critical part of a building's design. It contributes to occupiers' comfort and satisfaction. In the Netherlands health regulations forbid buildings where staff sit further than 6 m from a window. The BREEAM method of environmental assessment cites good daylight as a contribution to healthy building design, which in turn can have implications for absenteeism and productivity benefits. BREEAM design guidelines demand a daylight factor of 2% for 80% of the occupied space of the building. Computation of daylight factor will be introduced in Section 5.4.

Careful building design can produce comfortable levels of interior lighting without glare, and yield significant savings in electricity consumption through the reduced need for artificial lighting and the consequent reduced need for cooling. Perimeter daylighting uses glass in various locations to allow light to enter the perimeter rooms of a building. Daylighting offers dramatic reductions in the energy costs in buildings with the high lighting and cooling loads typical of commercial premises. Passive solar daylit spaces are popular with building occupants and daylighting systems can be fitted to existing buildings.

In this chapter a review of recent daylight research is undertaken. Additionally, software design tools will be presented to enable computation of daylight penetration through multi-glazing.

5.1 Daylighting fundamentals

The fundamental definitions presented in this section are primarily based on BS 4727, Part 4: Glossary of terms particular to lighting and colour.

5.1.1 Luminous flux (φ)

This is defined as the light emitted by a source, or received by a surface. The SI unit of luminous flux is lumen (lm). A lumen is the amount of light emitted in a unit solid angle by a source of one candela output. An alternative way of defining lumen is that it is the amount of light which falls on a unit area when the surface area is at unit distance from a source of one candela. The unit lumen-hour is usually associated with the science of illumination and it represents the quantity of light emitted by a one-lumen lamp operating for one hour.

5.1.2 Luminous intensity (I)

This is defined as the power of a source or illuminated surface to emit light in a given direction. It is measured in candela (cd) which is equal to one lumen per steradian. Candela is also defined as the luminous intensity of a monochromatic light source that emits radiation at a frequency of 540 THz and an emissive power of $1/683$ Watt per steradian.

The relationship between the flux ϕ (lumen) from a light source and the uniform intensity I (cd) in a solid angle ω (steradian) is given by

$$\phi = I.\omega \tag{5.1.1}$$

5.1.3 Illuminance (E)

This is the luminous flux incident per unit area. It is measured in lux (lx) which is equal to one lumen per square metre. Illuminance is inversely proportional to the square of the distance of the light source, and proportional to the cosine of the angle made by the normal to the surface with the direction of the light rays.

The direct illuminance at a point which results from a large source of a uniform diffusing surface may be obtained for a small element on the source surface. The result is then integrated for the whole source surface. The direct illuminance E (lx) at a point located at distance H, below the centre of a disc source of radius R, can be calculated from the following expression:

$$E = L\frac{R^2}{R^2 + H^2} \tag{5.1.2}$$

5.1.4 Luminance (L)

Luminance is a measure of brightness of a surface. It may also be defined as the intensity of light emitted in a given direction per projected area of a luminous or reflecting surface. The unit of luminance is cd/m² of a projected area. A non-SI unit, apostilb (asb), can also be used which expresses the light emitted in terms of lumens per unit area. The relationship between the two units is given by

$$\text{Luminance (asb)} = \pi \times \text{luminance (cd/m}^2) \tag{5.1.3}$$

5.1.5   Source of daylight

The sun provides the daylight in two ways. Part of the sun's energy reaches the earth's surface as direct sunlight. Some of the other part is scattered by the atmosphere and produces the blue sky. The latter can be considered as the effective source of daylight.

5.1.6   Luminance distribution of the sky

Originally it was assumed that the sky had a uniform luminance. Under this assumption and for a sky luminance of L cd/m², the horizontal illuminance due to an unobstructed sky hemisphere is given by

$$E = \pi L \tag{5.1.4}$$

Measurements have, however, shown that the sky has a non-uniform luminance. A more detailed discussion on the sky luminance distribution will be presented later in this chapter.

5.2   Windows as daylight providers

Recent developments in technology have shown that significant savings in electrical consumption within the building sector are possible through exploitation of daylight. Modern buildings frequently employ designs and equipment which enable maximum exploitation of solar heat and light with the added possibility of glare and overheat avoidance using weather-sensitive, controlled blinds. One such building is the new European Court of Human Rights in Strasbourg which, on demand, can provide up to 92% protection against solar heat. The most modern of daylight-assisted lighting controls have the capability to provide dimming up to 1% of the full range (TLC, 1998). The human eye is very sensitive in the 0–10% dimming range where any sudden change is uncomfortable. The latest equipment, using digital control technology provides a smooth logarithmic variation. The maximum possible dimming down results in an electrical power consumption saving of 85% (TLC, 1998).

Research has shown that daylight has an important bearing on the human brain chemistry. Light entering via eyes stimulates the nerve centres within the brain which controls daily rhythms and moods. With the advent of superinsulated windows it is possible to provide much larger glazed areas thus exploiting daylight and passive solar heat gains. Windows as energy providers are key elements in any solar energy building design and a more detailed discussion on their energetic impact is provided later in this chapter.

Research related to daylight quality and its effects on perceived comfort, work performance and general productivity varies. Lighting quality is characterised by many factors including quantity, content and contrast. It is dependent upon window size, construction and transmission properties, room characteristics, finishes applied to walls, ceilings and floors, building aspect, location and architecture, and ultimately must be suited to the tasks being carried out and the comfort of building occupants. Weir (1998) has undertaken an exhaustive literature review of the above factors and hence drawn a number of conclusions. These are summarised below.

- People prefer environments with windows and daylight conditions (Wyon and Nilsson, 1980; Collins, 1975), and may recover from operations and illness more quickly in environments which are daylit and afford an exterior view (Loe and Davidson, 1996).
- The average person receiving more than 1000 lx from natural daylight for less than one hour per day is not receiving sufficient levels to maintain optimal mood. A typical office worker could spend 50% or more of their time in environments of 0.1–100 lx (Espiritu, 1994). This could be improved by rethinking the office environment, and building construction.
- Buildings with low daylight factor create environments with homogenous lighting, having little contrast and holding limited interest for the occupant, whereas those with high daylight factor transmit more quality daylight, creating conditions likened to those found externally, maintaining optimal mood conditions for longer (Cawthorne, 1991).
- It is recognised that a holistic approach to lighting design is required to provide environments which are pleasing to the eye, comfortable for the occupant, and which do not limit work productivity (Loe and Davisdon, 1996).
- One unwanted aspect to the presence of windows is the generation of disability glare and discomfort glare. The impact of these can be minimised by appropriately sizing glazing areas in a facade, avoiding window proportions of 40–55% (Boubekri and Boyer, 1992). Discomfort glare occurs, however, when contrasting fields of brightness and darkness exist. Use of large window areas avoids this. A more detailed discussion on glare is provided in Section 5.5.
- On a window/floor area ratio basis, Christoffersen (1995) found that ratios much above 25% significantly reduced net energy savings for buildings, but that window/floor area ratios around 25% allowed quality daylight to be transmitted, maintaining potential for larger overall energy saving due to reduced lighting loads. The above limit will, however, increase with the use of superinsulated windows.

- Improvements in daylight penetration to the indoor environment can significantly lessen energy consumption on artificial lighting systems (Zeguers and Jacobs, 1997).

Research on the provision of daylight and its impact on work performance and productivity is still in its infancy. It is therefore difficult to produce confident relationships between daylight level and improvements/detriments to work output and quality. What is clear, however, is that people prefer daylit environments and enjoy the benefits associated with windows. Occupants who are contented with their environment find it easier to channel their attention to work tasks; distraction is reduced and work productivity is increased.

Admitting daylight into a building is an important function of windows. Daylight may save energy by reducing reliance on artificial lighting. This factor is more significant in commercial buildings compared to houses. Table 5.2.1 shows the importance of daylighting in reducing energy consumption due to using artificial lighting in an office building. Admitting daylight via windows and skylights can save up to half of the energy than could be consumed if there was no daylighting.

5.3 Design of daylighting systems

The introduction of natural light is a powerful architectural tool as it defines and shapes the interior spaces. The daylight admitted into a building should be balanced to provide visual comfort and to enable occupants to perform their visual tasks. The balance of light in a space depends on the overall number and size of windows, their location, and the average reflectance of the interior and exterior surfaces of a room. Using at least two windows on different walls or a skylight may improve the balance of the admitted light. Location of windows within a building shell can be selected so that direct sunlight reflects off interior walls and floors and provides more diffuse and even light. Reflective ground surfaces and walls may be used to increase daylight admitted through south- and north-facing windows.

The more light admitted, the better people can see. However, the daylight quantity should be controlled and only recommended values should be used. Light from the sky is cooler, gentler, and diffuse compared to the light from the sun. It has also more visible light with a significantly smaller infrared

Table 5.2.1 **Lighting energy costs (MWh) in an office building (Ander, 1995)**

	Atlanta	Chicago	Denver	Los Angeles	New York	Seattle
No daylighting	300	300	300	300	300	300
Sidelighting only	231	240	240	228	243	246
Side + toplighting	171	183	174	156	192	198

component. Thus, in situations where daylight is desired with minimal solar heat gain, north windows can provide the best quality of daylight of any orientation.

5.3.1 Design issues

When the design process of daylighting system is employed for a building, certain issues should be considered.

- *Sky conditions* Sky conditions vary the nature and quantity of the light entering a building. Three types of sky conditions are utilised to estimate illumination levels within a space.
  1 Overcast sky: defined as being a sky in which at least 80% of the sky dome is obscured by clouds. The illumination levels produced by the overcast sky may vary from a few hundred to several thousand lx, depending on the density of the clouds.
  2 Clear sky: defined as being a sky in which no more than 30% of the sky dome is obscured by clouds.
  3 Cloudy sky: defined as being a sky in which 30–80% of the sky dome is obscured by clouds. It usually includes widely varying luminance from one area of the sky to another and tends to change quite rapidly.

In Section 5.6 all-sky luminance distribution models and relevant Excel workbooks will be presented.

- *External obstructions and orientation* External obstructions that surround a window such as trees and other buildings may affect the amount of daylight entering a space. The awareness of the daylight pattern, contact with the outside world and the view out are important aspects of orientation.
- *Change and variety* Change and variety are at the heart of daylighting, and the window is the medium through which it delivered. These changes of daylight conditions are due to weather, season and time of day. They influence the appearance of the interior spaces within a building.
- *Sunlight* Optimisation of daylight increases the overall level of light and assists in providing change and variety. Sunlight is fundamentally good both therapeutically and visually.
- *Colour* Daylight is the colour reference. All other forms of light change the perceived colour to a greater or lesser degree. In buildings, the colour of a white wall will vary with time of day but it will always appear white due to human adaptation to the natural light.
- *View* Windows provide an important link to the outside world. View out depends to an extent upon location, size, shape and detailing of the window. Small windows, for example, break up a view. Windows also allow the view in. During the day the view in is difficult because the external light

is greater than that inside. At night the reverse occurs, allowing view in. Using curtains and blinds may, however, control the problem of privacy.

• *Glazing* The type of glazing can significantly affect daylighting. Clear glass, for instance, provides good visibility. Tinted or reflective glass helps reduce glare. Much of the solar gain is absorbed by the tinted glass and then released inside the building. Thus, tinted glass has less effect on reducing air conditioning. In addition, tinted glass produces conditions where the occupants switch on the lights, thus increasing energy use. Photochromic glass changes colour according to the ambient light conditions. This also helps reduce glare. Electrochromic glass becomes over opaque when a current is applied to it and thus can be used for privacy.

5.3.2 Design strategies

The strategies for an effective daylighting system may be summarised as follows.

• Extending the perimeter form of a building may improve the building's performance by increasing the total daylighting area.
• Locating an aperture high in a wall allows deeper penetration of daylight.
• Using the optimum glazing area to achieve daylight saturation, as additional glazing area will increase the cooling loads more than it will reduce the lighting loads.
• Reflecting daylight within space results in increasing room brightness by spreading and evening out brightness patterns.
• Sloping the ceiling from the fenestration area will help increase the brightness of the ceiling further into a space.
• Avoiding direct beam daylight on critical visual tasks. Poor visibility and discomfort will result if excessive brightness differences occur in the vicinity of critical tasks.
• When harshness of direct light is a potential problem, vegetation, curtains, or louvres can help soften and distribute light more uniformly.

5.3.3 Design elements

The most significant design determinant when implementing daylighting strategies is the geometry of a building's walls, ceilings, floors, windows, and how each relates to the other. An understanding of the effects of the various building elements will provide the basis for manipulating form to achieve adequate lighting levels.

• *Exterior elements* Exterior elements can be useful controls for fenestration. Examples are overhangs, light shelves, horizontal louvres, vertical louvres (fins), daylight tracking and reflecting systems.

- *In-wall and roof elements* The amount of daylight within a building can be increased by increasing the total amount of glazing area. However, admitting more light may bring in unwanted heat gain. Recent advances in glazing technology have reduced this liability. The emerging window technology has been discussed in the first chapter of this book.
- *Interior elements* These may be further categorised as room geometry, room surface reflectance and interior shading control. A brief discussion of these items follows.

The depth that daylight will penetrate is dependent on the ceiling height relative to the top of the window. A high window will allow daylight to strike the ceiling plane and be reflected into the interior space. In a typical building with a window height of 2.5 m and a room width of 3.7 m, daylight can penetrate about 6 m from the window elevation. The depth of the room has a direct effect on the intensity of illumination. With deeper rooms, the same quantity of incoming light is distributed over a larger area.

The ceiling is the most important surface in reflecting the daylight coming into a space onto the work plane. The next most important element is the back wall, followed by the sidewalls, and finally, the floor. Several types of manual interior control devices can be used to eliminate excessive bright spots and also get daylight where it is needed. Examples are venetian blinds, draperies, and roller shades.

5.3.4   Lighting controls

The demand for energy efficiency has led to an increasing application of intelligent lighting controls. These may be categorised as: Time-scheduling, Presence detection, Daylight linking, Manual switching, and Intelligent luminaires.

5.4   Daylight factor

In design studies it has become customary to specify interior daylighting in terms of daylight factor (DF). This is the ratio of the internal illuminance to the external illuminance, available simultaneously and is usually expressed as a percentage. The daylight factor is divided into three components: the direct skylight (sky component), SC, the externally reflected component, ERC, and the internally reflected component, IRC. Thus

$$DF = SC + ERC + IRC \tag{5.4.1}$$

The SC and ERC are both found by considering the geometry of the visible sky or the external reflected surfaces at a point on a horizontal plane within the room. They can be found from a Waldram diagram, BRE protractors, BRE tables, and Pilkington paper pot diagrams.

The IRC is based on inter-reflection theory and can be found from formulae, BRE tables, and BRE nomograms (Building Research Establishment, 1986).

5.4.1 Calculation of sky component (SC)

The sky component is the ratio of illuminance at any given point that is received from a sky of known luminance distribution to the horizontal illuminance under an unobstructed sky hemisphere. Likewise, the external and internal reflected components are, respectively, the ratios of the illuminance received after reflections from external and internal surfaces to the horizontal illuminance under an unobstructed sky hemisphere. An electronic lookup table for the sky component, based on the CIE standard overcast sky, is provided in Calc5-01.xls. This table was originally published by Hopkinson et al. (1966). The BRE protractor and the accompanying literature (Building Research Establishment, 1986) enable estimation of the above three components. It is worth mentioning that Calc5-01.xls requires the datafile In3-5.CSV which is included in the compact disc.

The BRE sky component tables may be used to obtain the daylight level at a reference point in a horizontal plane if the height and width of the window and the distance of the reference point from the window are known. Figure 5.4.1 shows these details. The electronic lookup table, Calc5-01.xls, gives the sky component at the intersections of the ratio H/D and W/D. The geometric construction has to be such that the horizontal and vertical planes drawn through the given point to meet the window wall perpendicularly form two bounding edges of the window. If the window sill is above the reference plane the height of the sill above the reference plane must also be taken into account. Example 5.4.1 demonstrates the use of Calc5-01.xls.

5.4.2 Calculation of externally reflected component (ERC)

If direct entry of sunlight or skylight is restricted through the window then it is necessary to calculate the ERC. In this case the obstruction's luminance is taken as a fraction of the obscured sky's luminance. Usually the reflectance of the obstruction is taken as 0.1–0.2. If a significant proportion of the sky is obscured then the value of the ERC is so small that daylighting is of little value. Further information on the computation of ERC is provided by Pritchard (1995).

5.4.3 Calculation of internally reflected component (IRC)

Figure 5.4.1 provides minimum values of the IRC. This information is based on the work undertaken by the UK Building Research Establishment. The design chart is for a 6 m square room with a 3 m ceiling and a single window.

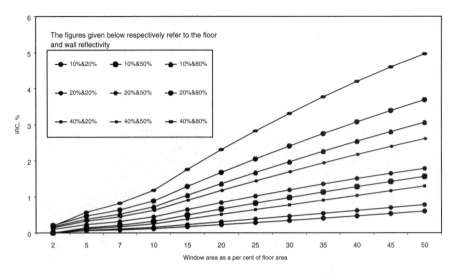

Figure 5.4.1 *Minimum value of the internally reflected component*

In summary the sky component, SC, is by far the dominant part of the daylight factor.

Example 5.4.1

Consider the case of a single-glazed rectangular window shown in Figure 5.4.2. The external obstruction runs along the entire length of the room. Obtain the sky component using Calc5-01.xls. Also obtain the ERC and IRC given the reflectance of the external and internal surfaces are respectively 0.1 and 0.5. The floor reflection factor may be taken as 20%, the wall reflection factor is 50% and the window/floor area = 0.2.

5.4.4   Calculation of SC

With reference to Figure 5.4.2, compute the following:

(a) $W/D = \text{Tan } 20° = 0.364$, $H_1/D = \text{Tan } 45° = 1.0$, and $H_2/D = \text{Tan } 35° = 0.7$

Note that the vertical portion of the window between H_1 and H_2 receives daylight from the sky canopy and the portion between H_2 and H_3 receives the wall-reflected component (ERC).

(b) Open workbook Calc5-01.xls. Notice that this includes a FORTRAN-based DLL program [Fr305.dll]. Therefore, Excel should be launched first and then Calc5-01.xls opened within Excel (see box below). Note the two relevant files In3-5.csv and Fr305.dll must be loaded in the same PC folder as Calc5-01.xls.

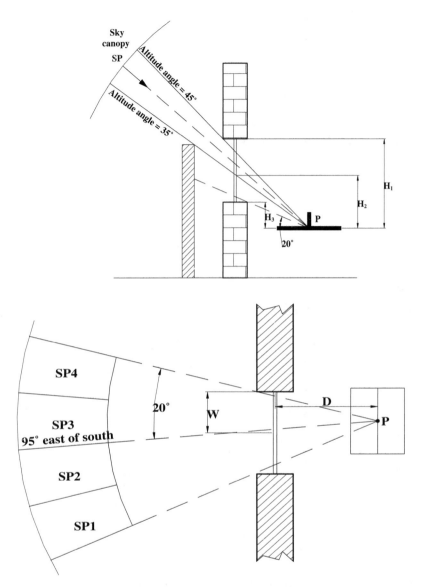

Figure 5.4.2 *Window schematic for Example 5.4.1 (Muneer, 1997)*

(c) Insert the values for the H_1/D, W/D pair in cells B4 and B5 respectively.

(d) Press Alt + F8. The Macro dialog box appears. Click on Run button to run the FORTRAN-based DLL program [Fr305.dll]. The sky component = 2.02 (cell B6).

For all DLL-based workbooks the following procedure **MUST** be used:
- Launch Excel software
- Open the DLL-based workbook
- Enter data in the relevant worksheet(s)
- Simultaneously press ALT + F8 keys
- Select the relevant macro from the dialog box
- Either click the Run button, or simultaneously press ALT + R keys

(e) Repeat steps (b) and (c) for the H_2/D, W/D pair. The value of 1.18 (cell B6) is obtained.
(f) The actual sky component is then obtained by subtraction of the above two values and then doubling the result (due to symmetry). Thus, sky component at point $P = 2 \times 0.84 = 1.68\%$.

5.4.5 Calculation of ERC

Note that $W/D = 0.364$ and $H_3/D = \text{Tan } 20° = 0.364$. For this combination Calc5-01.xls provides a SC value of 0.346. The actual sky component of the external obstruction is therefore, $2(1.18 - 0.346) = 1.67\%$. The ERC is now obtained as the product of its (subtended) SC and reflectance $= 1.67 \times 0.1 = 0.17\%$. The ERC in this case is thus of negligible value.

5.4.6 Calculation of IRC

Using the data provided for the wall and floor reflection factors and window/floor area the IRC is read off from Figure 5.4.1 as 0.85%. We note that for the given situation, $SC = 1.68\%$, $ERC = 0.17\%$ and $IRC = 0.85\%$. Thus, the daylight factor $= 2.7\%$.

It must be borne in mind that the above computation of sky component does not take into account the effects of window orientation, e.g. sun-facing or shaded aspects. It is therefore only an approximate method of obtaining internal illuminance. In later sections, more precise procedures are presented which take into account the window aspect and the real sky luminance distributions. However, due to its simplicity the above procedure for sky component estimation is widely used.

Hopkinson et al. (1966) have enumerated the advantages of daylight factor as follows. Firstly, it represents the effectiveness of the window as a lighting provider. Secondly, the daylight factor remains constant even though the outdoor illuminance may fluctuate. Constancy is associated with the concept of adaptation. Appreciation of brightness is governed not only by the actual luminance of the habitated environment but also by the brightness of the surroundings which govern the level of visual adaptation. As a result, visual appreciation of the interior of a room does not change radically even though the actual luminance will be higher as a result of the greater amount of daylight penetration resulting from brighter skies.

At any given point the daylight factor will result in wide variations in internal illuminance. Acceptance of a given illuminance level as the criterion of an appropriate visual environment poses a problem in relation to the variability of available daylight. One solution is to design in such a way that the recommended level of internal illuminance is attained during a certain agreed proportion of the working period throughout the year. An example of this type of approach is to be found in the work of Hunt (1979) for Bracknell and Kew in the UK. It is possible to undertake illuminance frequency analysis for other locations too using the procedure in the following section. Figure 5.4.3, extracted from Pilkington's (1993) design book and Kinghorn's work undertaken at Napier University, shows the illuminance frequency distributions for world-wide locations.

An average but 'loose' value of DF may also be calculated in a single step. The relevant material is presented in Section 5.8. Although easy to use, Eq. (5.8.1) provides a very rough estimate of DF and is therefore not recommended for serious design work.

5.5 Glare

Glare is the excessive brightness contrast within the field of view. The excessive contrast between foreground and background may disturb the eye's ability to distinguish objects from their background and to perceive detail. The human eye can function quite well over a wide range of luminous environments, but it cannot function well if extreme levels of brightness are present in the field of view at the same time. People orient windows toward an interesting view such as snow, water, or sand. Daylight reflection from such surfaces intensifies the glare problem, especially if the window faces east or west.

Windows may give rise to glare. The bright sky may be close to the line of view. It may cause reflections on work surfaces, e.g. display screens. Light from the sun may shine directly or by reflection to create glare.

Glare is a subjective phenomenon and difficult to quantify. A generalised form of glare quantification can be derived by studying the average response of a large number of people to the same glare situation. Glare can be classified into two types: discomfort and disability.

5.5.1 Discomfort glare

This is defined as glare which causes visual discomfort without necessarily impairing the vision. Discomfort glare, as presented by Baker et al. (1993), from a light source can be expressed as:

(a)

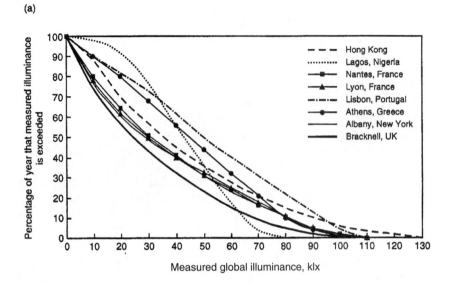

(b)

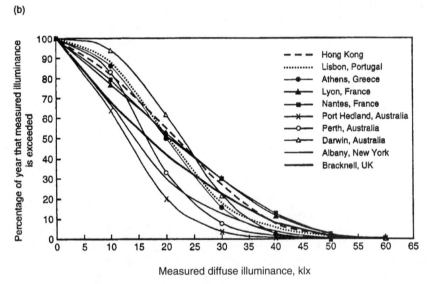

Figure 5.4.3 *Cumulative frequency of (a) global and (b) diffuse illuminance for world-wide locations*

$$\text{Discomfort glare} = \frac{L_s^{1.6} \times \omega^{0.8}}{L_b \times P^{1.6}} \times 0.45 \qquad (5.5.1)$$

where L_s is the luminance of the source, L_b is the average luminance of the background, ω is the angular size of the source and P is the position index which indicates the effect of the position of the source on glare.

5.5.2 Disability glare

This is defined as glare which impairs the ability to see detail without necessarily causing visual discomfort. Its effect can be expressed as a shift in the adaptation level of the eye.

Boubekri and Boyer (1992) studied the effect of window size on sunlight presence and glare and noted that the discomfort glare of sunshine can compete with the positive psychological effects of sunlight. A survey carried out in nine UK schools showed that 47% of teachers complained of thermal and/or visual discomfort from the sun, and that they were more tolerant towards the sun than pupils. Boubekri and Boyer found that window size accounts for less than 30% of variation in perceived glare. Figure 5.5.1 shows that perceived glare rises from 1.4 to 4.7 as the window area increases from 20% to 50% of the wall area, and then decreases as the window size increases beyond 50%. The occupant experiences discomfort when the perceived glare value rises above a value of 4. Perceived glare is in the tolerable range, except when the window size is 40–55% of the wall area. The reasons for this may be summarised as follows:

- Small windows – glaring source is small and perceived sensation is not disturbing.
- Medium windows – a high contrast between glare source and surrounding adjacent wall leads to a higher perceived glare level.

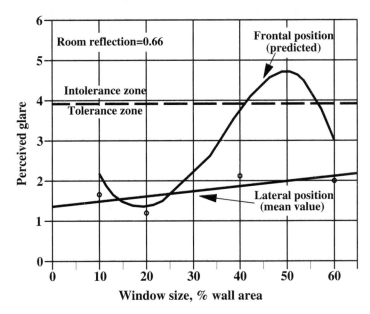

Figure 5.5.1 *Influence of window size on glare (Boubekri and Boyer, 1992)*

- Large windows – though the glare source is large, the contrast between the source and the surroundings is small, raising the adaptation level of the eye and reducing the glare sensation and the level of discomfort.

Boubekri and Boyer's (1992) work has shown that adequate space layout and optimum placement of furniture in the office have a large potential to reduce discomfort glare. Research has also indicated that a lateral viewing position keeps the levels of discomfort glare well within the acceptable comfort limits even for quite large window areas. Studies such as these open up the 'market' for large glazing facades with the obvious consequence of exploiting daylight as well as passive solar energy. With the growing use of daylight in office buildings, the issue of glare continues to receive widespread attention.

5.6 Availability of daylight

In the United Kingdom the latest update of the building regulations aims to improve the lighting efficiency (CIBSE, 1996). To meet the deemed to satisfy approach set out in the new regulation, the designer is prompted to encourage the maximum use of daylight. Efficient and more precise design of windows in buildings requires the development of inclined surface illuminance models. These in turn require values of horizontal global and diffuse illuminance. In the absence of measurements it is necessary to resort to luminous efficacy models to obtain an estimate of global and diffuse illuminance from other measured or estimated atmospheric parameters. Several approaches have been adopted, including the use of solar altitude, water vapour content, Linke turbidity factor and many other atmospheric parameters. Muneer (1997) has presented a survey of these models.

The global luminous efficacy of daylight, K_G, is expressed as the ratio of illuminance (lx) to irradiance (W/m^2) which can be found through the integration of the whole spectrum, i.e.

$$K_G = \left[680 \int_{x_1}^{x_2} V(\lambda) I_G(\lambda)\, d\lambda\right] \Big/ \left[\int_0^{\infty} I_G(\lambda)\, d\lambda\right] \qquad (5.6.1)$$

$V(\lambda)$ is the CIE spectral sensitivity of the human eye and $I_G(\lambda)$ is the solar spectral irradiance. x_1 and x_2 determine the lower and upper limits of the visible bandwidth.

5.6.1 Horizontal global and diffuse illuminance

The luminous efficacy of daylight depends upon the way in which the radiant energy is shared between the visible and invisible (infrared and ultraviolet) parts of the spectrum. This in turn depends upon a number of factors including the state of the sky (clear, overcast or average) and the altitude of the sun. In particular, the luminous efficacy is different for the sun alone, the sky alone and for the global radiation (sun plus sky).

5.6.1.1 Luminous efficacy

The human eyes are distinctly different from those of other animals. This difference is due to the proportion of rods and cones in the nerve endings of the human eye's retina, i.e. the human eye has a much larger proportion of cones. The cones respond over the 400–730 nm wavelength band with a varying strength of the output signal.

Determinations have been made by workers in different parts of the world of the luminous efficacy of daylight from simultaneous measurements of the illuminance and irradiance. Worthy of note among the earliest measurement efforts are Pleijel (1954) in Scandinavia, Blackwell (1954) at Kew, England, Dogniaux (1960) at Uccle, Belgium and Drummond (1958) at Pretoria in South Africa. Pleijel showed that clear and overcast skies vary little in luminous efficacy with solar altitude (and thus with time of year) but that there is a marked decrease in the efficacy of the sun's beam radiation at solar altitudes less than 30°. Blackwell's measurements were related to global radiation with clear, overcast and average skies. The mean efficacies were found to be 119, 120 and 116 lm/W respectively. With average skies, the global efficacy was found to vary between 105 and 128 lm/W. It is desirable to obtain luminous efficacies under all-sky conditions. Such models are presented in the following sections.

5.6.1.2 Perez model

The Perez model (Perez et al., 1990) for all-sky luminous efficacy is given as

$$K_G \text{ or } K_D = a_i + b_i l_w + c_i \cos z + d_i \ln(\Delta) \qquad (5.6.2)$$

K_D is the diffuse irradiance luminous efficacy and a_i, b_i, c_i and d_i are the coefficients which are functions of sky clarity. Δ denotes the optical transparency of the cloud cover and l_w is the atmospheric precipitable water content.

5.6.1.3 Muneer–Kinghorn model

The philosophy behind these models is that the luminous efficacy is most significantly influenced by the sky clearness index (Muneer and Kinghorn, 1997). Thus,

$$K_G = 136.6 - 74.51 K_t + 57.3421 K_t^2 \qquad (5.6.3)$$

and

$$K_D = 130.2 - 39.828K_t + 49.9797K_t^2 \tag{5.6.4}$$

The above models have been rigorously evaluated against an extensive set of measured data gathered from a variety of locations across the UK as part of the International Daylight Measurement Programme. Findings confirm that in the event of unavailability of long-term measured illuminance data, using measured irradiance values in conjunction with a luminous efficacy model is the most reliable method of synthetically generating an illuminance database. Figures 5.6.1(a) and (b) demonstrate this point, respectively depicting the calculated global and diffuse illuminance values against their corresponding measured counterparts. The similarity between the computed and measured traces is remarkable.

The workbooks Calc5-02.xls and Calc5-03.xls enable luminous efficacy and zenith luminance computations, respectively using the above mentioned Perez and Muneer–Kinghorn models. Note that Calc5-02.xls is a DLL-based file. Refer to the text box provided under Example 5.4.1 for getting help in the execution of this workbook.

Each of the above two workbooks contain three sheets, namely 'Site', 'Compute' and 'Graph'. Data related to the site location and surface geometry are to be provided within the 'Site' sheet. If a validation of any of the three models is required the user may enter the relevant measured data under the 'Measured data' columns within the 'Compute' sheet. The sheet named 'Graph' is dynamically linked and therefore will provide a visual means of evaluation, as shown presently.

During the preparation of the CIBSE Guide J, the Muneer–Kinghorn model was used to produce long-term illuminance data sets for a number of UK sites.

Average luminous efficacy models also show promise, at least for the temperate belt of the world. Muneer and Angus (1993) have shown that for UK locations the respective average luminous efficacies of 110 lm/W and 120 lm/W for global and diffuse components are comparable with other luminous efficacy models.

5.6.2 Frequency of occurrence of illuminance

Buildings are increasingly being designed today to exploit natural daylight availability as effectively as possible. Modern office complexes can now even incorporate the use of light-pipe technology to bring daylight to central cells within the structure that are remote from fenestration. Indeed, certain local county councils have adopted policies whereby commissioned new structures, such as school gymnasia, must incorporate daylighting into their design before being considered for approval. Not only is this advantageous from the energy-saving perspective, it also enhances corporate image and public perception towards environmental concern.

When considering the design of an integrated natural and artificial lighting system, it is of primary concern to recognise what quantity of daylight is

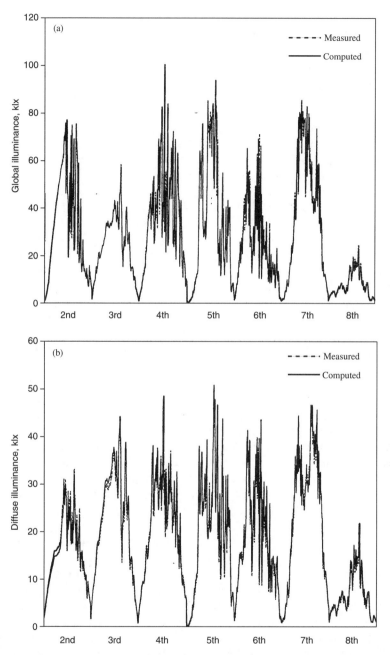

Figure 5.6.1 *Variation in (a) global and (b) diffuse illuminance derived from measured irradiance (Edinburgh, Napier University, April 1993 data)*

available. Due to the lack of long-term historical solar illuminance measurements, various researchers have developed techniques to mathematically model levels of illuminance at frequent intervals, i.e. hourly and sub-hourly. Through creation of a synthetically derived solar illuminance database the frequency of distribution, or cumulative frequency, of daylight can be determined. Access to such data enables the lighting designer to predict the frequency of occurrence of natural illuminance above, or below, a predetermined level.

Previous work in the field of irradiance modelling has focused on developing estimations based primarily on the availability of other meteorological data, such as prevailing cloud-cover and sunshine. Such data are routinely and reliably recorded at many more locations than solar irradiance. Hence, these data may be used to construct a widespread, yet accurate, network of synthesised solar irradiance datasets. A comprehensive review of procedures available that allow daylight frequency levels to be estimated from meteorological data is presented in the literature (Kinghorn and Muneer, 1998).

The most accurate method of enabling daylight estimations is by interlinking the luminous efficacy models with the corresponding irradiance measurements. Using such measurement data, recorded over periods of up to 20 years, Kinghorn and Muneer (1998) presented the data shown in Figures 5.6.2(a) and (b) for the cumulative frequency of global and diffuse illuminance for a number of locations in the UK.

5.6.2.1 Liu and Jordan's method

The background to this method was discussed earlier on in Chapter 4. Figures 4.2.2–4.2.4 showed the K_T distributions, respectively, for the USA, India and the UK. Recall that the dimensionless quantity K_T represents the ratio of global to extraterrestrial irradiation. It therefore provides an indication of the prevalent atmospheric clarity. The generalised K_T-curves present the insolation character for the respective regions. The curves enable querying the availability of solar energy above a given threshold. For example, for Indian locations, during a month for which $\overline{K_T} = 0.7$, $K_T \leq 0.73$ for 70% fractional time, and $K_T \leq 0.68$ for 20% of the time. In contrast the corresponding figures for the USA are, respectively, 56% and 30%. It is therefore evident that the distributions for the Indian locations are flatter. This means that for the Indian subcontinent the daily clearness index (K_T) varies in a narrower range and thus indicates a stable solar climate.

Strictly speaking the above insolation frequency distributions are for daily based quantities. However, Whillier (1953) has shown that the hourly and daily distribution curves are very similar to each other. Thus the above curves may also be used to obtain the frequency occurrence of hourly global irradiation. This type of information is a useful aid for daylight designers for exploring the potential for energy savings via modern photoelectric controls.

(a) Global illuminance, klx

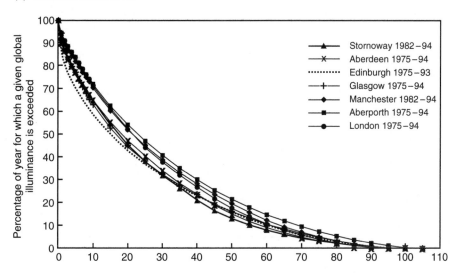

(b) Diffuse illuminance, klx

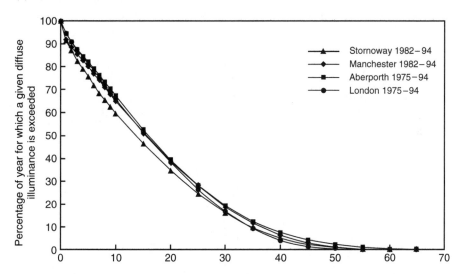

Figure 5.6.2 *Cumulative frequency of (a) global and (b) diffuse illuminance for UK locations (Kinghorn, 1999)*

5.6.3 Orientation factors

It is reasonable to assume that, even with overcast conditions, windows facing the direction of the sun will receive more light than those facing away. The

CIBSE Window Design Guide contains a set of orientation factors (see table below) which should be used when calculating the DF for energy-saving estimates, i.e. Orientation weighted DF = Orientation factor × Overcast sky DF.

This information was based on the work of D.R.G. Hunt carried out at the BRE, England during the 1970s. Since then improvements in orientation factor have been proposed by Littlefair (1990) and these are included in the table below.

Orientation factors

Direction	Orientation factor (Hunt, 1979)	Orientation factor (Littlefair, 1990)
North-facing window	0.77	0.97
East-facing window	1.04	1.15
South-facing window	1.20	1.55
West-facing window	1.00	1.21

5.6.4 Slope illuminance

In the previous section it was shown that orientation factors may be used to take account of a window's orientation with respect to the sun. In that respect orientation factors provide a slightly better assessment of daylight admittance than calculations based on the simple daylight factor approach. However, orientation factors fail to take account of the dynamic variations in daylight as pointed out by Haves and Littlefair (1988). The latter team have introduced a procedure to address the above-mentioned shortcomings of the daylight factor. Haves and Littlefair's (1988) procedure to obtain internal illuminance is summarised below:

$$IL_{in} = IL_{TLT}.r \qquad (5.6.5)$$

IL_{in} is the desired horizontal internal illuminance and IL_{TLT} the external slope illuminance. r is defined as the modified daylight factor, it being the ratio of the internal to external illuminance in the plane of the window with a tilt angle of TLT,

$$r = d/d_{TLT} \qquad (5.6.6)$$

where d is the standard CIE daylight factor (Section 5.4) and d_{TLT} is the ratio of the exterior illuminance in the plane of the window to the exterior horizontal illuminance under CIE overcast sky conditions. For an unshaded vertical window, $d_{TLT} = 0.396 + 0.5\rho$, where ρ is the albedo (reflectivity) of the underlying land mass. A model that enables the estimation of IL_{TLT} is presented below.

5.6.4.1 Muneer–Kinghorn model

This model (Kinghorn and Muneer, 1999) is along the lines of Muneer's (1990) work on solar irradiance modelling. Thus,

$$IL_{TLT} = (IL_G - IL_D).r_B + IL_D[(1 - F_{IL})TF + F_{IL}.r_B] \qquad (5.6.7)$$

Recall that r_B was defined in Chapter 4 (Eq. (4.2.23b)). The subscripts G and D in Eq. (5.6.7) refer to the global and diffuse components.

$$r_B = \text{Max}[0, \cos(\text{INC})/\sin(\text{SOLALT})]$$

$$F_{IL} = (IL_G - IL_D)/IL_E \qquad (5.6.8)$$

IL_E in Eq. (5.6.8) is the horizontal extraterrestrial illuminance, the product of extraterrestrial irradiance and its luminous efficacy of 96.8 1mW^{-1}.

The ratio TF is the tilt factor. For any sloped surface of angle β, TF represents the ratio of background-sky irradiance (or illuminance) on a slope to the horizontal diffuse irradiance (or illuminance):

$$TF = \frac{IL_{TLT}}{IL_D} = \cos^2\frac{\beta}{2} + \left\{ \frac{2b}{\pi(3 + 2b)} \left[\sin\beta - \beta\cos\beta - \pi\sin^2\frac{\beta}{2} \right] \right\} \qquad (5.6.9)$$

Kinghorn and Muneer have shown that for the respective cases, i.e. shaded (sh) and sun-facing (sf) components of the sky vault, the tilt factor varies with clearness index, K_t. The respective tilt factors are obtained from

$$TF_{sh} = 0.4 - 0.0014K_t - 0.0793K_t^2 \qquad (5.6.10)$$

$$TF_{sf} = 0.4 + 0.1991K_t + 0.4755K_t^2 \qquad (5.6.11)$$

Once TF values are obtained, values of b_{sf} and b_{sh} are routinely returned from Eq. (5.6.9). Note that b_{sf} and b_{sh} describe the radiance or luminance distribution of the sky vault thus,

$$\frac{L_\theta}{L_Z} = \frac{(1 + b\sin\theta)}{(1 + b)}$$

where L_θ is the luminance of a sky patch at an angle θ from the horizon, L_Z the zenith luminance and b the radiance or luminance distribution index.

Calc5-04.xls enables computation of slope illuminance based on the Muneer–Kinghorn model.

Example 5.6.1

Five-minute averaged horizontal global and diffuse irradiance and horizontal global and diffuse illuminance measured values are provided for Garston, UK

(51.71°N, 0.38°W) in Chapter 8. On 1 April 1992 at 0930 hours the global and diffuse irradiation on a horizontal surface were recorded as 392 W/m^2 and 245 W/m^2 respectively. The corresponding illuminances were recorded as 42.2 klx and 27.3 klx. Use the Kinghorn and Muneer (1999) model to obtain the diffuse slope illuminances on east- and north-facing windows.

Using the procedure highlighted in Eqs (5.6.5) and (5.6.6) obtain the internal illuminances for the above two aspects and hence compare the daylight factors obtained with this procedure against those obtained using the orientation factor weighted daylight factor.

(a) Open workbook Calc5-04.xls.
(b) Activate sheet 'Compute'. Insert the given site data LAT, LONG, and LSM in cells B4:B6. Insert the given Year and Month in cells B7:B8. Insert the given surface data in cells J4:J6. Aspect = 0° (north orientation), Tilt = 90° (vertical surface) and $\rho = 0.2$. The diffuse sky illuminance on the north-facing surface is thus obtained as 10.3 klx. A similar procedure for the east-facing surface will yield the corresponding value as 19.7 klx.
(c) Refer to Eq. (5.6.6). Note that d = 0.022 and $d_{TLT} = 0.396 + 0.5\rho$. Thus for $\rho = 0.2$, $d_{TLT} = 0.496$ and $r = 0.044$. Using Eq. (5.6.5) the internal illuminances are then obtained as 872 lx and 458 lx for the above respective cases.

Note that validation data and a corresponding linked graph are also included in the Calc5-04 workbook. The *x*- and *y*-axes in the 'Graph' sheet are respectively the measured and computed global slope illuminance.

The following table enables comparison between the present set of results, converted to daylight factor values, against the orientation-weighted daylight factors.

Comparison of daylight factor (DF) expressed as per cent

Overcast sky = 2.2	Hunt (1979)	Littlefair (1990)
Orientation-weighted (north)	1.7	2.1
Orientation-weighted (east)	2.3	2.5
Slope illuminance based (north)	1.7	
Slope illuminance based (east)	3.2	
Luminance distribution based*	3.8	

* To be discussed in Section 5.6.6

The above comparison shows that even the simple technique of orientation-weighted daylight factor produces reasonable accuracy for the above estimates. Note, however, that the slope illuminance-based computations produce in effect 'dynamic' values of orientation factors, i.e. the factors change with the sky clarity.

Table 5.6.1 Comparison of measured and computed illuminance for Example 5.6.1 for Garston, 1 August 1991

Year	Month	Day	Hour	Minute	I_G (W/m²)	I_D (W/m²)	IL_G (klx)	IL_D (klx)	Measured data (klx)				Computed data (klx)			
									IL_N	IL_E	IL_S	IL_W	IL_N	IL_E	IL_S	IL_W
1991	8	1	8	30	505	132	58.3	21.2	8.4	76.2	30.8	5.7	7.8	67.0	28.5	7.8
1991	8	1	9	30	653	217	73.2	31.3	10.0	63.0	46.4	10.8	11.3	58.7	44.5	11.3
1991	8	1	10	30	428	307	50.8	37.3	11.7	26.6	33.4	11.6	14.4	26.7	29.7	14.4
1991	8	1	11	30	309	286	37.6	35.0	11.8	21.9	22.2	12.8	13.8	17.4	19.1	13.8
1991	8	1	12	30	515	390	60.5	46.9	12.7	19.6	34.6	18.5	17.9	27.7	37.4	17.9
1991	8	1	13	30	98	88	13.0	12.1	5.4	5.3	6.0	7.1	4.8	4.8	5.7	5.5
1991	8	1	14	30	810	324	89.9	41.4	11.5	11.6	52.0	64.1	14.1	14.1	57.8	75.4
1991	8	1	15	30	229	219	27.4	26.1	10.6	9.2	11.2	15.0	10.2	10.2	13.5	14.9
1991	8	1	16	30	443	270	49.9	35.0	13.6	10.0	18.9	55.1	12.6	12.6	24.7	66.0

Table 5.6.1 shows a comparison of measured and estimated slope illuminance using the Kinghorn and Muneer (1999) model.

5.6.5   Zenith luminance

Daylight design for buildings requires knowledge not only of the total amount of external illuminance available but also of the distribution of luminance across the sky vault. This is of particular interest when considering external illuminance as a lighting provider in, say, a deep plan side-lit room which may receive daylight from only a small portion of the sky. Sky luminance distribution data are of great importance to the lighting designer considering daylighting as an option for the provision of internal illuminance. Previous studies have shown that the sky vault can be considered as a series of separate sky patches, each with its own individual degree of luminance. Such luminance values can be determined as a function of the corresponding zenith luminance. Once zenith luminance computations are available absolute luminance values of each sky patch can be easily determined.

A number of researchers have proposed zenith luminance models for clear skies. Notable among these are Kittler (1970), Krochmann (1970), Nagata (1970), Liebelt (1975), Dogniaux (1979), Karayel et al. (1983), Nakamura et al. (1985) and Rahim et al. (1993). Some of the above models are not applicable in the tropical belt as they use a tangent function of the solar altitude (Rahim et al., 1993). The latter team have also demonstrated the site-specific nature of many of the older models.

Hopkinson et al. (1966) and more recently Littlefair (1994) have shown that under dark, overcast skies the Moon and Spencer (1942) proposed CIE overcast-sky model shows good agreement with measurements. Under such conditions the zenith luminance (L_z) may be obtained as

$$L_z = \{9/(7\pi)\}IL_G \tag{5.6.12}$$

5.6.5.1   All-sky zenith luminance models

Perez et al. (1990) have developed an all-sky zenith luminance model which has been tested against extensive data from five locations in North America. The model is represented by

$$L_z/I_D = a_i + b_i \cos z + c_i \exp(-3z) + d_i\Delta \tag{5.6.13}$$

This model claims to be site and season independent. With an overall bias error around 1% and RMS errors ranging between 0.7 kcd/m^2 for clear skies to 1.5 kcd/m^2 for intermediate skies, it represents a significant improvement over the above models. Calc5-02.xls may be used to obtain Perez zenith luminance estimates given horizontal diffuse illuminance.

Example 5.6.2

Five-minute averaged horizontal global and diffuse irradiance, horizontal global and diffuse illuminance and zenith luminance data are provided for Garston, UK (51.71°N, 0.38°W) in Data8-02.xls. Use the Perez et al. (1990) procedure to compute horizontal global and diffuse illuminance and zenith luminance for 1 August 1991. Compare the estimates against the respective measurements.

(a) Open workbooks Calc5-02.xls and Data5-01a.xls. Notice that Calc5-02.xls includes a FORTRAN-based DLL program [Fr309b.dll]. Therefore, Calc5-02.xls cannot be opened by double-clicking it from the Windows Explorer. Excel should be launched first and then Calc5-02.xls opened within Excel (see box below).

For all DLL-based workbooks the following procedure **MUST** be used:
- Launch Excel software
- Open the DLL-based workbook
- Enter data in the relevant worksheet(s)
- Simultaneously press ALT + F8 keys
- Select the relevant macro from the dialog box
- Either click the Run button, or simultaneously press ALT + R keys

---

(b) Activate sheet 'Site' of Calc5-02 and insert the given LAT, LONG, LSM in cells A2:C2 as shown.
(c) Activate sheet 'Compute' of Calc5-02 and, manually, fill cells A6:A17 with year (1991), cells B6:B17 with month (8) and cells C6:C17 with day (1).
(d) Choose an hour's data from Data5-01a for the purpose of calculations, e.g. for the hour beginning 1100. Copy the Hour and Minute data (cells A75:B86) from Data5-01a and paste it in cells D6:E17 of sheet 'Compute' of Calc5-02. Copy the averaged horizontal global and diffuse irradiance data (cells I75:J86) from Data5-01a and paste it in cells F6:G17 of sheet 'Compute'. Copy the horizontal global and diffuse illuminance data (cells C75:D86) from Data5-01a and paste it in cells P6:Q17 of sheet 'Compute'. Copy the zenith luminance data (cells Q75:Q86) from Data5-01a and paste it in cells R6:R17 of sheet 'Compute'.
(e) The computed values of IL_G, IL_D and L_Z are shown in cells L6:N17 of sheet 'Compute'. Table 5.6.2 shows the results. Sheet 'Graph' of Calc5-02 shows a plot of the computed parameters against the corresponding measured values.

Table 5.6.2 Input/output data for Examples 5.6.2–3 for Garston, 1 August 1991

Year	Month	Day	Hour	Minute	Measured data					Muneer–Kinghorn			Perez		
					I_G (W/m²)	I_D (W/m²)	IL_G (klx)	IL_D (klx)	L_z (kcd/m²)	IL_G (klx)	IL_D (klx)	L_z (kcd/m²)	IL_G (klx)	IL_D (klx)	L_z (kcd/m²)
1991	8	1	11	0	500	355	59.5	42.3	16.9	57.2	43.5	13.1	55.8	41.3	12.9
1991	8	1	11	5	455	319	48.6	37.8	13.8	53.1	39.0	13.1	51.1	37.4	11.7
1991	8	1	11	10	364	307	44.8	36.7	14.8	43.5	37.7	13.5	40.8	35.3	12.8
1991	8	1	11	15	277	249	33.4	29.9	8.9	34.0	30.8	11.6	31.1	28.9	10.7
1991	8	1	11	20	205	193	25.0	23.5	11.2	25.8	24.1	9.3	24.8	23.5	9.7
1991	8	1	11	25	228	219	27.9	26.6	8.5	28.5	27.3	10.4	27.4	26.4	10.8
1991	8	1	11	30	309	286	37.6	35.0	8.4	37.6	35.3	13.1	34.7	33.0	12.3
1991	8	1	11	35	703	373	76.8	46.0	16.6	79.3	46.1	11.5	77.3	43.8	14.1
1991	8	1	11	40	592	283	67.8	36.5	9.4	67.6	34.7	10.3	65.0	35.9	11.0
1991	8	1	11	45	295	258	37.6	33.0	9.8	36.1	31.9	11.9	33.1	29.9	11.3
1991	8	1	11	50	350	299	43.7	37.0	12.5	42.1	36.8	13.4	39.3	34.5	12.8
1991	8	1	11	55	400	336	47.7	40.6	16.6	47.5	41.2	14.6	44.8	38.6	14.2

5.6.5.2 Muneer–Kinghorn model

As stated above the luminous distribution index, b, provides an indication of the relative brightness of the sky vault. Steven (1977) has shown b to vary from 1.23 to −0.62 when the sky condition changes from overcast to clear skies. It has been shown by Steven (1977) and Muneer (1987) that the radiance, or luminance, distribution of each half of the sky-vault, e.g. 'sun-facing' (by the sun) and 'shaded' (opposite sun), may be represented by a unique value of b. In this case, these indices are denoted by b_{sf} and b_{sh} respectively. Zenith luminance, L_z, is then calculated in the following manner as a function of these indices and the corresponding diffuse illuminance of the sky vault:

$$L_z = \frac{1.5 I L_D}{\pi}\left[\left(\frac{1 + b_{sh}}{3 + 2b_{sh}}\right) + \left(\frac{1 + b_{sf}}{3 + 2b_{sf}}\right)\right] \qquad (5.6.14)$$

Note that to enable zenith luminance computations, values of b_{sh} and b_{sf} have to be determined first (see Eqs (5.6.9)–(5.6.11)).

Example 5.6.3

Repeat Example 5.6.2 using the Muneer–Kinghorn (1997) and Kinghorn–Muneer (1999) models.

(a) Open workbooks Calc5-03.xls and Data5-01a.xls.
(b) Activate sheet 'Site' of Calc5-03 and insert the given LAT, LONG, LSM, AZIMUTH and SLOPE in cells A2:E2 as shown.
(c) Repeat step (c) from the above example.
(d) Repeat step (d) from the above example. Notice that the horizontal global and diffuse illuminance data should be pasted in cells U6:V17 of sheet 'Compute' and the zenith luminance data in cells W6:W17 of sheet 'Compute'.
(e) The computed values of $I L_G$, $I L_D$ and L_Z are shown in cells Q6:S17 of sheet 'Compute' of Calc5-03.xls. Table 5.6.2 presents the results. Sheet 'Graph' of Calc5-03.xls shows a comparison between the computed values and their corresponding measured values.

The reader may wish to try the above Examples 5.6.2 and 5.6.3 to obtain $I L_G$, $I L_D$ and L_Z for Garston or Fukuoka, Japan. Measured data for both locations are provided in Data5-01b and Data5-02 respectively.

5.6.6 Sky luminance distribution

On the daylighting front recent advances in computer graphics technology allow the realistic modelling of complex building interiors with a minimal training time. One such modelling and visualisation package is the

RADIANCE lighting simulation system (Ward, 1994). The main features of RADIANCE have been enumerated by Mardaljevic (1995) as follows:

(a) It is a physically based program which allows precise estimation of interior illuminance.
(b) It has the capability to model geometries with realistic, luminance distributions.
(c) It supports a wide variety of reflection and transmission models.
(d) It can import building scene descriptions from CAD systems.
(e) It can estimate daylight factors using real sky luminance distributions, rather than assuming the worst case scenario used by the CIE overcast sky model.

Mardaljevic (1995) has undertaken the first comparison of RADIANCE results to actual room illuminances under a real sky. Using 700 scans of measured sky luminance measurements, undertaken by the Building Research Establishment at Watford, illuminance predictions were found to agree quite favourably with the internal illuminances. A sample RADIANCE output of a simulation of the Queen's Building, DeMontfort University in Leicester, England is shown in Plate 5.1 (see colour plate section). This plot has been provided by John Mardaljevic, a building energy simulation expert at DeMontfort.

The RADIANCE system is free, copyrighted UNIX based software produced at the Lawrence Berkeley Laboratory in California. Details of acquiring this software have been given by Mardaljevic (1995).

Skylight is a non-uniform extended light source. Its intensity and spatial distribution vary as a function of prevailing sky conditions. In addition to direct sunlight, sky-luminance angular distribution is the necessary information required for calculating daylight penetration into any properly described environment. Because actual sky-luminance distribution data are available only in a handful of locations, it is essential to be able to estimate skylight distribution from routine measurements such as irradiance. In the following section luminance distributions for all-sky conditions are presented.

Perez et al. (1993) have presented an all-sky model which is a generalisation of the CIE standard clear-sky formula (CIE, 1973). This expression includes five coefficients that can be adjusted to account for luminance distributions ranging from totally overcast to clear skies. The relative luminance l_v, defined as the ratio between the sky luminance at the considered point L_v and the luminance of an arbitrary reference point is given by

$$l_v = f(\theta, \xi) = [1 + a\exp(b/\cos\theta)][1 + c\exp(d\xi) + e\cos\xi^2] \tag{5.6.15}$$

For $x = a, b, c, d$ and e,

$$x = x_1 + x_2 z + \Delta(x_3 + x_4 z), \text{ for } \varepsilon \text{ (sky clearness) bins 2–8} \tag{5.6.16a}$$

otherwise

$$c = \exp\{(\Delta[c_1 + c_2 z])_3^c\} - 1 \qquad\qquad (5.6.16b)$$

$$d = \exp\{\Delta[d_1 + d_2 z]\} + d_3 + \Delta d_4 \qquad\qquad (5.6.16c)$$

The coefficients a, b, c, d and e are adjustable functions of irradiance conditions. A listing of these coefficients has been provided by Muneer (1997). For further details the reader is, however, referred to the article by Perez et al. (1993).

Calc5-05.xls and Calc5-06.xls, which respectively use the absolute and relative co-ordinate scheme for the sky patch, enable computation of the sky luminance distribution. Presently, in Calc5-05.xls and Calc5-06.xls the dimensionless parameter l_v has been normalised against zenith luminance. In the relative co-ordinate scheme the azimuth of any given sky patch is its angular separation from the sun. The other co-ordinate scheme, i.e. the absolute framework, allows the user to obtain the luminance distribution of the sky with the north direction being the reference. Details of the sky element grid adopted for these computations are shown in Figure 5.6.3.

Example 5.6.4

In the electronic file Data8-07.xls measured luminance distribution data for Fukuoka, Japan, are presented. Use data for the sky scan for 6 June 1994 at 12 noon LCT to evaluate the Perez all-sky luminance distribution model (Eq. (5.6.15) refers). Use Calc5-05.xls to compute the above luminance distribution and compare it against measured dataset.

Note: The measured data for Fukuoka is transformed form due south to a due north reference using the workbook Calc8-01.xls . The following procedure is to be used:

(a) Launch the Calc8-07.xls workbook.
(b) Highlight and copy cell range D705:ER705.
(c) Launch the Calc8-01.xls workbook.
(d) Paste the above data in the cell range C2:C146 of sheet 'Measured data'.
(e) Highlight cell range A2:C146 and then use the Data, Sort command. The dialog box 'Sort' appears. Make sure that the 'Sort by' and 'Then by' boxes respectively contain 'Altitude' and 'Azimuth' and the corresponding 'Ascending' radio buttons are selected. Click OK to execute.
(f) Copy cell range C2:C146 to the corresponding column of the 'Sorted data' worksheet.
(g) Launch the Calc5-05.xls workbook.
(h) Copy cell range C2:C146 from step 'f' into cell range B4:B148 of sheet 'Sky_Lum data' of the Calc5-05.xls workbook.

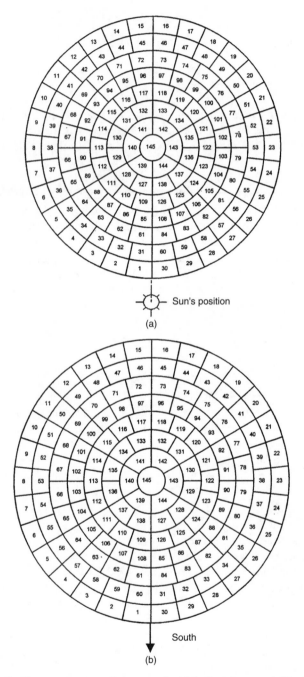

Figure 5.6.3 *Sky scan recording map for (a) Garston and Sheffield (PRC Krochmann scanner – relative co-ordinate system) and (b) Fukuoka (EKO scanner – absolute co-ordinate system)*

(i) Provide the site, time and solar data in cell range B5:B18 of the 'Main' worksheet.

(j) The final computed data is now available in cell range E4:E148 of 'Sky_Lum data' sheet.

(k) The measured and computed columns of measured and computed data are then saved in LD_Indat.csv file. A sample is provided in the 'Exe_files' folder. The file LD_Vals.exe (see the latter folder) may then be used (by double-clicking the file name icon from Windows Explorer) to produce plots of the sky scan.

A comparison of measured and computed sky scan plots is demonstrated in Figure 5.6.4. The plot shows numerical values of the luminance of each sky patch and a close similarity between the measured and computed values. Plots such as the one under discussion may be obtained simply by double-clicking the LD_Vals.exe file which is available in the **Exe_files** folder. The data required by the above exe file are to be provided in the LD_Indat.csv.

Plates 5.2 and 5.3 (see colour plate section) show colour luminance distribution plots for Garston (UK) data. These plots enable a better visual comparison between the measured and computed datasets. Once again the Perez model seems to produce reasonable estimates of the sky-luminance distribution. Colour plots such as these may be obtained by using the LD_Fill.exe file which is also available in the **Exe_files** folder. The data required are once again provided via the LD_Indat.csv file. Further validation work on luminance distribution has been undertaken by Chain et al. (1999) and plots similar to those present in Figure 5.6.4 included in the latter reference.

Note that the file LD_Numbr.exe produces a scheme of the UK sky scan system. A directly executable file 'Plot_XY.exe' for *x-y* plots is also included. This file draws data from the file Data_XY.txt. This versatile tool enables quick graphical review of very large data files, e.g. it is possible to plot several hundred thousand to a few million data points, such as those encountered in solar energy and daylight research.

Note that within Calc5-05 and Calc5-06.xls a doughnut diagram is also provided. This diagram, included within the sheet named 'Graph' enables a coarse method of validation. The inner sectors represent the measured and the outer ones the computed luminance data.

5.7 Luminance transmission

Hopkinson et al. (1966) have presented daylight transmission curves for single-, double- and triple-glazings of clear float glass design. The CIE sky component table, presented in Chapter 3, incorporates transmission loss for a single-glazing. For double- and triple-glazings the *BRE Digest* (Building Research Establishment, 1986) recommends respective correction factors of 0.9 and 0.8 to

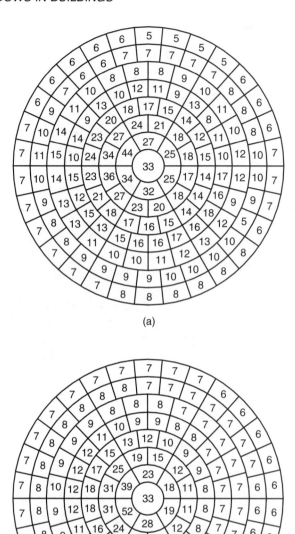

(a)

(b)

Figure 5.6.4 *Comparison of (a) measured and (b) computed sky luminance distribution for Fukuoka, 6 June 1994, 12 hours LCT*

be multiplied to the total daylight factor. This is certainly a simple but approximate approach. In the present context, it is possible to investigate the fine detail of daylight penetration through multiple glazings without any loss of accuracy by combining the above luminosity estimates with the glazing transmission characteristics. This material is presented in the following sections.

5.7.1 Incidence angle of luminance from a given sky patch and transmission through glazing

In order to obtain the transmission of luminance from any given sky patch discussed above, the angular separation of the sky patch and a normal to the window glazing is required. Calc5-05.xls enables such computations to be performed quite easily. This is demonstrated via Example 5.7.1.

Example 5.7.1

Refer to Figure 5.4.2 wherein four sky patches, SP1–SP4 are shown. Compute the incidence angle between a normal to the window and the luminance emanating from these sky patches. Also obtain the respective angular transmittances for a single-glazing assuming normal incidence transmittance, $\tau_o = 0.9$.

Refer to Figure 5.7.1 which provides computational details for any given sky patch and its angular separation from the sun's position. In this particular case the geometry for a normal to the window may be used instead of sun's position to obtain the desired solution. A step-by-step procedure using Calc5-05.xls is provided herein:

Enter $\tau = 0.9$ in cell B25.

Enter altitude and azimuth of the first point
The altitude and azimuth (measured from true north) of the centre of SP1 are to be provided in cells D13 and E13 as 40, 80. Note that the latter are the altitude and azimuth co-ordinates of the mid-point of SP1.
Enter altitude and azimuth of the second point
The altitude and azimuth of the normal to the window is provided in cells D8 and E8 as 0, 95.

The angle between the above two points is then read off from cell J13 as 42.3°. The transmittance is provided in cell N13 ($=0.88$).
Using a similar procedure the incidence angle for SP2 is obtained as 40.3° and transmittance as $=0.89$. SP3 and SP4 are then obtained from consideration of symmetry.
Caution: File Calc5-05.xls must **NOT** be saved after the above execution since the formulae for the sun's position are deleted by the entry of the above numerical data.

(a)

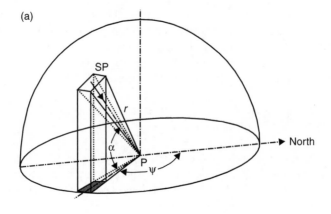

(b)

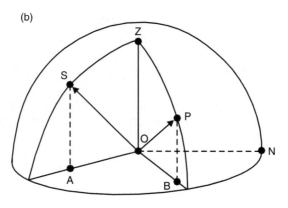

N = north
P = sky patch
S = position of sun in sky
Z = zenith of sky vault
∠ZOS = solar zenith angle
∠AOS = solar altitude angle
∠NOA = solar azimuth angle
∠NOB = sky patch azimuth angle
∠BOP = sky patch altitude angle
∠POS = elongation angle between P and S

Figure 5.7.1 *(a) Geometry of a given sky patch (SP) and (b) sky patch and solar geometry (Muneer, 1997)*

Example 5.7.2

Refer to Example 5.6.1 wherein illuminance data for Garston, UK were provided. Using Perez all-sky luminance distribution model (Eq. (5.6.15)) obtain the internal illuminance for the reference point shown in Figure 5.4.2. Use data obtained in the above example.

As mentioned above, Figure 5.7.1(a) shows a sketch of the sky hemisphere and the geometry for any given sky patch, SP. A derivation for estimating the illuminance on a horizontal surface due to the given sky patch is now presented:

Area of sky patch $= (r \, d\alpha)(r \, d\psi)$

where $d\alpha$ and $d\psi$ determine the size of the sky patch and r is the radial distance of the patch. In Calc5-05.xls these values may be reset at $10°$ ($\pi/18$ radians) intervals.

Let $\Delta(IL)$ represent the internal horizontal illuminance at the reference point P due to the given sky patch. The total internal illuminance due to sky may then be obtained by summing up the contributions of all relevant sky patches. It may easily be shown that

$$\Delta(IL) = \tau L (r \, d\alpha)(r \, d\psi) \sin \alpha / r^2 \qquad (5.7.1)$$

where L is the luminance of the sky patch in cd/m^2. Using the above fixed values of $\pi/18$ for $d\alpha$ and $d\psi$ used in Calc5-05.xls,

$$\Delta(IL) = \tau L (\pi/18)^2 \sin \alpha \qquad (5.7.2)$$

Based on Example 5.7.1, an average incidence angle of $41.30°$ and an average τ of 0.885 may be assumed for the above four sky patches. Using Calc5-02.xls $L_{Z,computed}$ is obtained as 5865 cd/m^2. The following table summarises the rest of the computations.

Sky patch (Figure 5.4.2)	L/L_Z Calc5-05.xls	$L = L_{Z,computed} \times (L/L_Z)$ cd/m²	lx Eq. (5.7.2)	$\Delta(IL)$
SP1	1.72	5865	10 090	179
SP2	2.19	5865	12 840	228
SP3	2.90	5865	17 010	302
SP4	3.95	5865	23 170	411
			Total internal illuminance =	1120

Note that this example indicates a daylight factor of 3.8%. A comparison with DF obtained from other simpler procedures was presented in Example 5.6.1. Of course the present procedure provides the most precise values of internal illuminances as it takes into account the detailed luminance distribution of the complete sky canopy. The RADIANCE software package undertakes this type of analysis for representation of the illuminance environment within buildings.

5.8   Optimisation of glazing area

Wilkinson (1992) has undertaken a study of the window area and the interaction of the costs of electric lighting and the penalty paid in increased heating costs. A simple formulation for the average daylight factor has been presented in Pritchard (1995):

$$DF_{av}(\%) = A_w\,\theta\tau/[2A_T(1 - \rho_{av})] \tag{5.8.1}$$

where A_w and A_T are respectively the window and total room surface area, θ is the angle subtended by the sky at the centre of the window and τ is the glazing transmittance. ρ_{av} is the average room reflectance. Note that Eq. (5.8.1) is very approximate and should be handled with care.

Using Eq. (5.8.1) a relationship for the total energy expenditure on electric lighting and heating was presented by Wilkinson (1992):

$$\text{Total energy costs} = [c_1/A_w] + [c_2 A_w] \tag{5.8.2}$$

The first term on the right-and side of the equation represents the costs associated with top-up electric lighting (inversely proportional to the window area) while the second term reflects the heating costs which linearly increase with glazing area. The c_1 and c_2 constants will respectively include the window daylight and thermal transmission characteristics. The constant c_1 will additionally include information related to the illuminance requirements for any given building application and the design data for the top-up electric lighting.

Equation (5.8.2) may be differentiated against the window area to provide an expression for an optimum value of A_w.

5.9   Innovative developments

A high density of urban structures can often lead to the loss of daylight amenity. Improper design of large glazed facades may also cause the problem of glare as has been pointed out above in this chapter. One innovative solution that has emerged in recent years is to capture daylight via a mirrored lightpipe and then direct it to those areas of building which are starved of daylight. Monodraught, an English company specialising in building services products, have patented a 'Sunpipe' system which can pipe daylight to internal spaces with the added advantage that excessive solar gains are avoided. The mirrored light transmission system is crudely analogous to the fibre optic cable, the difference being that in the latter device the transmission efficiency is much higher because the signal is carried through by means of a multiple refraction effect.

A schematic of the Monodraught system is shown in Figure 5.9.1. Daylight is gathered via a polycarbonate dome at roof level and then transmitted

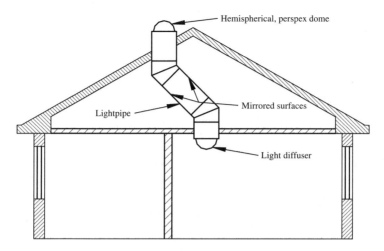

Figure 5.9.1 *A schematic of the Monodraught lightpipe system*

downwards to interior spaces within buildings. The internal surface of the sunpipe is coated with a highly reflective mirror finish material (typically with a reflectance in excess of 0.95) which helps in achieving a reasonable illuminance indoors when daylight is introduced via a light diffuser. The light-reflecting tube is adaptable to incorporate any bends around building structural components.

Measurements on a sunpipe system undertaken at Liverpool and Nottingham Universities have indicated that under hazy sunshine conditions a lighting level of 900 lx was recorded internally at approximately 2 m below the outlet light diffuser. In typical installations sunpipes of up to 6 m in length have been used, some with four pipe bends.

Although commonly used in the USA and Australia, lightpipes are a relatively new concept in Europe. However, Monodraught sunpipe systems have successfully been installed in buildings across the UK. The total number of buildings within the UK with mirrored lightpipes now exceeds 750. The building types have ranged from insurance companies to health clinics and from residential to university buildings.

A further innovation in the development of the sunpipe system is its integration with electric lighting within the sunpipe so that the device continues to function as a light source even during the hours of darkness (Payne, 1998). In another innovation the sunpipe has been combined with a natural ventilation system which draws air from the rooftop opening to provide cooling for the building fabric. Such systems are described in further detail in Chapter 4.

Shao et al. (1998) have presented simple design formulae for the design of mirror lightpipes. One such formula relates the transmittance (τ) of the lightpipe to ρ, the pipe surface reflectance, θ the angle between the incident light and the pipe axis, the length (L) of the lightpipe, and d_{eff}, the effective diameter of the pipe

$$\tau = \rho^x \qquad\qquad (5.9.1)$$

where

$$x = \frac{L \tan \theta}{d_{eff}}$$

Field monitoring of buildings installed with sunpipes was carried out by Shao et al. (1998). The broad conclusions that were drawn were that lightpipes can be effective devices for introducing daylight into buildings, provided an excessive number of bends or long pipe lengths are avoided. Use of as large a pipe diameter as possible was also recommended.

References

Ander, G.D. (1995) *Daylighting*. Van Nostrand Reinhold, New York.

Baker, N., Fanchiotti, A. and Steemers, K. (1993) *Daylighting in Architecture*. James and James Ltd, London.

Blackwell, M.J. (1954) Five years continuous recordings of total and diffuse solar radiation at Kew Observatory. Met. Res. Publication 895, Metorological Office, London.

Boubekri, M. and Boyer, L.L. (1992) Effect of window size and sunlight presence on glare. *LR&T* 24, 69–74.

Building Research Establishment (1986) *BRE Digest, Estimating daylight in buildings: Part 2*. Building Research Establishment, Watford, UK.

Cawthorne, D. (1991) *Buildings, Lighting and the Biological Clock*. The Martin Centre for Architectural and Urban Studies, University of Cambridge.

Chain, C., DuMortier, D. and Fontoynont, M. (1999) A comparative model of luminance, correlated colour temperature and spectral distribution of skylight: Comparison with experimental data. *Solar Energy* 65, 285–295.

Christoffersen, C. (1995) *Daylight Utilisation in Office Buildings*. PhD thesis, SBI report 258, Danish Building Research Institute (1995).

CIBSE (1996) *Building Services Supplement May 1996*. Chartered Institute of Building Services Engineers, London.

CIE (Commission Internationale de l'Eclairage) (1973) Standardisation of luminous distribution on clear skies. International Conference on Illumination, Paris.

Collins, B.L. (1975) Windows and people: a literature survey – psychological reaction to environments with and without windows. NBS Building Sience Series 70.

Dogniaux, R. (1960) Données météorologiques concernant l'ensoleillement et l'éclairage naturel. *Cah. Cent. Sci. Bâtim.* 44, 24.

Dogniaux, R. (1979) Variations qualitatives et quantitatives de composante du rayonment solaire sur une surface horizontale par ciel serein en fonction du trouble atmosphérique. Publication IRM, Serie b(62), Bruxelles.

Drummond, A.J. (1958) Notes on the measurement of natural illumination II. Daylight and skylight at Pretoria: The luminous efficacy of daylight. *Arch. Met. Wien, Series B* 9, 149.

Espiritu, R.C. (1994) Low illumination experienced by San Diego adults: association with atypical depressive symptoms. *Biological Psychiatry* 35, 403–407.

Haves, P. and Littlefair, P.J. (1988) Daylight in dynamic thermal modelling programs: Case study. *BSER&T* 9, 183.

Hopkinson, R.G., Petherbridge, P. and Longmore, J. (1966) *Daylighting.* Heinemann, London.

Hunt, D.R.G. (1979) Improved daylight data for predicting energy savings from photoelectric controls. *LR&T* 11, 9–23.

Karayel, M., Navvab, M., Neeman, E. and Selkowitz, S. (1983) Zenith luminance and sky luminance distribution for daylighting applications. *Energy and Buildings* 6, 3.

Kinghorn, D. and Muneer, T. (1998) Daylight illuminance frequency distribution: Review of computational techniques and new data for UK locations. *LR&T* 30, 139–150.

Kinghorn, D. and Muneer, T. (1999) All-sky zenith luminance models for the UK. *LR&T* (to be published).

Kittler, R. (1970) Some considerations concerning the zenith luminance of the cloudless sky. Circular No. 11, CIE E-3.2.

Krochmann, J. (1970) Uber die horizontal beleuchtungs-starke und die zenitleuchtdichte des klaren himmels. *Lichttechnik* B22, 551.

Liebelt, C. (1975) Leuchtdichte- und strahldichteverteilung durch tageslicht. *Gesundsheitsingenieur* 96, 127.

Littlefair, P.J. (1990) Predicted annual lighting use in daylit buildings. *Building and Environment* 25, pp 43–54

Littlefair, P.J. (1994) A comparison of sky luminance models with measured data from Garston, United Kingdom. *Solar Energy* 53, 315.

Loe, D. and Davidson, P. (1996) A holistic approach to lighting design. *Energy Management*, Sept./Oct. 16–18.

Mardaljevic, J. (1995) Validation of a lighting simulation program under real sky conditions. *LR&T* 27, 181.

Moon, P. and Spencer, D.E. (1942) Illumination from a non-uniform sky. *Trans. Illum. Engng. Soc. NY* 37, 707.

Muneer, T. (1987) *Solar Radiation Modelling for the United Kingdom.* PhD thesis, CNAA, London.

Muneer, T. (1990) Solar radiation model for Europe. *BSER&T* 11, 153.

Muneer, T. (1997) *Solar Radiation and Daylight Models.* Architectural Press, Oxford.

Muneer, T. and Angus, R. (1993) Daylight illuminance models for the United Kingdom. *LR&T* 27, 223.

Muneer, T. and Kinghorn, D. (1997) Luminous efficacy of solar irradiance: Improved models. *LR&T* 29, 185.

Nagata, T. (1970) Luminance distribution of clear skies, Part 2 – Theoretical considerations. *Trans. Arch. Inst. Japan* 186, 41.

Nakamura, H., Oki, M. and Hayashi, Y. (1985) Luminance distribution of intermediate sky. *J. Light & Visual Environment* 9, 6.

Payne, T. (1998) A brighter future for natural daylight. *M&E Design* November 1998.

Perez, R., Ineichen, P. and Seals R. (1990) Modelling daylight availability and irradiance components from direct and global irradiance. *Solar Energy* 44, 271.

Perez, R., Seals, R. and Michalsky, J. (1993) Modelling skylight angular luminance distribution from routine irradiance measurements. *J. Illum. Eng. Soc.* Winter, 10.

Pilkington (1993) *Glass in Building*. Architectural Press, Oxford.

Pleijel, G. (1954) The computation of natural radiation in architecture and town planning. *Meddelande Bull., Statens Namnd for Byggnadsforskning, Stockholm* 25, 30.

Pritchard, D.C. (1995) *Lighting*. Addison Wesley Longman Limited, Harlow.

Rahim, M.R., Nakamura, H., Koga, Y. and Matsuzawa, T. (1993) The modified equation for the zenith luminance of the clear sky. *Proc. 2nd Lux Pacifica Conf.*, Bangkok, 10–13 November 1993.

Shao, L., Elmualim, A.A. and Yohannes, I. (1998) Mirror lightpipes: Daylighting performance in real buildings. *LR&T* 30, 37.

Steven, M.D. (1977) Standard distribution of clear sky radiance. *Q. J. Roy. Met. Soc.* 103, 457.

TLC (1998) *Luxcontrol*. Tridonic Lighting Components, Basingstoke.

Ward, G.J. (1994) The RADIANCE lighting simulation and rendering system. *Computer Graphics Proceedings*, Annual Conference Series.

Weir, G. (1998) *Life Cycle Assessment of Multi-glazed Windows*. PhD thesis, Napier University, Edinburgh.

Whillier, A. (1953) *Solar Energy Collection and its Utilisation for House Heating*. PhD thesis, MIT, Cambridge, MA.

Wilkinson, M.A. (1992) The effect of glazing upon energy consumption within buildings. *LR&T* 24, 99.

Wyon, D.P. and Nilsson, I. (1980) Human experience of windowless environments in factories, offices, shops and colleges in Sweden. *Building Resources Worldwide, Proceedings of the 18th CIB conference*, 234–239.

Zeguers, J.D.M. and Jacobs, M.J.M. (1997) Energy saving and the perception of visual comfort. *Proceedings of Lux Europa*.

6 ACOUSTIC PROPERTIES OF WINDOWS

If the well-being of building occupants is not at the forefront of design criteria, the building, though well designed in terms of thermal performance and daylight transmission as discussed throughout Chapters 3–5, will still be deemed unsatisfactory by its occupants: work performance is also heavily influenced by the acoustics of the working environment. For this reason it is important to have correct acoustic properties of windows.

Sound is a form of wave energy. Noise is unwanted sound, and as such, may be described as pollution. This evokes a need for corrective action. Noise pollution manifests itself in many ways, including hearing damage, communication disruption and the creation of unnecessary stress. It may originate from transportation, industry, community life, and other sources. Annoyance very often occurs because the interference experienced by an individual is not the result of an action he or she benefits from, either immediately or directly.

Windows play an important role in attenuating exterior noise to an acceptable level for building occupancy. Achieving this is a function of three variables: the noise source, the receiver (the occupant) and the transmission medium (the window). Thus it may be deduced that

- Noise source variables concern the nature, composition and origin of the noise.
- Receiver variables focus upon tasks and activities being performed by the building's occupants.
- Window variables include the number and thickness of glazing panes, and the type of glass used.

This chapter will consider issues of aural comfort; exterior noise sources which impact upon the interior environment, the effect they have upon health and productivity of building occupants, and how windows can be designed to act as appropriate filters to attenuate noise.

6.1 Aural comfort

Attempts to apply consistent comfort principles of thermal comfort analysis to building acoustics have been explored in the recent past. If the definition of thermal comfort is *that condition where neither a warmer, nor cooler environment is desired,* then acoustic comfort can be paralleled as *that condition where neither too quiet nor too noisy an environment exists.*

Complaints about noise in general have increased over the past few decades. For example, a survey carried out in England and Wales on 14 000 households between 1985 and 1987 showed that 14% of the adult population suffer from domestic noise annoyance, 11% of the subjects were bothered by road traffic noise, and 7% by aircraft noise. The increase in complaints received is a combination of several factors. Increased public awareness about entitlement to quieter environments and a wider knowledge of the complaint procedure are partly responsible, but increases in general environmental noise levels also play a role.

There are thresholds of background noise level which should not be exceeded in order to establish conditions of comfort. Table 6.1.1 shows interior noise targets for some common building uses, while Figure 6.1.1 illustrates sound pressure and level for typical locations.

6.2   Noise sources

Most noise consists of a wide spectrum of frequencies. Before action can be taken to minimise the effect of noise, frequency levels and strengths must be identified. One of the dominant problems is traffic noise.

6.2.1   Road traffic noise

Road traffic noise is generally low frequency, and is a function of vehicle type, road surface, topography, and speed. Some typical road traffic noise levels are

Table 6.1.1 Interior noise targets

Location	Recommended maximum L_{Aeq} Level dB(A)
Dwellings	
Bedrooms	30–40
Living rooms	40–45
Offices	
Private/small conference rooms	40–45
Large offices	45–50
Educational	
Classrooms (15–35 people)	40
Classrooms (> 35 people)	35
Music/drama spaces	30
Health and Welfare	
General wards	55
Small consulting rooms	50
Diagnosis rooms	45

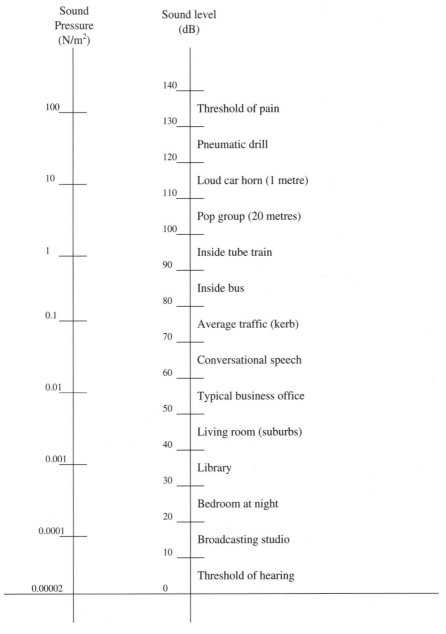

Figure 6.1.1 *Sound pressure and level*

shown in Table 6.2.1. Road traffic noise decreases by approximately 3 dB(A) with each doubling of the distance away from the road.

Table 6.2.1 Road traffic noise levels (Pilkington, 1995)

Situation	Noise level dB(A) L_{A10}	L_{Aeq}
20 m from busy motorway, average speed 62 mph, grassed terrain	80	77
20 m from busy main road, average speed 31 mph, paved	70	67
20 m from busy main road, average speed 31 mph, screened by houses	60	57

6.2.2 Rail traffic noise

Railway locomotive noise has a similar spectrum of frequency to road traffic noise, although electric trains have more emphasis towards middle frequencies, with higher frequencies decaying more quickly. Rail noise annoyance is generally more accepted than road traffic noise, despite higher noise levels, because it is more predictable and noise disturbance is shorter in period than the constancy of road traffic noise. The expression of rail noise is normally in terms of a 24-hour period since most traffic is regulated and timetabled. The noise levels associated with high-speed, diesel passenger trains and freight trains, averaging 120 trains per day are shown in Table 6.2.2.

6.2.3 Aircraft noise

Aircraft noise is a function of altitude, weather conditions, load and type of aircraft, with takeoff noise dominated by low frequencies, and landing with high-frequency reverse thrust noise. In the past, noise in areas surrounding airports has been assessed using the Noise and Number Index (NNI). This is a composite of the number of aircraft movements and the peak noises which they generate, and is generally plotted in contours around runways. NNI has since been replaced with L_{Aeq} (equivalent continuous A-weighted sound pressure level in decibels), in accordance with International Standard ISO 1996–1 (ISO, 1996a). Table 6.2.3 shows the probable community annoyance due to aircraft noise at varying levels of NNI and L_{Aeq}.

Table 6.2.2 Rail traffic noise levels (Pilkington, 1995)

Distance from track	Noise level dB(A)
Open grassland terrain	L_{Aeq}
25	67
50	64
100	59
200	54

Table 6.2.3 Aircraft noise levels (Pilkington, 1995)

NNI	L_{Aeq} (12 hour)	Probable community annoyance
35	57 +/−4	Low
45	66 +/−4	Moderate
55	75 +/−4	High
60	80 +/−4	Very high

Most conclusions concerning the ways in which people are affected by noise have been drawn from the results of subjective questionnaire-based surveys which are used to assess the number of people affected by traffic noise, and to what level. The problem of making definite conclusions from the surveys is that different types of noise have been assessed by different parameters; L_{Aeq}, L_{A10} (traffic noise level measured with standard 'A' scale weighting), NNI, and different measurement locations. The type of questionnaire used is also highly variable.

6.3 The acoustic environment

One problem experienced in assessing the exposure of an office worker to noise is that internally generated noise levels can often exceed those of external noise sources. Despite this, external annoyance may remain the focus of complaint, especially if the noise source is of a single tone or is impulsive in nature, as with an alarm or construction noise. The building occupant has a greater element of control over noise generated internally, compared with external noise where no control is available. This difference has psycho-acoustic implications. The traditional way of accounting for tonal or impulsive noise was to add a penalty value to the measured dB(A). BS 4142 (British Standards Institution, 1997) recommends a value of 5 dB(A) although this is regarded by some as in-accurate, as annoyance levels are so subjective in nature. A particular noise can cause annoyance at a level as much as 10 dB below background levels, parti-cularly where the noise is impulsive or tonal (Wilson et al., 1993).

Baker (1993) found that noise experienced by workers sitting just 2 m from a window wall affected by traffic noise averaged 60 dB. The background noise level in the office during unoccupied periods averaged 45–50 dB. Seventy per cent of workers seated within 7 m of the noise-affected window revealed the external noise disturbance unacceptable. A study of all office occupants re-vealed that 48% of workers regarded the internal noise level as unsatisfactory.

6.3.1 Speech

The range of frequency covered by adult speech lies between 500 and 2000 Hz. Suppression of higher frequencies is crucial in maintaining privacy of conversation, since aural intelligibility relies on these most. In addition to developing noise criterion curves Beranek (1989) defined the speech-interference level (SIL). This enabled the influence of background noise levels on speech to be quantified. The average sound pressure level is calculated for three octave bands: 600–1200 Hz, 1200–2400 Hz and 2400–4800 Hz, covering most frequencies of speech. In the 1960s this was altered to three bands with centres: 500, 1000 and 2000 Hz, with a fourth centred at 4000 Hz added later. The average sound pressure level in the four bands is termed the preferred octave speech interference level (PSIL). The PSIL levels shown in Table 6.3.1 are suggested for good speech communication. Prevailing values much in excess of those listed will render normal speech unintelligible, except at very close distances. Table 6.3.2 lists sound level/distance relationships for speech intelligibility, in terms of background noise level in dB(A), and background noise rating (NR, generally used for machinery and services noise), while Table 6.3.3

Table 6.3.1 Suggested maximum PSIL values for effective communication

Room type	Max. acceptable PSIL (dB)
Small private office	45
Conference room	30–35
Concert hall	25
Bedroom	30
Living room	45
Classroom/lecture theatre	30

Table 6.3.2 Sound level/distance relationship for speech intelligibility (Adams and McManus, 1994)

Background sound level dB(A)	NR	Max. distance for intelligibility (m)
48	40	7.0
53	45	4.0
58	50	2.2
63	55	1.2
68	60	0.7
73	65	0.4
77	70	0.2
Over 77	Over 70	Too noisy for speech

Table 6.3.3 Background sound levels for telephone conversations

Quality of conversation	Sound level dB(A)	NR
Satisfactory	58	50
Slightly difficult	68	60
Difficult	82	75
Unsatisfactory	Over 82	Over 75

shows the quality of conversation at various background sound levels for telephone conversations.

6.4 Health and productivity effects

Numerous studies have been carried out to investigate the effect of loud noise on human health, or prolonged exposure to higher levels of noise on hearing ability. The effect of noise upon human health is variant and a function of the nature, duration and location of the noise. The issue of personal susceptibility to noise remains a contentious one. In the office environment, however, exposure to loud noises is generally not experienced, and the problem is associated with longer exposure to lower sound levels. At lower sound levels, more general physiological, psychological and social effects occur. The impact of more moderate-intensity noise levels upon both human health and work productivity is, however, less well defined than for loud noise impacts. Problems in measurement and quantification of such effects mean that a relationship between noise discomfort and productivity loss is very difficult to develop. Studies to date have failed to identify any reliable formulation of the problem, but have led to a better understanding of its nature.

Sounds of only 20 dB(A) engender increased alertness during sleep. From 35 dB(A) the time required to fall asleep increases and the duration of sleep falls. Noise exposure can lead to a number of symptoms being experienced, including headaches, nausea, fatigue, nervousness, accentuated irritability and aggressiveness, activity disruption, reduced concentration, capacity for conversation and work efficiency, increased accident risk, and feelings of isolation.

Smith and Stansfield (1986) studied the effects of aircraft noise on self-reported everyday errors. The results of the study highlighted two points. Firstly, a positive relationship was found between aircraft noise exposure and the frequency in occurrence of minor errors; e.g. errors of memory, attention and action. Psychologists suggest that information is handled on different processing levels, with higher levels controlling the actions of lower levels, and decision-making criteria. Perception and memory are controlled by these higher processing levels. Environmental stressors like noise affect the operation of cognitive processes. Secondly, no correlation between sensitivity to noise and noise exposure was found, which contradicts the common belief that certain individuals are more sensitive to noise than others and experience exacerbated effects due to noise.

Interference with communication is one of the most common complaints of noise. In industry this can lead to inefficiency and possibly serious or even fatal accidents. High noise levels render speech unintelligible, and can restrict the understanding of warning signals. Increased agitation or annoyance can also result, which could affect emotional responses, making people less reasonable than they might otherwise be. Noise which is insufficient to mask speech signals can, however, increase the difficulty of the listener, requiring more effort, especially in telephone communication. Holloway (1969) suggests that if non-masking noise can cause problems in speech intelligibility, then it is possible that difficulties can arise in other tasks performed simultaneously with listening. This implies that the person listening acts as an information processor of limited capacity.

There is a need to interpret and understand noise signals, especially speech. Loudness of speech is also known to rise as difficulty in understanding increases. Adams and McManus (1994) summarised the effects on task performance and communication in four statements:

- Noise may stimulate people; raise level of arousal and improve concentration and performance in relation to simple tasks.
- Noise, particularly loud or monotonous ambient noise, may reduce arousal and have a detrimental effect on performance.
- Loud noise is inherently annoying and distracting.
- Loud noise interferes with physiological mechanisms which are essential to complex task performance.

Broadbent (1980) notes that it is the meaning of noise, not only its intensity, which produces annoyance. One suggestion for differences in personal response is that expectations differ between individuals. Two noises may have the same sound energy level, but one may be found more annoying than the other if it is *expected* to be quieter. Another reason may be the nature of the noise; impulsive tones are generally more annoying than constant noises of the same sound energy level. Annoyance due to noise is often associated with psychiatric ill-health. Annoyance was defined by the World Health Organisation (WHO) as *a feeling of displeasure evoked by noise*.

Shultz (1978) has made an attempt to quantify annoyance levels by way of noise level. His findings suggest that very few people are annoyed at noise levels below 45 dB(A). There is an increase in the number of people annoyed as the outside noise level rises above 60 dB(A). At 65 dB(A) approximately 25% of the population are highly annoyed.

Many studies have investigated the effects of infrasonic noise on people, yet the impact of low-frequency noise had received little or no attention (Broner, 1978). Reports of nausea, disorientation and general unpleasantness in response to infrasonic noise sources have been published, where the unknown element of low-frequency noise effects had been neglected. Man-made sources of noise at low frequency (20–100 Hz) include compressors, boilers, cars and ships. The focus of problems due to noise from these sources is annoyance, although responses to low-frequency sound have varied from sleep disturbance to threats of suicide in people who are otherwise disturbed.

Leventhall (1973) noted adverse effects on performance at noise levels lower than 80 dB(A), but that improvements in performance sometimes occurred at higher levels. This suggests that individuals are affected by the arousal effect, similar to that experienced in higher-frequency noise.

The complete elimination of noise is not encouraged either, except in conditions where this is required for short periods, e.g. recording studios. Complete silence for prolonged periods can be very disturbing due to the effects of sensory deprivation and feelings of isolation. Noise within the workplace can be beneficial to efficient operation of machinery and equipment, as it gives an indication of the state of working order. Reasonable noise levels penetrating from the exterior can also be beneficial to work productivity.

It is easily seen, then, that attenuation of external noise sources to an acceptable level via sound-reducing glazing solutions is beneficial to work performance. Findings may be summarised as follows:

- Noise exposure can lead to a number of symptoms being experienced, including headaches, nausea, fatigue, nervousness, irritability, aggressiveness, disruption to tasks, reduced concentration, reduced ability to converse, reduced efficiency, increased numbers of accidents, and feelings of isolation. All of these effects, whether directly or indirectly, limit an individual's capacity to focus on a specific task, negatively influencing work performance and productivity.
- A direct relationship is confirmed between noise exposure and frequency of minor errors. This reduces the efficiency of work tasks performed, and may eventually lead to serious errors in instances where workers experience fatigue.
- Interference with communication is one of the most common complaints associated with noise. Disturbances in communications is both inefficient and dangerous.
- Where the noise disturbance in an environment is deemed unsatisfactory, the main tasks being carried out may remain unaffected but at the expense of secondary tasks becoming inefficient, or containing errors. It may also lead to the early onset of fatigue in workers, reducing productivity and performance.
- A large number of factors influence noise perception, including personal health, personality, social habits and class, type of community, psychological well-being, and prejudice. It is therefore difficult to draw firm conclusions relating to noise and perceived aural comfort. What is certain, however, is that tonal, impulsive, loud and disturbing noises cause annoyance, which is detrimental to work task performance.
- Annoyance due to disturbance from noise sources is one of the most frequently received complaints. It cannot be measured using electronic equipment, and is only partially correlated with dB(A) measurements. Noises which are tonal or impulsive in nature are found to be most annoying.
- A substantial majority of workers sitting close to a window wall find disturbance from external noise sources to be unacceptable.

- Complete elimination of noise sources can be equally detrimental to work performance. Artificially suppressed acoustic environments could reduce arousal and distract concentration. An environment which is neither too noisy nor too quiet is optimal to work performance.

Adams and McManus (1994) conclude from a review of research techniques that the relationship between measured noise and noise level effects is extremely complex, and varies from person to person. There are a large number of influences on noise perception, including personal health, personality, social habits, social class, community type, psychological well-being, and prejudice.

There is a clear need to design windows such that annoyance and disturbances caused by unwanted sound sources are minimised, while ensuring that thermal and visual qualities are not compromised in terms of occupant comfort and potential environmental impact. The section which follows provides a method for assessing the sound attenuation properties provided by windows.

6.5   Noise transmission through glazing

This section is concerned with the noise that penetrates from the outside of a building (the source) to the working environment inside (the receiver), due to the attenuation properties of the window (the transmitting medium). The aim is to evaluate noise-attenuation properties for any given window construction. An office building will be considered by way of demonstrating the relevant analysis. The following assumptions are made regarding the office environment, location, orientation and construction:

- Each window configuration is installed within a typical open-plan office setup, with office location and orientation, wall construction, and window sash and frame construction remaining constant across all permutations.
- The example office is in a city-centre location, on an intermediate floor of a building and has one external wall.

The procedure for calculating aural performance of windows will be illustrated via Example 6.5.1. The following are the salient features of the computational procedure.

- Frequency-dependent values of sound insulation as a function of the thickness of glazing, cavity width and infill gas for a given window configuration are evaluated.
- Frequency-dependent sound reduction is then converted into a single number characterising the acoustical performance for the window.

The present analysis is based on the work of Pilkington (1995), Beranek and Ver (1992), ISO (1996b) and Weir (1998). The method is not suitable for evaluating triple-glazed window constructions. The mid-pane in such windows causes acoustic coupling, and the attenuation value of the overall window is reduced due to vibration. The noise reduction achievable using a triple-glazed window with two 8 mm cavities is less than that for a double-glazed window with a cavity width of 20 mm. It is assumed therefore that if noise attenuation is an important criterion in building design, double-glazed windows with a cavity greater than 50 mm would be preferred over triple-glazed options. To obtain data on triple-glazed windows, the manufacturer should be approached for a detailed breakdown of sound-insulation properties. By changing the prevailing noise spectrum and building construction details, this example can be adapted to calculate attenuation properties for other locations, varying noise sources and different building details. Calculations can be performed for any window/wall proportions or single-/double-glazed options.

Noise-reduction values for single-glazing panes and numerous double glazed windows are widely available through the literature and manufacturers' brochures. Sound reduction due to the cavity gas R_{gas} is a logarithmic function of C_0, the acoustic velocity within that medium. Values of C_0 for air, argon, krypton, xenon and SF_6 are presented below:

	C_0 (m/s)	Log C_0
Air	340	2.53
Argon	44	2.39
Krypton	169	2.23
Xenon	135	2.13
SF_6	128	2.11

No acoustic benefit is achieved through the use of argon in place of air in window cavities (Pilkington, 1997), due to their similar C_0 values. For this reason argon can be likened to air in acoustic calculations. Xenon was found to have a very similar C_0 value to sulphur hexafluoride, SF_6 ($C_0 = 128$ m/s), for which published data are available. Xenon is therefore likened to SF_6 for acoustic calculations. Performing a proportional analysis, based on acoustic velocity, it is possible to interpolate between data values for air/argon and xenon/SF_6 to produce data for krypton gas.

Figure 6.5.1 illustrates the frequency-dependent sound reduction for gas infill within cavity widths less than 50 mm. Generally speaking, there is no noticeable benefit below a cavity width of 50 mm. There is a sharp increase in sound reduction when the cavity width rises above 50 mm as shown in Figure 6.5.2.

Example 6.5.1 assesses the ability of window constructions to attenuate noise to an acceptable working level, whereby task operation is not detrimentally affected, and work performance is not compromised.

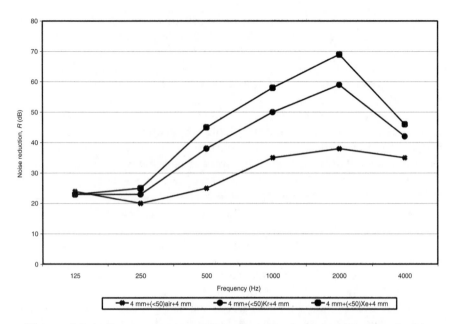

Figure 6.5.1 *Frequency-dependent sound-reduction values for double-glazed windows incorporating two 4 mm glass panes and a cavity of less than 50 mm*

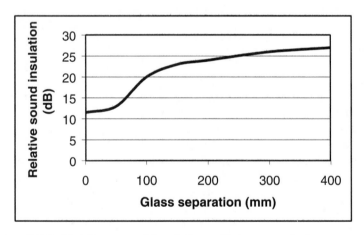

Figure 6.5.2 *Relative sound insulation with increased air space width*

Example 6.5.1

For the data given below find the Sound Reduction Index, R (dB) for the facade (composite wall) and also find the single-number rating which takes into account the given sound spectrum. The window to be used is a 12 mm krypton fill between two 4 mm panes of glass.

Given data
Office location: city centre
Window type: 4-12Kr-4
Window area, A_w (60% of facade) = 21 m^2
Wall area, A_{wall} (40% of facade) = 14 m^2
Glazing properties

Frequency, f (Hz)	125	250	500	1000	2000
Sound reduction, R_w (dB)	23	23	38	50	59

The first requirement is to evaluate the frequency-dependent values of airborne sound insulation for the selected window design, in this case a double-glazed, krypton filled window. The single-frequency sound reduction index, R, is calculated for the above frequencies. An example calculation is presented here for noise at 250 Hz frequency.

A summary of the sound-reduction values, R_w, for a number of single- and double-glazed windows is shown in worksheet Calc6-01. These data were reported by Weir (1998).

The frequency-dependent airborne sound insulation values may then be used to obtain single numbers characterising the acoustical performance for the given window configuration. The single-frequency sound reduction Index, R, for a composite wall, incorporating a glazed area, is given by (Pilkington, 1969)

$$R = 10 \, \text{Log} \frac{A_t}{\frac{A_{wall}}{10^{R_{wall}/10}} + \frac{A_w}{10^{R_w/10}}} \qquad (6.5.1)$$

where

A_t = total area of wall and window (facade area), m^2
A_{wall} = area of the masonry wall, m^2
A_w = window area (m^2)
R_{wall} = sound reduction index of masonry wall at 250 Hz, dB
R_w = sound reduction index of window at 250 Hz, dB

R_{wall} is taken for that of a masonry wall of minimum thickness 300 mm, and has frequency-dependent values as follows (Pilkington, 1969):

Frequency (Hz)	125	250	500	1000	2000
R_{wall} (dB)	40	45	53	59	64

Hence, using Eq. (6.5.1), R for a frequency of 250 Hz = 25 dB.

This calculation is repeated for noise frequencies in the range 125–2000 Hz. Next, the frequency-dependent noise-reduction values are compared to the

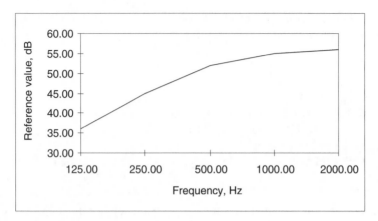

Figure 6.5.3 *Reference values for airborne sound reduction in octave bands (ISO, 1996b)*

relevant reference curve. The curve of reference values for airborne sound in octave bands is illustrated in Figure 6.5.3. The sum of unfavourable deviations is then obtained for the calculated and reference data. The term unfavourable deviation is defined as the difference between the reference and calculated value. If, for any given frequency, the calculated value is above the reference value, the difference is set to nil.

The reference curve is iteratively shifted downwards in steps of 1 dB towards the calculated curve until the sum of unfavourable deviations is just below the value of 10 dB. The value, in decibels, of the reference curve at 500 Hz, after shifting it in accordance with this procedure, gives the sound reduction index, $R_{weighted}$. In this example $R_{weighted} = 41$ dB.

Spectrum adaptation terms, given in dB, are added to the single-number rating to take account of the particular sound spectra. The predominant noise source in a city centre is the background outdoor noise and traffic noise. For this reason a single adaptation term is calculated respectively for background outdoor (C_0) and traffic noise (C_{tr}). ISO (1996b) provides a detailed account of the procedure to calculate C_0 and C_{tr}.

The workbook Calc6-01.xls automates the procedure of computing R, $R_{weighted}$, C_0 and C_{tr} thus characterising the acoustical performance of any given window. The procedure is as follows:

- Open the workbook Calc6-01.xls.
- Select the worksheet labelled 'Basic data'.
- Select the window type for which sound reduction properties are required.
- Copy and paste the sound reduction values for the given window construction, for each frequency, to sheet 'SRI calculation', cell range D9:H9. Note that the wall sound reduction data must be provided in the cell range D7:H7 of the latter sheet.

- Activate the 'Rweighted Calculation' sheet.
- Cell range B3:B5 provides the R_{weighted}, C and C_{tr} values.

Thus, $C = -4$ dB and $C_{\text{tr}} = -9$ dB.

The single-number quantity of the krypton cavity-filled double-glazed window is hence given as:

$$R_{\text{weighted}}(C : C_{\text{tr}}) = 41(-4 : -9)\,\text{dB}$$

This implies that the facade has a frequency-dependent airborne sound insulation value of 41 dB with an outdoor noise correction factor of –4 and a traffic noise correction factor of –9. In simpler terms, this means that the sound insulation value of the facade is 37 dB $(41-4=37)$ for outdoors and 32 dB $(41-9=32)$ for traffic noise.

The aural analysis presented above is important to the designer and architect in providing buildings which are pleasant and comfortable places for work, and which maximise employee productivity. As previously mentioned, a building that provides excellent thermal and visual conditions is of limited use if the aural performance is such that work tasks are compromised and building users are dissatisfied. The above example provides an efficient and simple-to-use procedure for analysing nose transmission through glazing systems.

References

Adams, M.S. and McManus, F. (1994) *Noise and Noise Law: A practical approach*. E&FN Spon, London.

Baker, N.V. (1993) Thermal comfort evaluation for passive cooling: a PASCOOL task. *Proc. of the 3rd European Conf. on Architecture*, p. 103.

Beranek, L.L. (1989) Balanced noise-criterion (NCB) curves. *J. Acoustical Soc. of America* 86, 650.

Beranek, L.L. and Ver, I.L. (1992) *Noise and Vibration Control: Principles and applications*. Wiley, New York.

British Standards Institution (1997) BS 4142: Rating industrial noise affecting mixed residential and industrial areas.

Broadbent, D.E. (1980) Noise in relation to annoyance, performance, and mental health. *J. of the Acoustical Soc. of America* 68, 15.

Broner, N. (1978) The effects of low frequency noise on people: a review. *J. of Sound and Vibration* 58, 483.

Holloway, C. (1969) Noise and efficiency: the spoken word. *New Scientist*.

ISO (1996a) 1996–1. Acoustics: description and measurement of environmental noise.

ISO (1996b) 717–1. Acoustics: rating of sound insulation in buildings and of building elements airborne sound insulation.

Leventhall, H.G. (1973) Man made infrasound, its occurrence and some subjective effects. *Proc. of the Colloq. on Infrasound*, Centre National de la Recherche Scientifique, Paris, 129.

Pilkington plc (1969) *Windows and Environment*. Pilkington Glass Ltd, St Helens, England.

Pilkington plc (1995) *Glass and Noise Control*. Pilkington Glass Products, CI/ SfB (31), July, 1995.

Pilkington plc (1997) *Glass and noise control*. Technical Bulletin, Pilkington Glass Products, May, 1997.

Shultz, T.J. (1978) Synthesis of social surveys on noise annoyance. *J. of the Acoustical Soc. of America* 64, 377.

Smith, A. and Stansfield, S. (1986) Aircraft noise exposure, noise sensitivity, and everyday errors. *Environment and Behaviour* 18, 214.

Weir, G. (1998) *Life Cycle Assessment of Multi-glazed Windows*. PhD thesis, Napier University, UK.

Wilson, M., Nicol, F. and Singh, R. (1993) Measurements of background noise levels in naturally ventilated buildings. *Proc. of the Institute of Acoustics* 15.

7 WINDOWS AND THEIR LIFE CYCLE

Since the late 1960s life cycle assessment (LCA) has become an increasingly important tool for engineers, technologists, scientists, designers, managers and environmentalists alike. LCA enables the effects which products, processes and activities have on local, regional or global environments to be assessed. It is necessary to consider the impact which raw material extraction, energy production, manufacturing processes, transportation needs and waste disposal requirements have on both social and natural environments. Impacts on the environment include effects on the atmosphere and the world's natural resources, in addition to human health factors, animal habitats, fuel depletion, noise pollution, and the availability of raw materials and primary fuel for the future.

Carbon dioxide (CO_2) has many influences on the environment, and has a very large part to play in global warming issues. In the building and construction trade CO_2 is the largest environmental concern, accounting for over 50% of the UK's total CO_2 emissions. This has prompted research into new material production, product design, manufacturing methods, recycling technology, use patterns, and waste disposal management. Table 7.0.1, extracted from Buchanan and Honey (1994), shows the carbon emissions resulting from the production of some commonly used building materials.

Greenhouse gases absorb infrared radiation from the sun's heat which would normally be reflected back into space. This retained heat in the atmosphere is reported to be very slowly increasing the earth's temperature. The natural greenhouse effect maintains the surface of the earth at a temperature which enables inhabitation, and is caused by important natural gases; CO_2, water vapour, methane (CH_4), and ozone (O_3). The effects of rising concentrations of CO_2, methane, nitrous oxides (NO_x), and ozone in the atmosphere, manifested in rising global temperatures, was first noted at the beginning of the nineteenth century by Jean-Baptiste Fourier. Other gases, not found naturally in the atmosphere, such as chlorofluorocarbons (CFCs), have also increased in concentration since the commencement of industrialisation. A world-wide rise in temperature, estimated at 2°–6°C over the next century could result from these changes. Warming of this magnitude would alter climates throughout the world, cause sea levels to rise and affect crop production. Much of the CO_2 in the atmosphere is a direct result of fossil fuel burning, which accounts for about 5 billion tonnes of CO_2 pro-

Table 7.0.1 Carbon emissions resulting from the production of commonly used building materials. All units in kg carbon per m³ of material (Buchanan and Honey, 1994)

	Carbon released	Carbon stored	Nett carbon emitted
Treated timber	22	250	−228
Glue laminated timber	82	250	−168
Structural steel	8132	15	8117
Reinforced concrete	182	0	182
Aluminium	6325	0	6325

duction annually. This alone is responsible for a yearly CO_2 concentration rise of 0.4% (Callander, 1995). The other two major influences on CO_2 production are cement manufacturing and changes in tropical land use, accounting for about 1 and 2 billion tonnes respectively (Callander, 1995). The development of products with low embodied energy contents, which use reduced quantities of energy and which contribute reduced amounts of greenhouse gases to the atmosphere in their use phase, has become of prime importance.

7.1   Definition of life cycle assessment

LCA takes a holistic view of the entire lifecycle of a product, process or activity with a view to identifying those stages of the life cycle which have the greatest adverse effect on the environment. Field et al. (1994) state that LCA has become one of the most actively considered techniques for the study and analysis of strategies to meet environmental challenges, and conclude that it is one of the most promising approaches to integrate environmental knowledge and data into a framework for action. The life cycle of a product is not simply its period of useful employment, but includes each stage from raw material extraction, manufacturing, retailing, use and maintenance to disposal or recycling. A simplified illustration of the LCA process is shown in Figure 7.1.1. At each stage, the transportation effects must be accounted for, in addition to the underlying requirements of administration and workforce services. There are four main stages to an LCA:

- Planning
- Inventory analysis
- Impact assessment
- Improvement analysis

Each LCA stage is discussed in detail throughout this chapter, specific to the LCA of multi-glazed windows.

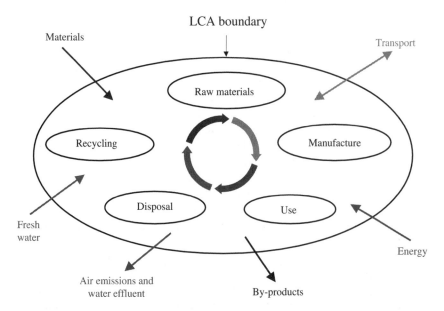

Figure 7.1.1 *Input/output data requirements for a comprehensive life cycle assessment (Weir, 1998)*

7.2 Planning

The main purpose of the planning phase is to define the investigation boundaries. LCA may be used for many different purposes, including the comparison of a range of products, identification of harmful stages in a product life cycle, new product development, allocation of process resources, categorising of research and development needs or aggregation of total product environmental burdens. During the planning of an LCA the objective must be clearly borne in mind while the system limitations are defined and the methods for data collection and evaluation are set out. System limitations may include such considerations as data availability, future environmental effects and technology development requirements.

Throughout all stages of the window life cycle it is necessary to be in close communication with production managers, transportation managers, windows users, technical staff, design engineers and building construction experts, such that the most up-to-date and relevant information is included in the analysis. Without close liaison with such personnel it is easy for the LCA to be mis-directed.

LCA is a very specific tool and whereas it can be applied to almost any product, process or activity, care must be taken not to generalise the results too far. LCA is a relatively new science and its application to window design is even more recent (Weir, 1998). Thus, LCA results for very many window designs are not readily available. The example LCA which follows is based upon a specific window type, manufactured in a specific location and used within a specific building type, in a defined location. The principles and techniques used in this analysis can easily be generalised and used to perform subsequent LCA studies on different window types and constructions, in alternative building types, based in any location desired.

The objective of this LCA is to outline the key sources of environmental impact throughout the life cycle of a multi-glazed window, and to identify realistic improvements which can be made to the window design, production processes, manufacturing techniques and life cycle activities to reduce this burden over the holistic life of a window.

The LCA used in this chapter is subject to the following conditions. The window considered is of timber frame construction, measuring 1.2 m by 1.2 m and manufactured in Norway using Scandinavian pine from well-managed tree plantations. It is transported by sea and road to an Edinburgh location where it is installed within a typical three-story office building. A plan of the office space is shown in Figure 7.2.1. A comparison of 18 multi-glazed window constructions is presented showing the difference between single-, double- and triple-glazed windows, with and without the use of low-emissivity glazing coatings, and the use of air, argon, krypton and xenon cavity gases. The useful life of the window is considered to be 20 years.

A clear definition of investigation inclusions and exclusions and the methods of data retrieval must also be set out during the planning phase. The setting of these have a significant influence on the results generated. The following set the boundaries for most general LCAs, and therefore form the investigation boundaries here:

Inclusions	*Exclusions*
• raw material extraction	• manufacture of capital equipment
• manufacturing processes	• maintenance of capital equipment
• packaging requirements	• manufacture of services
• transportation requirements	• maintenance of services
• in-use repairs and maintenance	• energy required to raise capital for
• waste disposal and recycling	production
• fuel production and use	
• energy generation	

Figure 7.2.1 *Example office dimensions and layout (Weir, 1998)*

It may be necessary to change the objectives of the LCA if no method can be found to obtain the data required. It is acceptable to do this, as LCA is an iterative process. The first LCA of a product, process or activity provides further data, information and knowledge for the second, third, etc. iterations of the LCA procedures. The overall objective of the LCA may be achieved through a fifth or sixth iteration of the process. This may be a lengthy procedure, but points to the fact that LCA is a commitment to ongoing environmental improvement, and is not something which is carried out as a 'one-off' exercise. It may be helpful to reduce the data acquired from many different sources to the same common unit. This is termed the 'functional unit', and simplifies the process of turning data into meaningful information. The functional unit adopted here is Joules per unit output (J/window).

The LCA of multi-glazed windows requires several data-acquisition methods to be adopted. For simplicity this is divided into the following sections.

7.2.1   Raw material extraction

In order to quantify the environmental burden associated with raw material extraction it is first necessary to identify all major raw materials required for the production of multi-glazed windows. This is done by examining and listing the main components which comprise a finished window. Secondly, each of these raw materials requires to be quantified in terms of mass or volume. This can be done by dismantling a finished window and weighing or measuring the volume of each component. Thirdly, the production and manufacturing processes need to be observed such that raw material wastage can be assessed and quantified. This can be achieved by close examination and measurement of manufacturing operations. Fourthly, and finally, the energy content or 'embodied energy' of the raw materials must be quantified. Embodied energy is a measure of the total energy required to extract, process and manufacture a raw material into a finished product, or a component product which may be used as part of a larger product. It would be very time intensive to assess each raw material prior to it arriving at the factory door. There are several sources of literature which provide this information. Care must be taken, however, to ensure that the basis of this information is in keeping with the objectives and boundaries of the LCA.

7.2.2   Manufacturing

The total energy consumed within the manufacturing plant is not limited to the consumption of energy for electricity and machinery power, but also includes all administrative, technical, building services and support facilities. Assessment is made by detailed measurement of individual processes, or by averaging energy consumption over the number of window units manufactured annually.

7.2.3   Transportation

All stages and methods of transportation should be assessed and aggregated. Consideration must be given to the transportation of raw materials to the factory site, of finished windows to the construction site, and of disposal/ recycling of windows at the end of their useful life.

7.2.4   Use

The utilisation phase of a number of products has little impact on energy consumption and environmental impact. The design and construction of windows do, however, impact heavily on energy consumption. Windows which are designed to high thermal performance specifications significantly reduce the requirement for space heating over a lifetime of use. This is discussed at length in Chapter 3. Additionally, windows, which are designed to permit quality daylight into an occupied space, reduce the need for electric lighting and thus reduce the electricity requirement over a lifetime of use. It is necessary to calculate the energy consumption associated with space heating and electric lighting, using the transmission properties of windows, as discussed in Chapters 3–5, to gain a holistic view of window performance.

7.2.5   Recycling or disposal

The energy associated with recycling or disposing of windows once their useful life within the building envelope is over is very difficult to assess. As the number of LCAs being performed increases, available information on recycling and disposal will become more readily accessible, enabling engineers and environmentalists to make better and more informed judgements on the recycling and/or disposal of multi-glazed windows.

7.3   Inventory analysis

The inventory analysis is a methodical quantification of inputs and outputs. This is a measure of all matter which crosses the boundary defined in the planning phase. Energy, raw materials, air emissions, water-borne effluent and solid waste are examined and measured. This may employ several different data-acquisition methods, from physical measurements to database searches, surveys, questionnaires, analysis of historical data, theoretical calculations and individual interviews, as briefly outlined in the planning phase above.

To simplify the process, the life cycle is divided into a number of stages:

- materials and manufacture
- transportation
- use
- disposal and recycling

7.3.1 Materials and manufacture

Material requirements and manufacturing processes are simpler for some products than for others; the window requires detailed inventory analysis work due to the number of components involved and the complex processes required to manufacture a finished window. Timber processing, aluminium optimising, assembly, glazing unit production, painting, lighting, heating, administration, services, and technical design needs are all analysed individually, with a final aggregation to sum the data collected. Administration and services needs are accounted for in the factory as a separate but necessary issue. For the product to be produced, marketed and sold there must be administration personnel, a design team, factory workers, and management. To sustain a workforce requires services, heating, lighting and materials. Each of these has implications for energy consumption, material use and environmental impact. Each main material or component part within the finished window is discussed below.

7.3.1.1 Inert infill gas

There are two issues to be dealt with when considering the environmental impact of cavity infill gases. The first of these is the associated benefits, in terms of improved thermal properties and reduced heat loss from the window. These issues are discussed in full in Chapter 4. The second issue concerns the consequences which must be addressed regarding the energy input and environmental burdens created as a result of production. In this analysis three infill gases are investigated, and compared to the use of air in cavities.

- Argon
- Krypton
- Xenon

Argon, krypton and xenon are all present in the atmosphere, and production of the pure gases is a process of separation from other components present. Table 7.3.1 shows the percentage content of gases in air. Trace gases include

Table 7.3.1 Percentage composition of air by volume (Fernie and Muneer, 1996)

Component	Percentage
Nitrogen	78
Oxygen	21
CO_2	0.03
Argon	0.9
Krypton	0.000114
Xenon	0.0000087
Trace gases	0.069

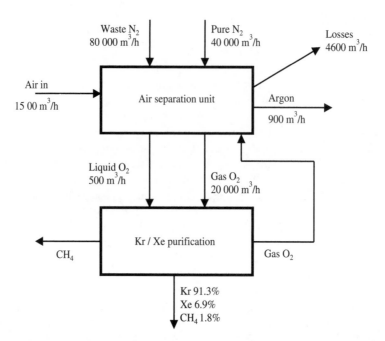

Figure 7.3.1 *Gas production schematic for BOC Middlesborough plant (Fernie and Muneer, 1996)*

water vapour, hydrogen, ozone, methane, carbon monoxide, helium, and neon. The process of separating inert gases from air is shown in Figure 7.3.1, extracted from Fernie and Muneer (1996).

The equipment required for the separation of gases from air was reported by BOC in Middlesborough, UK, to have a power rating of 12 MW. This is the only equipment required for extracting argon gas. Krypton and xenon, however, require the running of a crude krypton/xenon column, consisting of a reactor (4 kW), heater (10.8 kW), flash vaporiser (4 kW), liquid oxygen pump (2.3 kW), and purification column (2.4 kW). The actual yield of gas from the column is between 31% and 54%. Production rate data is based on an average yield rate of 42%.

For a window measuring 1.2 m by 1.2 m the area of glazing is 1.1 m², and the cavity gap for argon, krypton and xenon would be of 16, 12 and 8 mm respectively, requiring a gas volume of 17.6, 13.2 and 8.8 litres. The energy requirement to produce argon, krypton and xenon gases to fill this gap is 12 kJ, 508 MJ and 4.5 GJ respectively (Fernie and Muneer, 1996). Filling the glazing units with inert gas is a carefully monitored and controlled process. The panes are filled via filling and control holes drilled in the spacer, and the amount of gas flow is regulated using flow valves. The gas quantities and pressure regulation ensure that the mixing of gas with the displaced air is minimised, such that there is no 'flushing' process taking place. Gas is detected using special probes, and the gas flow is stopped by the closing of a solenoid valve, once the correct concentration is achieved in the pane. Exact levels of gas wastage are not known, but are minimal due to the use of efficient controls.

7.3.1.2 Low-emissivity coating

Float glass is produced 24 hours a day, and requires a weekly input of 5000 tonnes of materials for a typical float glass production plant. The annealing lehr works at a speed of 870 m/hour. The glass ribbon produced is 3.56 m wide, and can be produced in a variety of thicknesses. The gross area of glass produced is 3097 m^2/hour (Liggett, 1996). The net yield of glass allowing for breakage and trimming of the glazing edges has been accounted for in the calculations. Details of the energy analysis are as follows (Weir and Muneer, 1997):

Natural gas load	3165 kW	Energy input	1.7 kWh/m² low-e coating
Electrical load	783 kW	Energy input	0.4 kWh/m² low-e coating
Total load	3948 kW	Total input	2.1 kWh/m² low-e coating

Therefore, for the production of low-e coating for a window measuring 1.1 m^2, the energy content is 2.3 kWh per pane, or 8.4 MJ per pane.

7.3.1.3 Timber sash and frame

The timber used in the window manufacturing process is 100% softwood, and is obtained from organised, well-established tree management programmes in Scandinavia (Finland 30%, Norway 30%, Sweden 40%), whereby two trees are planted to replace the felling of one. Plantation forestry accounts for approximately 10% of timber requirements world-wide. About 2 billion tonnes of CO_2 enters the atmosphere as a direct result of forest destruction each year (Callander, 1995). Timber has a high strength to weight ratio, and is easily formed for many applications. It possesses good thermal and sound-insulating properties, does not corrode, and given the right conditions and treatment will not rot. One very popular treatment applied to softwoods is preservative impregnation. All timber components are impregnated with a white spirit-based solution, which soaks into the timber pores, and slows down the process of decay in the timber, thus lengthening the window life cycle. To achieve impregnation all timber sections are enclosed in a designated chamber and a vacuum is created. The preservative tank is then opened and the chamber is filled. The vacuum is maintained for a few minutes before a discharge pump is operated and the vacuum is lost. The loss of vacuum ensures that each timber pore is filled with preservative. The chamber is then emptied of preservative, and a new vacuum at a higher pressure is created over a longer period of time. A final discharge completes the impregnation process, and the timber remains within the drying chamber for 1–2 days.

There are many different uses for timber, requiring differing treatment processes and having varying energy contents. Energy content is a measure of the total energy input required to extract raw materials and manufacture them into useful materials or finished articles, and normally includes the energy associated with packaging and transportation, but excludes use and recycling. Table 7.3.2, extracted from Buchanan and Honey (1994), shows the energy content for some popular forms of timber used in construction; softwood having an energy content of 15.5 GJ/m^3. This information must be used within the boundaries of the analysis. Research has shown energy contents which are both higher and lower than the figures shown in Table 7.3.2. Analysis by West et al. (1994) produced data for indigenous softwood which includes entries for transportation, material extraction, processing and manufacture. This indicates an energy content of 2.6 GJ/m^3. Further studies by Hollinger and Hunt (1990), Halliday (1991) and Dinesen and Trabergy-Borup (1994) arrived at figures of 0.51 GJ/m^3, 1.77 GJ/m^3, and 4.03 GJ/m^3 respectively. These final values are widely dispersed due to wide variance in the underlying analyses. The working boundaries, as set out in the planning phase of an LCA, must be kept central to all decision making in the analysis. Varying boundary inclusions can cause energy content valuations to differ greatly. Manufacturing methods may be widely varying in nature, incorporating many differences in procedure, machinery and available technology. Work by West et al. (1994) was found to be most closely related to the LCA boundaries under Section 7.2, and hence an energy content of 2.6 GJ/m^3 of softwood timber is used in this analysis.

Allowing for the waste within the window production process and given the window dimensions and type, a total mass of 37 kg of timber is used (frame 14.94 kg, sash 10.01 kg, waste 12.05 kg). The density of softwood varies greatly, according to the water content in the timber, but an average of 500 kg/m^3 is used. This gives an energy content for the timber component, exclusive of machining, of 192 MJ.

To provide material for the window sash, timber must pass through a laminating process where two or three sections of timber are glued and compressed together. Therefore, to complete the analysis for the embodied energy of timber, a contribution for the glue involved in laminating must be added. Honey and Buchanan (1992), in their analysis, estimated that 0.5 kg of glue is

Table 7.3.2 Energy content for some popular forms of timber used in construction (Buchanan and Honey, 1994)

Timber type	Energy content (MJ/m^3)
Rough timber	848
Glulam timber	4 500
Hardboard	20 600
Softwood	15 500
Particleboard	12 900

required per square metre of laminate surface. Twenty-five per cent of timber laminated involves one layer of glue and two sections of timber, while the remaining job requires two layers of glue and three sections of timber. Each layer covers an area of 0.07 m². Therefore, taking into account the fact that only 30% of sashes are laminated, an average of 0.04 m² of glue is applied to each sash (expressing this in mass terms gives 0.02 kg of laminate glue). The glue is assumed to have an energy intensity of 160 MJ/kg, which equates to 3 MJ per sash. The total embodied energy for the timber sash and frame, inclusive of timber processes and laminating glue, is hence 195 MJ.

7.3.1.4 Aluminium

The processes involved in cutting and assembling the aluminium components for the window construction involve minimal quantities of energy. The main consideration for material consumption and energy use comes at the aluminium manufacturing stage. Aluminium smelting and forming is a highly energy-intensive procedure, and must be considered in the LCA of the window unit. The process of manufacturing aluminium components from raw bauxite is a multi-stage procedure, as illustrated in Figure 7.3.2. The most energy-intensive stages in the procedure include the crushing of raw bauxite, electrolysis of alumina, to produce soluble aluminium, and the casting of ingot. The final processing is performed in the window factory, whereby lengths of formed aluminium are cut to the desired size. All other processing is performed at the aluminium plant. Again, the energy content of aluminium production is much debated. Buchanan and Honey (1994) quote a content of 130 MJ/kg for general aluminium, while Saito and Shukuya (1995) quote a content of 503 MJ/kg for pressed and finished aluminium window frames. Further work by Young and Vanderburg (1995) produced data for both primary and secondary aluminium. Primary aluminium is produced from raw bauxite, and secondary aluminum is recycled material, having gross energy requirements of 225 MJ/kg and 50 MJ/kg respectively.

Aluminium is used for many different purposes within the window construction. Aluminium profiles are fitted along the bottom edge of the sash to protect the timber from water penetration. The window-opening mechanism, various sections of the ventilation grills, and the glazing unit spacer are also made of aluminium to ensure a light-weight design. The total mass of aluminium used in a standard window of 1.2 m by 1.2 m, and the total waste from each process was calculated as shown in Table 7.3.3.

The total waste at the window factory site, of 0.306 kg per window, is not discarded but sold to a metal merchant for recycling as secondary aluminium. The total energy input required to produce and process the aluminium for one window, assuming that 100% primary aluminium is used, is estimated to be 518 MJ. As noted previously, melting and reprocessing secondary aluminium uses a fraction of the energy to produce 1 kg of formed aluminium (50 MJ/kg compared to 225 MJ/kg for primary aluminium). This is because the energy-

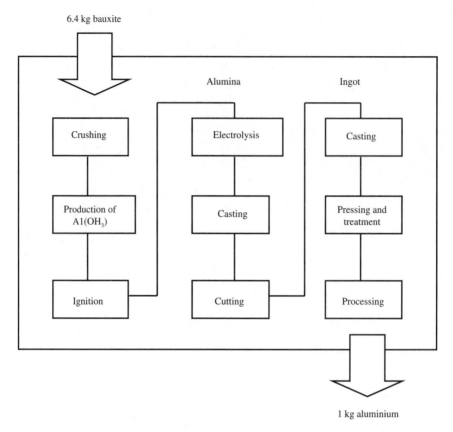

Figure 7.3.2 *Production of aluminium from raw bauxite (Saito and Shukuya, 1995)*

intensive processes of smelting and electrolysis are not required for secondary aluminium. UNIDO (1989) estimate that 27% of the world's total aluminium production comes from recycling aluminium. This percentage is likely to be lower for building materials due to design for long life spans in construction

Table 7.3.3 Estimate of total aluminium mass incorporated into one window measuring 1.2 m by 1.2 m (Weir, 1998)

Window component	Aluminium mass (kg)	% Waste	Total aluminium mass (kg)
Glazing unit spacer	0.24	3	0.25
Frame ventilation	0.16	17	0.19
Outer protection	1.42	17	1.66
Window mechanism	0.17	17	0.20
Total	1.99		2.30

components. If the assumption is made that about a quarter of the aluminium used is recycled, then the energy intensity for the aluminium used in the window becomes 409 MJ.

7.3.1.5 Sealed glazing unit

The production of large glass panes supplied to the factory is also an energy-intensive process, which must be accounted for in the LCA study. West et al. (1994), Saito and Shukuya (1995), and Dinesen and Trabergy-Borup (1994) report the energy content per kg of sheet glass manufactured to be 13 MJ/kg, 16.9 MJ/kg, and 18.6 MJ/kg respectively. There is less discrepancy between these values than for aluminium and timber. This is perhaps because the technology used is standardised, and fewer differences between manufacturing methods exist. Again, the work of West et al. (1994) was found to be compatible with the aims of LCA, and an energy content of 13 MJ/kg of sheet glass is used.

An energy and material analysis for the glass sheet manufacturing was carried out. The mass of glass required for a double-glazed unit of 1.1 m² was measured to be 21.2 kg in the finished product. A small amount of material is wasted due to breakages, and small offcuts which are not able to be used. Wastage is minimised due to the high levels of technology implemented and amounts to approximately 5.5% of the total glass utility. Taking this into account means that the average glass consumption for one unit is 22.26 kg having an energy content of 289 MJ.

7.3.1.6 Components

A number of components are assembled into the window construction; handles, security mechanisms, seals and ventilation grills are fitted to the completed sash and frame. All components are bought as finished products, requiring minimal processing on the factory site. Table 7.3.4 lists the mass of materials used, and associated embodied energy values. The total embodied energy of materials used for components was calculated to be 144 MJ.

7.3.2 Manufacturing

Having discussed the major material inputs to the window system, the manufacturing process itself must be considered and the energy consumption for production, administration, services, lighting and heating estimated. Again this is sub-divided for simplicity.

7.3.2.1 Timber sash and frame production

Sections of timber are first moulded using an energy-intensive sequence of mills and saws which provide the necessary profiling. Further milling is required to

Table 7.3.4 Materials and embodied energy of components

Material	Mass incorporated in frame (kg)	Mass incorporated in sash (kg)	Embodied energy (MJ/kg)	Total embodied energy (MJ)
Zinc	0.74	0.11	68.4*	57.6
Steel	0.05	0.17	34.9*	7.7
Plastic	0.03	0.04	160.0*	11.5
Rubber	0.45	–	148.0*	67.0
Total				143.8

* Extracted from Buchanan and Honey (1994)

shape each sash and frame for the ironmongery and accessories added later. The final two stages of production for the sash and frame include assembly and impregnation. The average energy consumption for the production of one sash and one frame were estimated to be 16.9 MJ and 16.3 MJ respectively (Weir, 1998).

7.3.2.2 Sealed glass unit production

The production process for the manufacturing of sealed glazing units is shown in Figure 7.3.3. The first task in the glass production procedure is to plan the cutting schedule. The glass sheets are precision cut on large, programmed cutting tables. Secondly, the edges around low-e coated glass sheets are ground to ensure that the adhesive seals the unit adequately. Glass panes are then washed to remove dirt and dust particles from the interior of the unit. An aluminium spacer is fitted to separate the glazings, and is kept in place by a butile compound. Before the unit is sealed it is filled with inert gas. Finally, the unit is sealed with a butile compound, and is ready for assembly into the window sash and frame.

The equipment used in these processes has a relatively constant load. It is possible therefore to divide the annual energy consumption by the number of units manufactured. Approximately 6 MJ of energy are consumed per finished window.

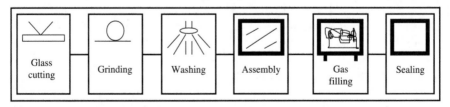

Figure 7.3.3 *Sealed glazing unit production line process (Weir, 1998)*

7.3.2.3 Aluminium processing

The cutting machinery for aluminium uses very little energy, and has a load power of approximately 4 kW. For a typical finished window, the factory processing of aluminium consumes a very small quantity of energy, approximately 0.2 MJ per finished window. This is negligible, and it is clear that the energy of production to produce aluminium from raw bauxite is of a greater concern.

7.3.2.4 Lighting and factory services

Lighting and factory services are not directly related to the manufacturing of the finished window, but are an essential element of the overall production process. Without these elements, production would be impossible. They are, however, not so easily subdivided into manufacturing stages, and must be accounted for in a unit overhead. Included in these are the factory services of administration, technical design, heating, lighting, and weekend and night-time loads. The average power load, annual energy consumption, and energy consumed per window is shown in Table 7.3.5.

Maintenance and repairs are kept outside the investigation boundaries for all stages of production, including machining, lighting, services and transportation. During the product use phase, maintenance and repairs become important, as the length of useful life for a window is a direct function of the treatment it receives while *in-situ*.

7.3.3 Transportation

Assessing transportation requirements throughout a product life cycle demands detailed inventory analysis based on the source and destination of all materials, fuels and components. In addition, information on the final destinations of finished products must be known, and the means by which they are transported. Different modes of transport have varying energy consumption

Table 7.3.5 Average electrical power load and energy consumption for non-machining requirements per window (Weir, 1998)

Energy use	Average power load (kW)	Annual energy consumption (GJ)	Energy consumption per unit production (MJ)
Administration	70	463	2.1
Technical design	57	380	1.7
Heating	49	1558	11.3
Lighting	256	3390	24.5
Night-time use	378	5006	36.2
Weekends	338	3036	21.9
Total			97.7

Table 7.3.6 Energy consumption associated with various modes of transport for given distances and loads (Buchanan and Honey, 1994)

Mode of transport	Energy consumption (MJ/Kg)
Road 30 km	0.11
Road 50 km	0.19
Rail 100 km	0.23
Rail 200 km	0.15
Rail 500 km	0.37

implications. Table 7.3.6 lists the energy consumption associated with various modes of transport, for given distances and loads.

Materials are sourced from a number of locations and countries throughout the world. Raw bauxite for the production of aluminium is shipped 12 000 km from Argentina, while timber is transported by rail from Norway, Sweden and Finland. Glass sheets are bought from a variety of locations, depending upon market availability, currency changes and manufacturing needs. Components are sourced from all over Europe, again according to market and currency variations.

Accurate measurement of energy consumption used in transporting these materials to the factory would require thorough analysis and reliable data on market sourcing and transportation systems, and would warrant an independent LCA study of its own. Therefore, literature and past research is extensively used. An estimation of transportation requirements associated with the main material sourcing for the production of one window unit is shown in Table 7.3.7. Energy of transportation of materials was estimated to be 65 MJ per window (Weir, 1998).

Window deliveries to the UK are made in a series of stages. Firstly, units are transported by road to Stavanger, where they are transferred to a shed, prior to

Table 7.3.7 Energy consumption associated with transporting materials to factory site per window (Weir, 1998)

Material	Source location	Average distance (km)	Mode of transport	Material mass per window (kg)	Total energy consumption per window (MJ)
Bauxite	Argentina	12 000	Ship	14.7	52.5
Aluminium	Norway	80	Road	2.3	0.1
Timber	Norway	100	Rail	11.1	2.6
Timber	Sweden	200	Rail	14.8	2.2
Timber	Finland	400	Rail	11.1	3.2
Glass	UK	600	Ship	21.2	3.8
Components	Norway	100	Road	1.6	0.4
Total					64.8

shipping. Orders are shipped to Aberdeen once per week. Aberdeen is used as the shipping point for the whole of the UK. Units are again stored before being transported, by road, to site. The number of handling exercises involved with this transport system means that breakages are a more common occurrence. It is not cost effective to transport windows in individual units, but the functional unit of this LCA is measured in J/window, and to this end, on a mass basis, the transportation analysis is the same. For example, a tilt and turn window weighing 37.5 kg and transported from the factory to an Edinburgh city centre location consumes fuel energy as follows:

80 km by road, Moi–Stavanger	0.304 MJ/kg	11.4 MJ
525 km by ship Stavanger–Aberdeen	0.03 MJ/kg	1.1 MJ
200 km by road Aberdeen–Edinburgh	0.76 MJ/kg	28.5 MJ
Total		41.0 MJ

The total energy consumption per window unit for transportation of raw materials and finishing is therefore estimated to be 106 MJ.

7.3.4 Use

In any LCA, certain phases of the life cycle will be highlighted as having a greater or lesser impact on the environment than others. Raw material sourcing, manufacturing, transportation and recycling/disposal of most products have the greatest impact on the environment, with little or no consideration being required for their general use. Windows differ greatly in their LCA. Their use phase impacts heavily on the environment. Window performance affects the indoor environment, building services operation, energy consumption of buildings and the well-being of occupants. Thermal insulating properties impact upon indoor air temperatures, draught sensation, radiant temperatures, and building user comfort, influencing energy use for heating and ventilation. No analysis would be complete without designing to optimise the well-being of occupants, while simultaneously minimising environmental impact generated from the life cycle. If the well-being of building occupants is not at the forefront of design criteria, the building, though well designed in terms of thermal performance, aesthetics and light transmission, will be unsatisfactory to its occupants. Work performance is heavily influenced by the working environment.

Energy consumption used for space heating over a lifetime of use is calculated for a number of window constructions. To consider the energy analysis of a window in isolation of the building of which it is a part would be both misleading and of limited use. For this reason the example office, having dimensions and layout as shown in Figure 7.2.1, is used to compare the space heating energy requirement associated with each of 18 windows used in construction. The following assumptions are made regarding the office environment, location, orientation and construction:

- The office environment is maintained at an environmental temperature which is high enough to meet thermal comfort needs, yet low enough to inhibit the early onset of fatigue in workers. It is therefore reasonable to assume that under normal operating conditions, a setpoint temperature of 19°C is maintained, using building controls and/or energy management systems.
- Each window configuration is installed within a typical office setup, with office location and orientation, wall construction, and window sash and frame construction remaining constant across all permutations.
- The example office is on an intermediate floor of a building and has one external wall. It is surrounded above, below and on all internal sides by spaces at the same temperature.

It is assumed that the space is heated throughout the heating season (1 October to 30 April in the northern hemisphere), over the hours 8 a.m. to 6 p.m., the windows are openable during summer months to provide natural ventilation, and that no artificial cooling is provided. The analysis is performed over a period of one year using a typical one year sample of weather data. The analysis is based on a glazed area equivalent to 60% of the external facade requiring 18 example-sized windows to cover this area. Annual space heating consumption for the office space, using each of 18 window constructions over the facade is illustrated in Figure 7.3.4. Refer to Table 7.3.8 for a definition of window types.

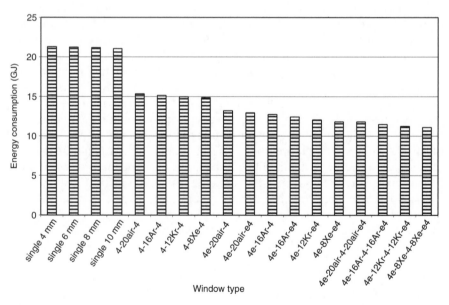

Figure 7.3.4 *Annual space heating energy consumption for example office for a glazed facade proportion of 60% (Weir, 1998). See Table 7.3.8 for window type definitions*

Table 7.3.8 Definition of window types used in this chapter (Weir, 1998)

Window type	Definition
Single 4 mm	Single glazed, 4 mm thick glass
Single 6 mm	Single glazed, 6 mm thick glass
Single 8 mm	Single glazed, 8 mm thick glass
Single 10 mm	Single glazed, 10 mm thick glass
4-20air-4	Double glazed, 4 mm thick glass, 20 mm air cavity
4-16Ar-4	Double glazed, 4 mm thick glass, 16 mm argon cavity
4-12Kr-4	Double glazed, 4 mm thick glass, 12 mm krypton cavity
4-8Xe-4	Double glazed, 4 mm thick glass, 8 mm xenon cavity
4e-20air-4	Double glazed, 4 mm thick glass, 20 mm air cavity, one low-emissivity coating
4e-20air-e4	Double glazed, 4 mm thick glass, 20 mm air cavity, two low-emissivity coatings
4e-16Ar-4	Double glazed, 4 mm thick glass, 16 mm argon cavity, one low-emissivity coating
4e-16Ar-e4	Double glazed, 4 mm thick glass, 16 mm argon cavity, two low-emissivity coatings
4e-12Kr-e4	Double glazed, 4 mm thick glass, 12 mm krypton cavity, two low-emissivity coatings
4e-8Xe-e4	Double glazed, 4 mm thick glass, 8 mm xenon cavity, two low-emissivity coatings
4e-20air-4-20air-e4	Triple glazed, 4 mm thick glass, two 20 mm air cavities, two low-emissivity coatings
4e-16Ar-4-16Ar-e4	Triple glazed, 4 mm thick glass, two 16 mm argon cavities, two low-emissivity coatings
4e-12Kr-4-12Kr-e4	Triple glazed, 4 mm thick glass, two 12 mm krypton cavities, two low-emissivity coatings
4e-8Xe-4-8Xe-e4	Triple glazed, 4 mm thick glass, two 8 mm xenon cavities, two low-emissivity coatings

Like the thermal characteristics of windows, the visual performance is important to building user satisfaction and influences the electricity consumption used for artificial lighting. Good lighting in a building may be defined as the provision of 'adequate' light, in the right place, at the right time, enabling occupants to perform tasks in comfort, to a high degree of efficiency, without suffering eyestrain or fatigue. Guidelines have been in place for many years to aid designers in the provision of sufficient lighting. What is less well documented is the definition of 'adequate' lighting. Use of appropriate luminaires, lighting control strategies, energy-saving schemes, exploitation of daylight, and the impact which environments have upon building occupants must be considered in the standard of service provided. Windows which permit light to enter an office space in a manner which is comfortable and satisfactory to its occupants, and which help create environments that permit maximum work productivity to be achieved, are sought.

Energy consumption used for electric lighting, based on a top-up lighting control strategy, for each window construction is calculated. To do this requires that the light transmitted through windows, onto the working plane within a building structure, is assessed. The extent to which light is transmitted through windows is a function of the optical properties of the material used, as discussed throughout Chapter 5.

A number of assumptions are made with regard to lighting control strategies within the office environment:

- Occupants do not override the lighting controls.
- Dimming control is linear in nature and does not employ step functions.
- Both lamps and control units are suitably maintained to ensure good performance.
- Building occupants do not object to gradation in daylight/artificial light throughout the passage of a day.

Annual energy consumption on artificial lighting for each of the 18 window constructions is illustrated in Figure 7.3.5, based again on a glazed area covering 60% of the external facade. The analysis is performed over a period of one year.

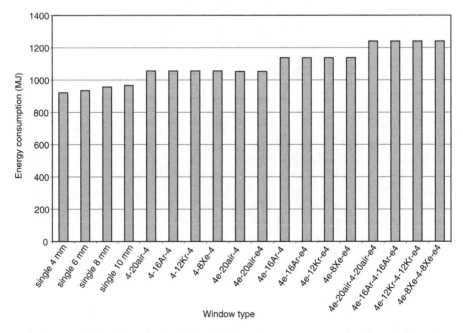

Figure 7.3.5 *Annual artificial lighting energy consumption for a glazed facade proportion of 60% and a top-up lighting control strategy (Weir, 1998). See Table 7.3.8 for window type definitions*

7.3.5 *Disposal and recycling*

Waste handling and management must also be considered in a thorough LCA. When a product reaches the end of its useful life it is tempting to focus attention on its successor, or to forget that the product requires disposing of and/ or recycling. Ninety five per cent of household, commercial and industrial wastes end up in landfill sites (Jones, 1993). This equates to 8 tonnes of waste per person annually. After more than five decades of profligate use of resources and badly managed waste disposal, attention has been turned to reduction of waste at source, re-use, recycling and use of waste to generate energy. These four management solutions, in addition to environmentally sensitive disposal of waste, form the framework of sustainable development, with the emphasis on reducing waste at source. The Scottish Office Development Department produced a planning policy guideline on waste management in March 1996, which is heavily focused on sustainable development solutions (Scottish Office, 1996). A Best Practicable Environmental Option (BPEO) that imposes least damage on the environment as a whole is sought. Research is ongoing and coincides well with the aims of LCA. The need to plan for disposal and re-cycling in the product conception phase is emphasised, and remains the only sustainable solution in the long term.

During the past decades there has been considerable interest in recycling products and materials. Public-awareness campaigns have raised the issue, enabling consumers to make more informed decisions about disposal and re-cycling of household and commercial waste. Bottle banks, paperless offices, textile re-use, newspaper reclaims and other initiatives make the public more aware of recycling possibilities, and place each community member in a position of responsibility. Beyond the issue of personal responsibility, corporations and industries have a responsibility too. Re-use and recycling of demolition and construction waste is no exception. However, little progress has been made in the practical implementation of research findings and government recommendations. The British Building Research Establishment (BRE) carried out a recent research programme to demonstrate the re-use and recycling of materials (Hobbs and Collins, 1997). It was found that around 96% by volume of the waste generated from the demolition of an existing building was re-usable or recyclable. Only a small percentage (4%) was sent to landfill sites. In the construction industry, the largest proportion of embodied energy for a given product is predominantly in material extraction and processing. Re-using materials omits this embodied energy in new constructions, while recycling of materials significantly reduces environmental impact.

Embodied energy of materials for a double-glazed window, in this LCA, was found to be of the order of 1500 MJ (excluding choice of cavity gas and low-emissivity coatings); approximately 85% of total energy consumption used in extracting raw materials, manufacturing and transportation. Re-use, or re-cycling, of window units would therefore show significant benefits in terms of material sourcing, energy generation and environmental emissions. However, no on-going construction activity could be found to support this initiative to date. Transportation of waste to processing centres remains a stumbling block to recycling initiatives, and development work to find reliable, economic markets for recycled materials is in its infancy.

A summary of all energy requirements involved in the extraction of materials, manufacture of finished window units, packing and transportation of both materials and finished products is illustrated in Figure 7.3.6. Used in conjunction with the energy consumption calculated for space heating and artificial lighting, presented in Figures 7.3.4 and 7.3.5, this summary of inventory analysis data forms the basis of the impact assessment which follows. The quantitative analysis does not include the disposal and recycling of materials due to a lack of quality data relating to this. LCA is, however, an iterative process, and as data quality improves, these elements may be included in the analysis with confidence. The total energy consumption throughout the life cycle (20 years) of each of 18 window constructions is illustrated in Figure 7.3.7.

7.4   Impact assessment

Impact assessment focuses on how the product affects the environment. This requires a qualitative and quantitative approach to analyse how raw material use, energy generation, water production, effluent output, air emissions and solid waste affect the environment. It is a question of defining and characterising the consequences which result from the inputs and outputs quantified in the inventory analysis. The World Resource Foundation (1995) considers LCA to be a vital, on-going tool, in combination with the trend towards more open disclosure of environmental information by companies, and the desire by consumers to be guided towards the least harmful products.

The energy content of material requirements and manufacturing processes is defined above in the inventory analysis. Each unit of energy consumed in developing materials, and in turning them into finished window products and in providing adequate space heating and artificial lighting, has its own implications for greenhouse gas production and the environment, as outlined in the introductory paragraphs.

To begin analysing the greenhouse gases emitted due to the burning of fossil fuels, an analysis of the methods of energy production must be made. It is assumed that all energy used to produce raw materials and to manufacture them into finished components or window units, and all energy used for artificial lighting, is electrical energy, generated using a mix of renewable energy, fossil fuels and nuclear power. All space heating energy requirements are assumed to be provided for by the combustion of natural gas in conventional central heating networks. The data shown in Table 7.4.1 show the emissions created for each MJ of electrical energy generated, relative to the average UK plant mix, and those emissions generated from the combustion of natural gas.

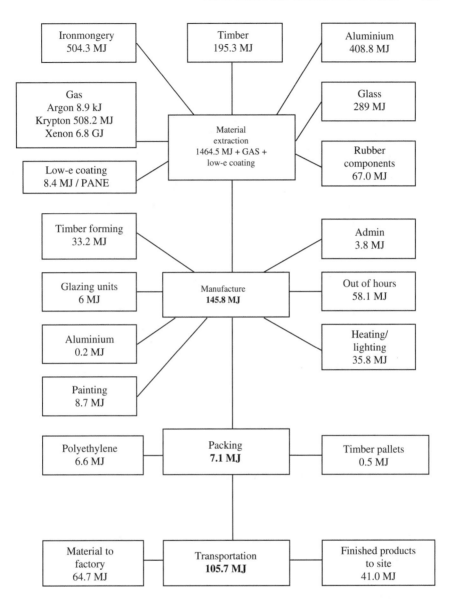

Figure 7.3.6 *Summary of energy consumption per finished window unit (raw material extraction to site arrival) for a window measuring 1.2 m by 1.2 m (Weir, 1998)*

The UK plant mix seems to be in a state of change. In 1997 the electricity supply mix was 42% coal, 2.5% oil, 21% natural gas, and 28.5% nuclear. However, during 1998 the above mix had changed to 39% coal, 2% oil, 27% natural gas, and 32% nuclear (DTI, 1997, 1998).

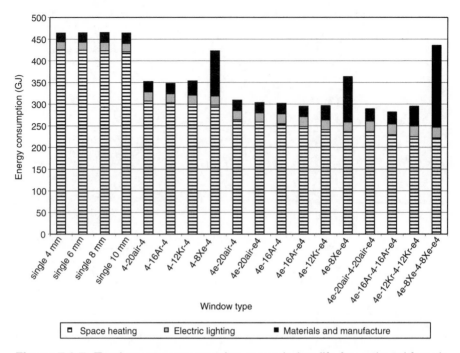

Figure 7.3.7 *Total energy consumption over window life for a glazed facade proportion of 60%, based on a top-up lighting control strategy (Weir, 1998). See Table 7.3.8 for window type definitions*

7.4.1   Transportation

Where transportation of materials, finished products, waste or recycled resources is necessary, there are several environmental impacts to be considered. Reduced air pollution and emissions result directly from maximising vehicle capacity, and in back-hauling materials, eliminating empty journeys. Ensuring that products are properly contained reduces the risk of waste due to breakages on a journey, and consideration should be given to the most appropriate route,

Table 7.4.1 Emissions generated as a result of producing 1 MJ of electricity in the USA and UK, and from burning natural gas (Weir, 1998)

	USA emissions			UK emissions		
	CO_2	SO_2	NO_x	CO_2	SO_2	NO_x
Electricity generation (UK Plant mix)	0.189 kg	1.60 g	0.694 g	0.2 kg	2.778 g	0.945 g
Natural gas combustion				0.058 kg	–	4.02 mg

in addition to the locating of manufacturing and production plants in relation to market places.

Weir (1998) has presented a case for the importance of transportation in a range of LCA studies, drawing a number of conclusions. In none of the LCAs did transport contribute less than 5% of the energy-related interventions or impacts, whereas contributions with more than 10% occurred regularly. Research work by Buchanan and Honey (1994) was used to evaluate emissions generated for various modes of transport on a distance and load basis. Table 7.4.2 shows the quantities of carbon dioxide, carbon monoxide, nitrous oxides, and hydrocarbons which result from road, rail and ship transport. For the distances and loads listed above, the generation of greenhouse gas emissions, as a result of transportation of materials and finished window units, was evaluated. The results are illustrated in Table 7.4.3.

Adding the impact associated with electrical energy generation, the combustion of natural gas and transportation requirements throughout the life cycle of a multi-glazed window unit, again related to our example case where 60% of the example office facade is glazed and a top-up lighting control strategy is adopted, the greenhouse gas emissions generated over a lifetime of use are illustrated in Figure 7.4.1. The major impact is easily identified as carbon dioxide, but other greenhouse gases are also emitted as pollution. These

Table 7.4.2 Transportation emissions per kg load, per km travelled (Buchanan and Honey, 1994)

Mode of transport	CO_2 (G)	CO (MG)	NO_X (MG)	Hydrocarbons (MG)
Road 30 km	0.28	16.7	2.7	2.0
Road 50 km	0.28	16.7	2.7	2.0
Road 100 km	0.17	10.1	1.6	1.2
Rail 200 km	0.05	3.2	5.1	0.4
Rail 500 km	0.05	3.2	5.1	0.4
Ship	0.03	1.6	2.6	0.2

Table 7.4.3 Greenhouse gas and hydrocarbon emissions generated as a result of transportation of materials and finished window units (Weir, 1998)

Material		CO_2 (kg)	CO (kg)	NO_X (kg)	Hydrocarbons (kg)
Bauxite	Transported to factory	472.20	28.30	45.00	3.500
Aluminium	Transported to factory	0.05	3.1×10^{-3}	4.9×10^{-3}	3.8×10^{-4}
Timber	Transported to factory	1.40	0.08	0.13	0.01
Glass	Transported to factory	0.34	0.02	0.03	2.5×10^{-3}
Components	Transported to factory	0.03	1.6×10^{-3}	2.6×10^{-4}	2.0×10^{-4}
Finished window units	Transported to site	2.64	0.16	0.07	0.03
Total		477	29	45	4

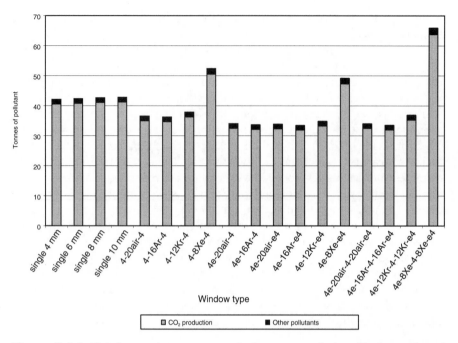

Figure 7.4.1 *Total greenhouse gas emissions over window life for a glazed facade proportion of 60%, based on a top-up lighting control strategy (Weir, 1998). See Table 7.3.8 for window type definitions*

other gases include sulphur dioxide (SO_2), nitrous oxides (NO_x), carbon monoxide (CO) and hydrocarbons.

7.5 Improvement analysis

Improvement analysis involves decision making to reduce environmental burdens. This requires taking an objective view of a product life cycle and assessing the impact which changes would make on the environment. The conclusion of any analytical study is borne out of underlying scope and goal definitions. The outcome of an LCA study is no different. The conditions fixed during the introductory stages of an assessment set the limits for possible improvements.

Using the information presented in Figures 7.3.7 and 7.4.1 as a guide towards selecting and designing windows which use reduced quantities of energy throughout their life cycle provides one source of improvement. If windows were selected according to their life cycle energy use or total environmental burden, rather than purely for aesthetics, or thermal performance properties, then this presents an improvement. It is seen that an energy saving of more than 150 GJ can be made over a lifetime of use by selecting a triple-glazed window with two low-emissivity glazing coatings and argon gas cavities (4e-16Ar-4-16Ar-e4), rather than a similar window having xenon gas cavities (4e-8Xe-4-8Xe-e4), which actually possesses better thermal transmission properties. This is because the energy associated with producing pure xenon gas is so great that the benefit of reduced space heating requirements can never be gained. The energy savings calculated in the example presented are for a specific building construction, orientation and use, but the same general principles would extend to many building types. Single-glazed windows do not possess sufficient thermal insulation properties, while windows incorporating xenon-filled cavities are too energy intensive in their manufacture stage.

Further improvements to the LCA results presented could, however, be achieved. Product design changes, raw material substitutions, manufacturing process changes, improved waste management facilities, or suggested consumer use changes, could be made as part of a long-term, proactive and strategic response to necessary and sustainable environmental initiatives. Little room is allowed for defensive, pragmatic assertions, based solely on the consequences upon human interest in the short term. The most common definition of sustainable development stems initially from the Brundtland Report, expressed as 'an approach to progress which meets the needs of the present without compromising the ability of future generations to meet their own needs' (WCED, 1987).

Improvement analyses which aim merely to improve environmental accountability with approaches which are not sustainable do not display sufficient initiative. To this end, the aims of the improvement analysis should focus on meeting the requirements of the present without compromising the ability of future generations to meet their own needs. Environmental sustainability provides a benchmark on which to base criteria for life cycle improvement analysis; a purposeful and challenging goal which is more rewarding than abstract and ambiguous attempts to 'lessen environmental burdens'. An unrestrained improvement analysis leaves too much scope for individual interpretation and poor judgement values.

The following recommendations, relating to the product, materials and management issues, seek to outline future improvements which may be practically and realistically implemented, highlighting problems which, as yet, remain unresolved. Much of the following discussion, rather than providing definitive solutions, poses questions to which the answers demand further research activity. No LCA, in its generic form, aims to answer all possible questions arising. LCA is a commitment to on-going improvement, and in some instances merely provides the researcher with the 'right' questions to ask; questions which may be addressed in a second, third, or fourth iteration of research techniques.

7.5.1 Products

Extending the useful life of a product means that fewer units are required over a given period of time to satisfy the same consumer need. The useful life of a product can be extended in a number of ways, all of which are dependent upon design criteria and quality of manufacture.

7.5.1.1 Durability

Durable items can withstand wear, stress and environmental degradation over long life cycles. The quality of finish and wood treatments applied throughout the manufacture stages are critical in creating windows which are durable.

7.5.1.2 Adaptability

Adaptable products make allowances for continual improvement and up-grading and/or may be used for more than one function. This is less applicable to windows, but standardisation of components would ensure easy maintenance and longer life cycles.

7.5.1.3 Reliability

Reliable products are able to meet performance criteria for a defined period of time, in an environment for which they were designed, without failing. Windows with high-quality seals, components and finishes will remain reliable for many decades, and will need to be replaced less frequently.

7.5.1.4 Maintenance

Windows which are easily and practically maintained reduce the time required for repairs and preventative work, and have better longevity.

7.5.1.5 Repairs

Products which allow the replacement of dysfunctional parts with ease, speed the return of systems to normal operating conditions, limiting down-time, and having little impact on operating efficiency. Again, standardisation of window components makes repairs quicker and simpler.

7.5.1.6 Re-use

Re-use of a product or part, once retired from a clearly defined duty, employs efficient use of resources but poses many questions about collection, transportation, processing and waste. Windows are one building component which lend themselves well to re-use. This has been demonstrated by Hobbs and Collins (1997).

7.5.1.7 Remanufacture

Remanufacture of parts is an industrial process which restores worn units to as-new condition. Again this would increase the longevity of windows requiring fewer replacements over a building life cycle.

7.5.2 Materials

Extending the useful life of materials used to manufacture products and components can have a significant effect on the outcome of an LCA study. Energy embodied in material sourcing and processing, prior to manufacturing, is often the dominant source of environmental burdens in an LCA, either directly or indirectly via fuel extraction and combustion to generate energy. There are several means by which the useful life of materials can be extended.

7.5.2.1 Substitution

Material substitution may be restricted by the need to use existing operating plant, but having capital equipment that may be adapted for a number of working materials enables a wider choice of markets to be sourced and more informed decisions about the environmental impact of materials to be made.

7.5.2.2 Recycling

Complete products or component parts may be regenerated in one of two ways. Closed-loop recycling recovers materials that are suitable substitutes for virgin materials, and which are used to manufacture the same product or component again. Open-loop recycling recovers materials a finite number of times before final disposal. Timber, glass and aluminium components within the window structure lend themselves well to recycling initiatives.

7.5.2.3 Reduced material intensiveness

Conservation of material resources can result in less waste and reduced environmental impact. A material which is manufactured from smaller quantities of material is likely to be lighter in weight, and therefore requires less packaging and reduced transportation energy.

7.5.3 Management issues

Product design factors and material selection issues are important to improvement analysis work. Additionally, management issues are central to environmental improvements. The planned use of materials and energy, and associated efficiency with which processes are carried out, impact heavily on LCA results.

7.5.3.1 Process substitution

Designers should be aware of the best available technology to perform a manufacturing requirement. Processes which create major environmental burdens should be replaced by more benign ones. Application of the best available technology limits material waste and inefficiencies in product and resource handling.

7.5.3.2 Process control

Control processes which suppress the influence of external disturbances and which ensure good performance stability should be adopted where practicable. Consideration should also be given to the layout of processes, such that output is consistent and efficient, and accident risks are reduced to a minimum.

7.5.3.3 Energy efficiency

Use of energy throughout the production process should be viewed holistically. Wherever possible heat losses from one system should be used to perform work in other processes. The provision of services should also be energy efficient, adopting the best available technology.

7.5.3.4 Inventory handling

Appropriately controlled resource and material handling whereby overstocking is eliminated limits waste due to spills and deterioration.

7.5.3.5 Facilities management

Flexible manufacturing principles can extend the useful life of facilities and equipment.

7.5.3.6 Packaging

The same principles of material substitution, recycling, re-use, product changes and use of reduced material intensiveness apply to packaging as well as finished products. Packaging and products should be designed to complement each other, and wherever practically possible, the use of packaging should be eliminated.

7.5.3.7 Transportation

Where transportation of materials, finished products, waste or recycled resources is necessary, a number of considerations are offered. Reduced air pollution and emissions result directly from maximising vehicle capacity and in back-hauling materials, eliminating empty journeys. Ensuring that products are properly contained reduces the risk of waste due to breakages on a journey, and consideration should be given as to the most appropriate route.

7.5.3.8 Selection of suppliers

Selection of environmentally responsible suppliers can significantly influence the environmental impact of a product's life cycle. Processes, activities and selection of materials further up the product development and component manufacturing tree can have a larger detrimental effect upon local and global environments than the final product itself.

7.5.3.9 Product labelling

Once a full LCA has been carried out, product labelling provides the consumer and retailer with information which allows them to make an informed choice. Provision of information on window U-values and the embodied energy of materials and manufacture would allow window specifiers and designers to make informed decisions regarding energy consumption and building performance.

7.6 Selection of the 'optimum' window type

For the range of single-, double- and triple-glazed window options analysed, and for the example building shown in Figure 7.2.1, where the window area is 60% of the south-facing facade, and the window life is assumed to be 20 years, the optimal window construction, in terms of energy consumption and greenhouse gas emissions was found to be:

4e-16Ar-4-16Ar-e4   triple-glazed window with two 16 mm cavities, filled with argon gas, and two low-emissivity coatings.

It can be seen, however, in Figure 7.3.7 that a number of window constructions consume very similar quantities of energy throughout their lifecycle. The example LCA shown in this chapter is not detailed enough to make a definitive selection, but does indicate that a number of window constructions consume smaller quantities of energy throughout their life cycle. Furthermore, the present analysis is subject to uncertainties and therefore it may only be used to indicate trends. These windows are generally of double- or triple-glazed construction, incorporating low-emissivity glazing coatings, and having air, argon or krypton gas-filled cavities.

A general trend is seen throughout the assessment of energy consumption and global environment impact, relating to material selection and window design. Windows which possess poor thermal insulating properties are characterised by a predominant energy requirement for space heating over window life. Windows which provide superior thermal insulating properties by use of highly energy intensive materials in construction are characterised by a predominant energy requirement in material sourcing and manufacture.

Design life is also seen to be critical to window selection. Windows designed for longevity should possess good thermal insulating and daylight transmission properties, as the impact of using materials with higher energy contents is offset by reduced requirements for space heating and artificial lighting energy consumption.

References

Buchanan, A. and Honey, B. (1994) Energy and carbon dioxide implications of building construction. *Energy and Buildings* 20, 205.

Callander, B. (1995) Scientific aspects of the framework convention on climatic change and national greenhouse gas inventories. *Environmental Monitoring and Assessment* 38, 129.

Dinesen, J. and Trabergy-Borup, T. (1994) An energy life cycle assessment model for building design. Danish Building Research Institute. Proceedings of the 1st International Conference on Buildings and the Environment, CIB 16–20 May 1994.

DTI (Department of Trade and Industry) (1997) *Digest of United Kingdom Energy Statistics.* The Stationery Office, London.

DTI (Department of Trade and Industry) (1998) *Digest of United Kingdom Energy Statistics.* The Stationery Office, London.

Fernie, D. and Muneer, T. (1996) Monetary, energy and environmental cost of infill gases for double glazings. *Building Services Engineering Research and Technology* 17, 43.

Field III, F.R., Isaacs, J.A. and Clark, J.P. (1994) Life-cycle analysis of automobiles: a critical review of methodologies. *Journal of Minerals, Metals and Materials Society* 46, 12.

Halliday, M. (1991) Feasibility of using timber for medium rise office structures. Research Report 91-3, Department of Civil Engineering, University of Canterbury.

Hobbs, G. and Collins, R. (1997) Demonstration of reuse and recycling of materials: BRE energy efficient office of the future. Building Research Establishment, IP3/97.

Hollinger, D. and Hunt, J. (1990) Anthropogenis emissions of carbon dioxide and methane in New Zealand. *Journal of the Royal Society, New Zealand* 20, 337.

Honey, B. and Buchanan, B. (1992) Environmental impacts of the New Zealand building industry. Research Report 92-2, Department of Civil Engineering, University of Canterbury.

Jones, P.T. (1993) *Underlying Trends in the UK Waste Sector, Waste: Handling, processing and recycling.* IMechE, Mechanical Engineering Publications Ltd, London.

Liggett, P. (1996) *Energy and Emissions per Square Metre of Pilkington K Glass.* Pilkington Glass Products.

Saito, M. and Shukuya, M. (1995) Energy and material use in the production of architectural windows for passive solar heating, ISES '95 Congress, Harare, Zimbabwe.

Scottish Office (1996) National planning policy guideline, NPPG10: Planning and waste management. March, 1996.

UNIDO (1989) United Nations Industrial Development Organisation, Industry and Development – Global Report 1989/90, Vienna.

WCED (1987) World Commission on Environment and Development, *Our Common Future*, Oxford Press, Suffolk.

Weir, G. (1998) *Life Cycle Assessment of Multi-glazed Windows.* PhD thesis, Napier University.

Weir, G. and Muneer, T. (1997) Low-emissivity coatings in high-performance double-glazed windows: Energy, monetary and environmental costs. *Building Services Engineering Research and Technology* 18, 125.

West, J., Atkinson, J. and Howard, N. (1994) Embodied energy and carbon dioxide emissions for building materials. *Proceedings of the First International Conference of Buildings and the Environment*, CIB 16–20 May 1994.

World Resource Foundation (1995) Information sheet, Warmer Bulletin, August 1995.

Young, S.B. and Vanderburg, W.H. (1995) Applying environmental life cycle analysis to materials. *Journal of Minerals, Metals and Materials* 46, 4.

8 SOLAR RADIATION AND DAYLIGHT DATA

8.1 International daylight measurement programme

The Commission International de l'Eclairage (CIE) declared the year 1991 as the International Daylight Measurement Year (IDMY). As a result, new activity commenced in the field of daylight measurement on a world-wide scale. This activity was later named the International Daylight Measurement Programme (IDMP). In the UK as a result of the CIE call, horizontal and vertical illuminance and irradiance (solar radiation) measurements have been carried out for four sites, i.e. Garston, Manchester, Sheffield and Edinburgh. The measurements at Edinburgh were respectively undertaken at Napier and Heriot-Watt universities. In Japan daylight data were recorded at 14 stations. Muneer (1997) has presented details of IDMP stations throughout the world. This information is shown in Table 8.1.1.

Measured solar irradiance and illuminance IDMP data for the UK and Japan have been compiled on a CD-ROM and duly reported (Muneer and Kinghorn, 1998). A selection of data is included in the CD-ROM accompanying this publication. Since the data gathered from the IDMP were reported by research parties from a variety of world-wide monitoring stations, the entire solar irradiance and illuminance dataset could not be included with this book. However, should more extensive data, other than that supplied be required, the reader is referred to the following websites; http://idmp.entpe.fr/ and http://www.cie.co.at/cie/home.html.

Most IDMP data are quality controlled in accordance with the rules set out by CIE (1994). The UK quality-controlled data provided to the authors have been rigorously checked, initially by the respective station managers and then by the overall co-ordinator, Professor P. R. Tregenza as part of an EPSRC-funded project (Tregenza, 1995). Japanese data were checked for quality by the research team headed by Professor H. Nakamura at Kyushu University.

The purpose of collating the measured solar data is to provide a quality-controlled daylight and solar radiation database which will, hopefully, satisfy a long-standing need.

8.2 Slope data

Daylight is a highly variable resource and therefore warrants measurement at a short time interval. The slope data are presented here in Excel format. The data

Table 8.1.1 World-wide IDMP stations (Muneer, 1997)

Country	Location	Latitude	Longitude	Type*
Australia	Sydney	33.87°S	151.27°E	R
Canada	Calgary	51.05°N	114.07°W	G
China	Beijing	39.80°N	116.50°E	R
China	Chongquing	29.58°N	106.47°E	G
France	Chanbery	45.57°N	5.92°E	S
France	Grenoble	45.12°N	5.72°E	S
France	Nantes	47.15°N	1.32°W	G
France	Strasbourg	48.57°N	7.75°E	S
France	Vaulx en Velin	45.77°N	4.92°E	G
Germany	Freiburg	46.80°N	7.15°E	S
Germany	Hamburg	53.55°N	9.97°E	G
Greece	Athens	37.97°N	23.72°E	G
India	Roorkee	29.85°N	77.90°E	R
Israel	Bet Dagan	32.00°N	34.82°E	S
Japan	Ashikaga	36.33°N	139.38°E	SR
Japan	Chofu	35.63°N	139.55°E	R
Japan	Fukuoka	33.52°N	130.48°E	R
Japan	Garston	51.71°N	0.38°W	R
Japan	Kiyose	35.77°N	139.53°E	S
Japan	Kyoto	35.02°N	135.78°E	R
Japan	Nagoya (Daido)	35.12°N	136.97°E	G
Japan	Nagoya (Meijo)	35.07°N	136.90°E	G
Japan	Osaka	34.58°N	135.50°E	S
Japan	Sapporo	43.05°N	141.33°E	R
Japan	Suita	34.83°N	135.50°E	S
Japan	Tokyo	35.67°N	139.82°E	R
Japan	Toyota	35.17°N	137.10°E	G
Japan	Tsukaba	36.15°N	140.05°E	R
Japan	Uozu	36.78°N	137.38°E	G
Netherlands	Eindhoven	51.42°N	5.47°E	R
Portugal	Lisbon	38.75°N	9.13°E	G
Russia	Moscow	52.70°N	37.57°E	S
Russia	Voeikovo	59.90°N	30.70°E	G
Singapore	Singapore	1.50°N	103.78°E	G
Sweden	Gavle	60.67°N	17.12°E	G
Sweden	Kiruna	67.85°N	20.27°E	G
Sweden	Norrkoping	58.60°N	16.12°E	R
Switzerland	Geneva	46.20°N	6.15°E	R
Ukraine	Karadag	40.27°N	49.57°E	S
United Kingdom	Edinburgh (Napier)	55.95°N	3.20°W	G
United Kingdom	Edinburgh (Heriot-Watt)	55.93°N	3.30°W	G
United Kingdom	Manchester	53.50°N	2.25°W	G
United Kingdom	Sheffield	53.38°N	1.50°W	R
United Kingdom	Garston	51.71°N	0.38°W	R
USA	Albany	42.70°N	73.85°W	G
USA	Ann Arbor	42.27°N	83.72°W	R
USA	Cape Canaveral	28.40°N	80.60°W	R

*Station classification as follows:
R: research class
SR: simplified research class
G: general class
S: simplified general class

Table 8.2.1 Illuminance thresholds (lx)

Sun at zenith	103 000
Clear sky, under sunlight (10 h solar time)	65 000
Clear sky, under sunlight (15 h solar time)	35 000
Sun at horizon	355
Flashlight at 1 m distance	250
Streetlights at night	175
Candlelight at 0.2 m distance	10
End of civil twilight	4.3
End of astronomical twilight	0.001
Full moon at zenith	0.215

included varies from a frequency of 5 minutes for three UK stations, i.e. Edinburgh, Napier (55.95°N, 3.20°W) and Heriot-Watt (55.93°N, 3.20°W) Universities and Garston (51.71°N, 0.38°W) to half-hourly time series for Manchester (53.50°N, 2.25°W) and Sheffield (53.38°N, 1.50°W). Fukuoka (33.52°N, 130.48°E) data are presented as 10-minute averages of 1-minute spot readings.

Table 8.2.1 provides approximate threshold values of illuminance. This information may be useful in acquiring a sense of the prevailing daylight illuminance levels for the locations under discussion.

A summary of the UK and Japanese slope data included in the accompanying CD-ROM is presented in Table 8.2.2. Further, Tables 8.2.3–8.2.4 respectively provide details of the notation, format and structure of the files provided on the CD-ROM. Approximately one week of data per month is included for each site considered. An attempt has been made to supply these data using the mean day of each month as a centre point for each weekly period. In accordance with the work of Klein (1977), the mean days of each month are reported as those for which daily horizontal extraterrestrial irradiance values are approximately equal to the mean monthly values. This approach provides a simple, yet reliable, method for determination of monthly average radiation values required in a multitude of solar energy engineering applications. In instances where no measured data are available for the mean day of each month, data for the nearest period to the mean day have been selected.

8.3 Sky scan data

Sky luminance and radiance distribution data from one Japanese and two UK sites are provided on the accompanying CD-ROM. A list of the electronic data files is provided in the front section of the book. Table 8.3.1 presents a summary of radiance and luminance data recorded by sky scanners at Sheffield, Garston and Fukuoka. Since these data are comparatively more scarce than,

Table 8.2.2 Slope illuminance database

Month	Mean day (Julian day)	Fukuoka (1994) Data8-01.xls Dates	Garston (1992, 1991*) Data8-02.xls Dates	Heriot-Watt (1994, 1993*) Data8-03.xls Dates	Manchester (1993) Data8-04.xls Julian days	Napier (1993, 1992*) Data8-05.xls Dates	Sheffield (1994) Data8-06.xls Julian days
January	17 (17)	11–15	15–21	15–21	19–25	19–26	15–21
February	16 (47)	3–7	13–19	14–20	45–51	No data available	45–51
March	16 (75)	1–5	16–22	No data available	73–79	14–20	73–79
April	15 (105)	1–5	No data available	13–19	103–109	13–19	103–109
May	15 (135)	1–5	13–19	13–19	133–139	13–19	133–139
June	11 (162)	2–6	9–15	9–15	162–168	9–15	162–168
July	17 (198)	5–9	15–21	19–23	196–202	15–21	196–202
August	16 (228)	1–5	14–20	14–20	225–231	14–20	225–231
September	15 (258)	1–5	13–19	No data available	256–262	13–19	256–262
October	15 (288)	1–5	13–19	No data available	288–294	13–19*	288–294
November	14 (318)	1–5	12–18*	No data available	314–320	12–18*	314–320
December	16 (344)	1–5	14–20*	14–20*	348–354	No data available	348–354

*Indicates data substituted from another year to produce a complete year of information

Table 8.2.3 Format of slope illuminance data files

Column	Edinburgh sites	Fukuoka	Garston	Manchester	Sheffield
A	Month	Date	Month	Year	Year
B	Day	Time	Day	Julian day	Julian day
C	Year	SOLALT	Year	Hour	Hour
D	Hour	SOLAZM	Hour	E_{eg}	E_{eg}
E	Minute	E_{vg}	Minute	E_{ed}	E_{ed}
F	E_{vg}	E_{vd}	E_{vg}	E_{egn}	E_{egn}
G	E_{vd}	E_{vb}	E_{vd}	E_{ege}	E_{ege}
H	E_{vgn}	E_{vgn}	E_{vgn}	E_{egs}	E_{egs}
I	E_{vge}	E_{vge}	E_{vge}	E_{egw}	E_{egw}
J	E_{vgs}	E_{vgs}	E_{vgs}	E_{vg}	E_{vg}
K	E_{vgw}	E_{vgw}	E_{vgw}	E_{vd}	E_{vd}
L	E_{eg}	E_{eg}	E_{eg}	E_{vgn}	E_{vgn}
M	E_{ed}	E_{ed}	E_{ed}	E_{vge}	E_{vge}
N	E_{egn}	E_{eb}	E_{egn}	E_{vgw}	E_{vgs}
O	E_{ege}	E_{edn}	E_{ege}	E_{vgs}	E_{vgw}
P	E_{egs}	E_{ede}	E_{egs}	RH	L_{vz}
Q	E_{egw}	E_{eds}	E_{egw}	T_{db}	RH
R	SOLALT	E_{edw}	SOLALT		T_{db}
S	SOLAZM	T_{db}	SOLAZM		
T	$C_{ef}C_{vf}$	T_{dp}	$C_{ef}C_{vf}$		
U			L_{vz}		
V			RH		
W			T_{db}		
X			E_{vs}		
Y			E_{es}		

say, slope data, the information contained on the accompanying CD-ROM comes in approximately 5-day blocks around the mean day of each month. Modelling procedures may be used to synthetically generate Table 8.3.1 data from that given in Table 8.2.2. To ensure concurrency between comparative data, the sky scanner data are presented (as far as practicable) in accordance with the slope data measurement period.

Sky luminance and radiance distribution data recorded at Fukuoka are respectively contained in the files Data8-07.xls and Data8-10.xls. In the case of the UK data, sky luminance distribution data are respectively contained in files Data8-08 and Data8-09 for Garston and Sheffield. The UK data were measured using a PRC Krochmann sky scanner. The Japanese data were recorded using a twin-headed sensor, capable of concurrent luminance and radiance recording, purposely developed by the EKO Company of Tokyo. A comparative evaluation of these instruments has previously been conducted against IDMP data from Geneva, Switzerland (Ineichen and Molineaux, 1993). Both instruments measure their required parameters by considering individual elements, or patches, of the sky. Each sky patch can be recognised in terms of its solar geometry, i.e. the altitudinal and azimuthal co-ordinates individual to

Table 8.2.4 Nomenclature used in slope illuminance data files

CIE abbreviation	Parameter	Units
C_{ef}	Shade ring correction factor for horizontal diffuse irradiance	Dimensionless
C_{vf}	Shade ring correction factor for horizontal diffuse illuminance	Dimensionless
E_{eb}	Direct (beam normal) irradiance	W/m^2
E_{ed}	Diffuse horizontal irradiance	W/m^2
E_{eg}	Global horizontal irradiance	W/m^2
E_{ege}	Vertical irradiance, east-facing surface	W/m^2
E_{egn}	Vertical irradiance, north-facing surface	W/m^2
E_{egs}	Vertical irradiance, south-facing surface	W/m^2
E_{egw}	Vertical irradiance, west-facing surface	W/m^2
E_{vb}	Direct (beam normal) illuminance	lx
E_{vd}	Diffuse horizontal illuminance	lx
E_{vg}	Global horizontal illuminance	lx
E_{vge}	Vertical illuminance, east-facing surface	lx
E_{vgn}	Vertical illuminance, north-facing surface	lx
E_{vgw}	Vertical illuminance, south-facing surface	lx
E_{vgs}	Vertical illuminance, west-facing surface	lx
L_{vz}	Zenith luminance	Cd/m^2
RH	Relative humidity	%
SOLALT	Solar altitude angle	°
SOLAZM	Solar azimuth angle	°
T_{db}	Dry bulb temperature	°C
T_{dp}	Dew point temperature	°C

Table 8.3.1 Sky scan database

		Luminance		Radiance
	Fukuoka (1994)	Garston (1992)	Sheffield (1993)	Fukuoka (1994)
	Data8-07.xls	Data8-08.xls	Data8-09.xls	Data8-10.xls
Month	Days	Julian days	Days	Days
January	11–15	15–21	No data available	11–15
February	3–7	44–50	No data available	3–7
March	1–5	76–81	14–20	1–5
April	1–5	103–109	14–17	1–5
May	1–5	133–138	18–19	1–5
June	2–6	162–168	No data available	2–6
July	5–9	191–197	No data available	5–9
August	1–5	230–236	No data available	1–5
September	1–5	256–262	17–19	1–5
October	1–5	288–294	15–21	1–5
November	1–5	314–320	18–24	1–5
December	1–5	348–354	20–26	1–5

Table 8.3.2 Sky patch geometry for UK locations (sun-relative co-ordinate system)*

Patch no.	1	2	3	4	5	6	7	8	9	10
Altitude (°)	6	6	6	6	6	6	6	6	6	6
Azimuth (°)	0	12	24	36	48	60	72	84	96	108
Patch no.	11	12	13	14	15	16	17	18	19	20
Altitude (°)	6	6	6	6	6	6	6	6	6	6
Azimuth (°)	120	132	144	156	168	180	192	204	216	228
Patch no.	21	22	23	24	25	26	27	28	29	30
Altitude (°)	6	6	6	6	6	6	6	6	6	6
Azimuth (°)	240	252	264	276	288	300	312	324	336	348
Patch no.	31	32	33	34	35	36	37	38	39	40
Altitude (°)	18	18	18	18	18	18	18	18	18	18
Azimuth (°)	0	12	24	36	48	60	72	84	96	108
Patch no.	41	42	43	44	45	46	47	48	49	50
Altitude (°)	18	18	18	18	18	18	18	18	18	18
Azimuth (°)	120	132	144	156	168	180	192	204	216	228
Patch no.	51	52	53	54	55	56	57	58	59	60
Altitude (°)	18	18	18	18	18	18	18	18	18	18
Azimuth (°)	240	252	264	276	288	300	312	324	336	348
Patch no.	61	62	63	64	65	66	67	68	69	70
Altitude (°)	30	30	30	30	30	30	30	30	30	30
Azimuth (°)	0	15	30	45	60	75	90	105	120	135
Patch no.	71	72	73	74	75	76	77	78	79	80
Altitude (°)	30	30	30	30	30	30	30	30	30	30
Azimuth (°)	150	165	180	195	210	225	240	255	270	285
Patch no.	81	82	83	84	85	86	87	88	89	90
Altitude (°)	30	30	30	30	42	42	42	42	42	42
Azimuth (°)	300	315	330	345	0	15	30	45	60	75
Patch no.	91	92	93	94	95	96	97	98	99	100
Altitude (°)	42	42	42	42	42	42	42	42	42	42
Azimuth (°)	90	105	120	135	150	165	180	195	210	225
Patch no.	101	102	103	104	105	106	107	108	109	110
Altitude (°)	42	42	42	42	42	42	42	42	54	54
Azimuth (°)	240	255	270	285	300	315	330	345	0	20
Patch no.	111	112	113	114	115	116	117	118	119	120
Altitude (°)	54	54	54	54	54	54	54	54	54	54
Azimuth (°)	40	60	80	100	120	140	160	180	200	220
Patch no.	121	122	123	124	125	126	127	128	129	130
Altitude (°)	54	54	54	54	54	54	66	66	66	66
Azimuth (°)	240	260	280	300	320	340	0	30	60	90
Patch no.	131	132	133	134	135	136	137	138	139	140
Altitude (°)	66	66	66	66	66	66	66	66	78	78
Azimuth (°)	120	150	180	210	240	270	300	330	0	60
Patch no.	141	142	143	144	145	146	147	148	149	150
Altitude (°)	78	78	78	78	90	90	90	90	90	90
Azimuth (°)	120	180	240	300	–	–	–	–	–	–

*See Figure 5.6.3(a)

each patch. Note that the geometric relationship between sky patches, solar position and sky zenith was shown in Figure 5.7.1.

Both PRC Krochmann and EKO instruments operate on the following principle. A hemisphere, representing the sky canopy, can be divided into bands of solar altitude. These bands lie parallel to the horizon and represent increments in solar altitude of 12°. Further, each band is azimuthally sub-divided to produce an array of sky patches. A short note on the merit of this technique of sky subdivision is available in the literature (Tregenza, 1987). The azimuthal increments of each band are shown in Table 8.3.2.

Figure 5.6.3 represents the individual sky patches as respectively measured by the PRC Krochmann (German) and EKO (Japanese) sensors. The outer bandwidths are those at the horizon, while the centre point (number 145) relates to the zenith of the sky hemisphere. There exists a slight difference between the numbering of each sky patch. This is due to the data collection techniques of the respective sky scanners. The EKO sensor used for Japanese data collection operates in the following manner. Starting at a southerly vector, the sensor is elevated to an angle of 6°. Rotating clockwise, the sensor records the properties of each sky patch at 12° intervals until it has returned to its initial starting point. The sensor then rotates counter-clockwise to the next elevation of 18° and records sky patch properties at 12° until again returning to due south. This clockwise-counter clockwise rotation continues through the further altitudinal and azimuthal divisions of the sky, as shown in Figure 5.6.3(b), until the sensor is finally vertical. At this point, the sensor is measuring the properties of the zenith of the sky canopy.

Though only 145 sky patches are considered by both sky scanners, it is seen that 150 patches are reported during each complete sky recorded by the PRC Krochmann instrument at both UK locations. This is due to this scanner recording an additional five values of zenith luminance during each complete sky scan. The sky scans at Garston and Sheffield sites are respec-tively reported at 15- and 30-minute intervals. Also, zenith luminance is the last patch to be measured. Therefore, when the sensor reaches a vertical position the zenith luminance may have changed since initialisation of that scan. Thus, the reported value may not be representative of the sky during the time-scale the scan was conducted. Data for patches 145–150 should be averaged to obtain zenith luminance in files Data8-08.xls and Data8-09.xls. For comparative purposes, Fukuoka sky luminance distribution data may be transposed into the same format as Data8-08.xls and Data8-09.xls via Calc8-01.xls workbook.

References

CIE (1994) Guide to recommended practice of daylight measurement. Technical Report CIE 108-1994. Commission International de l'Eclairage, TC 3.09.

Ineichen, P. and Molineaux, B. (1993) Characterisation and comparison of two sky scanners: PRC Krochmann and EKO instruments IEA Task XVII expert meeting Geneva.

Klein, S.A. (1977) Calculation of monthly average insolation on tilted surfaces. *Solar Energy* 19, 325.

Muneer, T. (1997) *Solar Radiation and Daylight models*. Architectural Press, Oxford.

Muneer, T. and Kinghorn, D. (1998) Solar irradiance and daylight illuminance data for the United Kingdom and Japan. *Renewable Energy* 15, 318.

Tregenza, P.R. (1987) Subdivision of the sky hemisphere for luminance measurements. *Lighting Research and Technology* 19, 13.

Tregenza, P.R. (1995) Standardisation of UK daylight data. Final report for EPSRC research grant GR/K07829, May 1995.

APPENDIX
Web-based and other software material

http://www.dialog.com/ or http://www.fiz-karlsruhe.de/stn/html
Energy Technology Data Exchange (ETDE). An International Energy Agency (IEA) database which provides bibliographic information on energy publications.

http://www.ncdc.noaa.gov/
The website for the US-based National Climatic Data Centre provides details of the protocol to be used for downloading solar and meteorological data for many US and global sites. Included in the list is a wide range of CD products.

http://www.BADC.RL.AC.UK
The Rutherford Appleton Laboratory based website provides the UK Meteorological Office data for the UK and the EU. The updates are made daily thus enabling access to recent solar radiation, temperature, cloud-cover, sunshine and wind data. The network is fairly exhaustive and a listing of the concerned stations may be obtained from: http://www.badc.rl.ac.uk/data/synoptic-new/radtlist.html

http://EETD.LBL.gov/CBS/NEWSLETTER/NL10/windows.html, and
http://www.efficientwindows.org
LBL window research-related websites.

http://solstice.crest.org/staff/ceg/sunangle/index.html, and
http://solstice.crest.org/software-central/html/forum.shtml
Websites which provide a calculator for solar geometry.

http://rredc.nrel.gov/solar/, and
http://eosweb.larc.nasa.gov/DATDOCS/Surface_Solar_Energy.html
Websites for obtaining solar radiation data for US sites.

www.ecbcs.org
International Energy Agency website for Energy Conservation in Buildings.

http://www.susdesign.com/windowheatgain
A shareware program that calculates the solar heat gain through vertical windows in temperate climates.

http://idmp.entpe.fr/
Information on a world-wide network of 48 stations measuring daylight and solar radiation under the CIE-International Daylight Measurement Programme.

http://SATELLIGHT.entpe.fr/
A database for daylight and solar radiation for a quarter of a million locations within Western and Central Europe. The data were collected by the Meteosat satellite.

www.iesd.dmu.ac.uk/~jm
Website that provides validation data for RADIANCE daylight simulation package using measured sky scan luminance distributions.

ASHRAE Handbook CD
ASHRAE Customer Services, Atlanta Tel: + 1-404-636 8400
Contains three volumes: HVAC Equipment and systems (1995), HVAC Applications (1996), and Fundamentals (1997).

Autoevaluator
Micro Surveys property Systems Ltd, London. Tel: + 44-181-395 3512
A PC software which allows enables cost evaluation of energy-efficiency measures for buildings.

FRAME (1992)
Developed by Enermodal Engineering Limited of Waterloo, Ontario, this program analyses heat transfer through frame, sash, divider and window edge.

RESFEN 3.0 (1997)
Available from the Lawrence Berkeley National Laboratory (LBL) in California, RESFEN 3.0 is a PC program for calculating the heating and cooling energy use of windows in residential buildings. The program comes on a suite of five floppy discs with a brief and easy-to-read manual.

Solar radiation data
Solar radiation data for the United Kingdom. Available from the UK Meteorological Office, London Road, Bracknell, England.

Solar radiation data for the United States and its territories. Available from National Renewable Energy Laboratory (NREL), 1617 Cole Boulevard, Golden–Colorado, this database provides information for 239 stations.

International Solar Irradiation Database. Prepared under the auspices of the University of Lowell Photovoltaic program, this compendium provides information for 55 countries.

THERM 2.0 (1998)

Available from LBL, THERM 2.0 is a PC program for analysing two-dimensional heat transfer through building products including multi-glazed windows. A detailed manual is accompanied by software, which may be loaded, on PCs from a set of two floppy discs.

VISION (1992)

A computer program to be used as a design and rating tool for evaluating the heat transfer, solar gain and temperature profile through glazing. The program is available from the Advanced Glazing System Laboratory, University of Waterloo in Canada.

WINDOW 4.1 (1994)

Developed at the Lawrence Berkeley Laboratory (LBL) in California this is a PC program for analysing the thermal performance of fenestration products. The software is downloadable via the website: http://windows.lbl.gov/materials/materials.html. Staff at LBL may be contacted at Plross@lbl.gov. The program is capable of analysing thermal and daylight transmission characteristics of any combination of glazing layers, gas layers, frames and spacers. Optical data for over a thousand glazing products is included in its library.

INDEX